PRAISE FOR *THE SAVAGE SHORE*

'Informed, measured and very readable.' —*Sydney Morning Herald*

'A fascinating, entertainingly written voyage on what have often been rough and murky seas.' —*Daily Telegraph*

'Tells colourful stories about the spirit of navigation and exploration, and of courageous and miserable adventures at sea.' —*Australian Geographic*

'Ripping yarns.' —*South Coast Register*

'To anyone that thought Australia had a boring history—read *The Savage Shore*.' —James Cripps, *Goodreads*

The SAVAGE SHORE

Extraordinary stories
of survival and tragedy
from the early voyages
of discovery

GRAHAM SEAL

YALE UNIVERSITY PRESS
NEW HAVEN AND LONDON

For information about this and other Yale University Press publications, please contact:

U.S. Office: sales.press@yale.edu   www.yalebooks.com
Europe Office: sales@yaleup.co.uk   www.yalebooks.co.uk

Internal design by Lisa White
Map by MAPgraphics
Index by Puddingburn Publishing Services
Set in 12/16 pt Minion Pro by Midland Typesetters, Australia
Printed and bound in Great Britain by Gomer Press Ltd, Llandysul, Ceredigion, Wales

Library of Congress Cataloging-in-Publication Data

Seal, Graham, 1950- author.
Title: The savage shore : extraordinary stories of survival and tragedy from the early
    voyages of discovery / Graham Seal.
Description: New Haven : Yale University Press, 2016. | Originial edition has subtitle:
    extraordinary stories of survival and tragedy from the early voyages of discovery to
    Australia. | Includes bibliographical references and index.
LCCN 2015043240 | ISBN 9780300220414 (alk. paper)
LCSH: Folklore—Australia—Bibliography. | Australia—Social life and customs—
    Bibliography. | Australia—Discovery and exploration.
Classification: LCC GR365 .S45 2016 | DDC 398.20994—dc23
LC record available at http://lccn.loc.gov/2015043240

A catalogue record for this book is available from the British Library.

10 9 8 7 6 5 4 3 2 1

CONTENTS

Batavia (Jakarta)

Christmas Island

Careening Bay
Prince Regent River

Montebello Islands
Barrow Island

Gascoyne River

Dirk Hartog Island
Turtle Bay
Shark Bay
Zuytdorp Cliffs

Wooramel River
Murchison River

Wittecarra Gully •Kalbarri
Abrolhos Islands
(also called Houtman Abrolhos)
•Mullewa
Irwin River
•Three Springs
Leeman
Dynamite Bay
Moore River

Karakin Lakes

Swan River •**Perth**

Cape Leeuwin •Busselton
Vasse River

•Middle Island

•Bald Island
King George Sound

AUSTRALIA

Raffles Bay

Inskip Banks

Darwin

Pennefather River   Wenlock River

Arnhem
Land

Kirke River
Gulf of   Edward River
Carpentaria
                                      Endeavour River

•Sweers Island

Finke Gorge•

•Brisbane

Blue
Mountains   •Sydney
Coffin Bay
•Adelaide
Marion Bay   •Canberra

Hopkins River
Glenelg River   •Melbourne
Middle Island
•Mount Singapore

Hobart•
Recherche Bay• Storm Bay

INTRODUCTION

Captain Cook did not discover Australia, despite what generations of school children were once taught and many still believe. The fact is that Cook only charted the east coast of the continent then claimed it in the name of the British Crown. Modern Australia was not discovered at all. It was revealed. Very slowly, through the mists of time and space and the explorations of many, the location, size and shape of the great southern land was uncovered.

This book is not so much about discovery as about encounters— first contacts with the landmass we now know as Australia. As the unknown continent at the end of the world emerged from myth into history and from speculation into geography, so it was found to have further secrets to reveal. These were not only about strange plants, animals and insects but also about its people and their beliefs and customs.

The southern landmass was first settled over 50,000 years ago by the peoples now called 'Aborigines'. Over this extensive time they evolved a diverse and complex society, linked by mythology and profound spiritual connection to the land. Then, perhaps 2000 to 3000 years or more ago, another group of people occupied the Torres Strait Islands, and they, too, developed into a defined society.

When Europeans did arrive in the south, the consequences for these groups of first Australians were almost unrelievedly bad. Compared with European society, indigenous Australia was seen as primitive and, initially at least, as having little of worth for trade or colonisation. For their part, the indigenous people were often uninterested in almost everything that Europeans handed them in the form of trade goods, trinkets and clothing. The gap between these cultures was immense. But subsequent history meant that the indigenous and colonialist story would inevitably become the same story.

Although this book is about the continent—and island—of Australia, its scope is global. It begins in ancient pagan, Christian and Muslim legends about a great landmass at the far end of the earth. It embraces the epic voyages and migrations from the old world to the new worlds of the East Indies and the Americas then, finally, to modern Australia. The effects of these many acts of exploration and colonisation by mariners in search of trade, treasure and scientific glory are still being worked out today. As new discoveries come to light, unexpected possibilities arise that reveal a very different view of the past. Surprising connections of trade, culture and even genetics are being found, or credibly suggested, between peoples previously thought to have had no contact with each other.

The consequences of these collisions and connections have not always been happy ones. The lure of rich trade and possession of new lands that energised the extraordinary mercantile expansion of Europe through the sixteenth to the eighteenth centuries led often to violence against indigenous peoples, including abduction, murder and, most ruinously, the destruction of age-old cultures and the languages that carried them.

On the other side of the unbalanced ledger, 300 or more Europeans were unlucky enough to be cast away on the alien shores of the southern land, and this was more than two centuries before the First Fleet anchored at Botany Bay in 1788. There may well have been many more. A few of these hardy souls were lucky enough to escape. Most did not, and the only notions we have of what their fates might have been are bound up in mystery and legend. In part, this book tells some remarkable stories of endurance and survival. But extreme as the fates of those still-missing castaways are likely to have been, their sufferings contributed to the gradual revelation of the unknown southern land from the ignorance and myth that had kept it hidden it for so long.

Through this larger narrative run many other threads. One, illustrated here in some magnificent cartography, is the development of 'the secret atlas'. Ships' masters and navigators laboured to chart the southern coasts and waters in which they found themselves, sometimes catastrophically. These carefully preserved charts, logs and journals were sent back to Europe where an efficient cottage industry produced new maps of the world, including all these hard-won details of cliffs, bays, estuaries, rivers, reefs and islands, to help other mariners plot safer courses to wherever their destinations might have been. In an important sense, modern Australia is the product of those immensely risky labours by so many people over many centuries.

Another, perhaps unforeseen, thread of the tale is the role of religious belief. Until relatively recent times, the large majority of human beings have worshipped one or more gods, along with attending to whatever practices and expressions of dogma were required of such beliefs. Here, we are brought hard up against the powerful faiths of Catholics, various forms of Protestantism, as well as a unique indigenous belief system. In those times and in those places, such beliefs controlled and shaped the way people saw the world and their place in it. As always, such beliefs also determined to a great extent how they would deal with those 'others' who were not of their faith but so obviously different in appearance, language, manner and almost all other vestiges of human identity.

This worked in both directions. Not only did Aboriginal peoples coming into contact with questing Europeans react to them in ways consistent with their spiritual beliefs, so of course did Europeans react to the ways of the 'natives' or 'indians', as they often called them. In ships' journals, official records and private documents, we read continually of the chasms of mutual incomprehension that separated those already in occupation and the newcomers. We also read how Europeans often justified their actions in the name of their god. These activities included 'the skin trade', the matter-of-fact abduction of indigenous men and women and the souveniring, display and study of their body parts. They also included the appropriation of anything the indigenous people held that the explorers thought valuable, as well as the legal possessioning of their lands by proclamations, pieces of paper and parchment, and a range of inscribed pewter plates, wooden plaques and messages in bottles.

Religion was also important in other ways. This was a time of European religious reform, even revolution, in which the new Protestant beliefs were challenging the orthodox views and practices of the established church of Rome. In these circumstances, people tended to adopt—sometimes under coercion—especially firm convictions of one kind or another. They were often sustained by these beliefs and prayers through incredible hardship and seemingly hopeless circumstances. As well as having a positive result, overzealous adherence to a particular creed produced one of the world's most horrific sagas of shipwreck, mutiny, rape, murder and bloody retribution. The consequences of that same belief system have also played into a remarkable pre-1788 genetic connection between Australian Aboriginal people and those escaping to North America from religious persecution in reformation Europe.

The baser end of the human spectrum is also represented in the form of greed for sunken treasures and exploitation of natural resources. But tales of dynamiting, arson and shadowy syndicates intent on plundering wrecks of their valuable cargoes are counter-pointed by the efforts of those wishing to study and preserve these heritage sites for future generations and for research. These activities are ongoing and are continually throwing up intriguing new possibilities in the story of the 'Southland'.

And in the end, there remain the legends. These include shipwrecks and pirates, sunken and buried treasures and their sometimes colourful hunters, lost colonies of Europeans wandering in the arid outback, as well as mysterious stone circles and other objects, inscriptions and artefacts allegedly stumbled upon by early and latter-day explorers, escaped convicts or pioneers. All these yarns are part of the largely untold story of Australia's hidden pre-1788 history. Together, they tell how the southern continent was, as poet Bernard O'Dowd wrote in his 1900 poem 'Australia', the 'Last sea-thing dredged by sailor Time from Space'.

NOTES ON USAGE

The timespan of this book and the numerous nations and cultures which appear in it means that many systems of writing and measuring time, distance and weight were in use. For the sake of readability, these have usually been standardised in the closest possible approximation to current usage in accordance with the following notes.

Spelling
During the period covered by this book, the spelling of almost every word of more than a few syllables could be wildly divergent, even when written by the same hand in the same document. Generally, variant spellings in quotations from primary sources have been regularised and correlated with any other mention of that word or name, other than in verbatim quotations from original documents.

Time
In 1582 it was finally decided that the prevailing Christian calendar, originally introduced by Julius Caesar, was unacceptably inaccurate. The modern, or Gregorian, calendar of 365 days, with

a leap year every fourth year, was adopted. As with most innovations, effective change was a long time coming and there was a lengthy transition period in which both systems were in use. (The Julian calendar is still used by many orthodox churches.) Unless otherwise noted, all dates from this period have been regularised in accordance with the modern calendar.

Personal names

Dutch male surnames were usually ended in 'soon' or 'zoon', meaning 'son of', as in the English language 'Johnson' and so on. Thus, the first European thought to have walked on Australia was Willem Janszoon, though his name is usually rendered as 'Jansz' in modern usage. It was common practice for the suffix to be dropped, except in official usage (and even then the practice was not consistent). Generally, I have retained the most common version of the name that appears in quotations from the primary source documents on which this book is substantially based (though these can vary wildly as well, even within the same document). Unless the longer form has become closely associated with a particular individual, the shorter form is used.

The names of many French and some British navigators were sometimes extravagantly lengthy. I have usually preferred the short versions by which they are generally known to history.

'Australia'

Names for what we now know as 'Australia' were many. They included *Terra Australis* (southern land), *Terra Australis Incognita* (the unknown south land), 'Beach', the 'Great South Land of the Holy Spirit' (*Espíritu Santo*), the 'Great South Land', 'New Holland', even 'Terre Napoléon', as well as others bestowed by various navigators from Willem Jansz to Matthew Flinders. Unless referring specifically to one or more of these original designations, the form 'Southland' is generally used to refer to the whole island continent.

Van Diemen's Land was renamed Tasmania in 1856, an official recognition of its European discoverer, Abel Janszoon Tasman.

Ships and boats

Readers may be slightly bewildered by the many different types of ships and boats mentioned in primary sources quoted here, particularly those related to the Dutch East India Company (VOC). There are yachts, galiots, skiffs, flutes, pinnaces and a host of others. There is no point trying to regularise these as they were not used consistently either by sailors or VOC officials at the time, nor by anyone since, including translators. It is not uncommon to find the same ship referred to by two different types in the same document, and sailors themselves would often use more than one term to describe their craft. Worse, few of the Dutch-type terms coincide with any English language equivalents, contributing to the confusion.

Here is a rough guide to the styles of vessel mentioned in the text:

flute (fleut, fluyt)—a merchant ship, usually with three square-rigged masts and multiple decks

caravelle—a small and manoeuvrable Portuguese sailing ship

corvette—a small to medium armed sailing ship, probably of French origin

retourschip—not a type of ship so much as a term for larger VOC ships that made the outward and homeward journey from the Netherlands to the East Indies and back; *Zeewijk*, *Batavia* and the *Zuytdorp* were of this class.

jacht (jagt)—a smaller and faster vessel than the retourships; the *Vergulde Draeck* was classed as a jacht.

Smaller boats belonging to the ships were of similarly varied types and are also described inconsistently. They included:

cock-boat—usually a small ship's boat

longboat—often, but not always, the same as a whale boat, both being open boats with oars and, sometimes, sails

galiot—originally a vessel with oars as well as sails, later a general term for a smaller trade ship

gig—a term that could be used for almost any small boat used to convey people to and from larger vessels

pinnace—usually a smaller sailing ship, but the term could also be used to describe a rowboat or small sailing boat

skiff—a small boat, much like a dinghy

skow or **scow**—improvised vessel, or raft.

Dutch weights, measures and distances

Dutch documents mention many different terms for the carrying capacity of ships, bottles, crates, casks and so forth. Not only could these terms vary from region to region, they could also vary from occupation to occupation. Where there is a need to indicate any of these weights and measures, I have given the approximate equivalent in modern metric form (though interpretations of these can vary).

Distance was usually measured, by Dutch mariners at least, in *miljen*, known in English as a 'Dutch mile' (*milj*). This is usually said to be roughly 5 kilometres, though some sources say it is as short as 1 kilometre. Such measurements have been left as they appear in the primary sources. In general discussion, they are approximately converted to their modern metric equivalents, as are English miles.

Longitude and latitude

It was not until the end of the period covered by this book, and even later in some instances, that mariners had reasonably accurate chronometers. The deficiencies of earlier instruments meant that otherwise carefully calculated degrees of longitude were wrong, sometimes fatally, as the number of apparently avoidable ship-wrecks attests. Unless there is a need to do otherwise, on those occasions where a position of longitude and latitude is given, it is in the corrected form.

Charts and maps

A 'chart' is usually defined as a nautical representation of coasts and waters, including conditions beneath the water, and used for navigation purposes. It is distinguished from a 'map' which mainly locates surface physical features of land. It is often said that a chart is a working document by which a course can be plotted, while a map is a static representation of places, topography and distances and so cannot be used for finding one's way.

Generally, the terms 'chart' and 'map' are used interchangeably in this book, though there are occasions, such as in the VOC and other cartographical works, where charts have been used to construct large-scale maps and atlases.

Nationalities

At the beginning of the period covered by this book, and quite far into it, the idea of a 'nation' is generally anachronistic. Apart from Britain and France, much of Europe had not yet been 'unified' into the countries we are mostly familiar with today. When the VOC was formed, it operated within a loose confederation of independent provinces. While many of its employees came from these areas, there were also many from other parts of Europe, with different languages, customs and ethnic histories. Even within these areas there were groups—sometimes large and numerous—with different traditions. While recognising these issues, the term 'Dutch' is generally used in this book to mean those who worked aboard or were carried by VOC ships. When it is necessary to make distinctions of ethnicity, culture or nationality, this is made clear in the text.

Indigenous group names

The indigenous names of local peoples are, as far as possible, those given in the primary sources. These names are often contested by anthropologists, linguists and by indigenous people themselves. For a long time, Norman Tindale's map of Aboriginal Australia was the most authoritative source for group names but is now often considered inaccurate to a greater or lesser extent. More recent attempts to map territories and languages allow for a large degree of flexibility. Sometimes, lack of precise information means it is only possible to refer to the 'local people' or 'indigenous inhabitants'. In modern times, many indigenous groups have formed collectivities under names such as Koori, Nyungar, Yamadji and Murri, among others (mostly variously spelled).

Terms for indigenous people

At the time covered by this book, European words for indigenous people encountered through colonial expansionism are nearly all objectionable today. They included 'indians', 'natives', 'moors', 'savages' and, occasionally, 'kaffirs'. As much of this book is based on original documents from the time, these terms inevitably appear in quotations from the sources. In writing about these matters, some of the period terms are occasionally used to maintain the appropriate sense of time and place in the narrative. In other cases, terms generally acceptable today are used, such as 'Aboriginal', 'indigenes', 'Islanders' (for Torres Strait Islanders) and occasionally 'first Australians'. In some cases I have followed the geographic precedents set by those who made first contact, such as François Péron who referred to the people he met as 'Diemenlanders'.

The names of deceased Aboriginal people will inevitably appear, hopefully causing no distress.

Place names

Many places—bays, islands, peninsulas, rivers, etc.—have had different names at different times. For instance, King George Sound was named by Europeans 'King George the Third's Sound' and is also sometimes called 'King George's Sound'. This book generally uses what are today the most common names and their rendering.

In this book the terms 'Spice Islands', the 'East Indies' or sometimes the 'Dutch East Indies' refer generally to the region now known as Indonesia and the Malay Archipelago.

PROLOGUE

It is March 1658. Upper steersman Abraham Leeman and thirteen sailors are cast away on the far side of the earth in a vast emptiness called by many 'the unknown south land.' Searching for the Dutch East India Company's *Vergulde Draeck*, lost two years earlier, Leeman and his men are separated from their ship. The captain has sent them ashore in a small boat to search for survivors, despite the foul weather bearing down on them. The storm hits. Leeman and his crew are trapped overnight on the beach. When the rain clouds clear away next morning, their ship is nowhere to be seen in the infinity of ocean to their north, south and west.

Leeman has one small boat, hardly any food or fresh water and little equipment. His men are terrified. They look to him and his navigator's skills to save them. Through the wind and waves, Leeman calls out to his god, time and time again. The choice for him and his men is a lingering death or a desperate dash for survival through treacherous waters along savage shores. After days of prayer and soul-searching, Abraham Leeman decides what he will do.

1

Imagining the
unknown Southland

A fabled southern landmass has existed in the world's imagination from ancient times. A mysterious continent was seemingly conjured from the earliest human attempts to record the world and its geography. The blurred lines between legend and fact were the first feature of the Southland and continue to influence our understanding of it. Sometimes, the myths turned out to be not so far from the truth. But even if not factual, the myths have persisted anyway.

Ancient myths

From at least the fifth century BC, the Greeks were aware that the world was a globe and speculated about a large landmass in the extreme south to balance the lands they knew in the northern hemisphere. Around the late fourth century BC, a writer known as Euhemeris claimed to have travelled to a mysterious island in the Indian Ocean known as Panchaea, a land rich with precious metals and the home of a people born of the soil. Also living on the island were said to be a number of different ethnic groups from the ancient world. One of these groups had been led from Crete to Panchaea by the Greek god Zeus, an early version of the lost tribe legend. Euhemeris was perhaps the first writer of travel fiction, but he was not the last. His fantasies were refined and embroidered down the following centuries, feeding into a vast mythology of unknown lands somewhere to the south.

The Romans followed the Greeks but embroidered the legend of a lost land by imagining it was peopled by strange beings who survived in great heat and necessarily walked upside down. By the second century AD, it was widely accepted that there was a southern landmass, probably inhabited, and laying at the bottom of the world—somewhere. Ptolemy (Klaudius Ptolemaios) drew a map at that time on which a large southern section appeared. Then, in the fifth century, a Roman known as Macrobius wrote about an uninhabited world to the south.

The ancient Muslim world also believed in the existence of the southern continent and maps that seem to represent some of its northern coastline were produced in the ninth century AD. These documents have led to suggestions that Arab explorers discovered the mysterious 'fifth continent', even as early as 1300AD.[1]

But recent research suggests an even earlier contact. In 2013 a scientific study provided genetic evidence suggesting that Australia may have been colonised by Dravidian people from India as early as 23,000 BC. As well as the genetic evidence, there are some indications of technological and biological changes at this time, including the possible introduction of the dingo to Australia.[2] Not surprisingly, these suggestions have been controversial, especially as the genetic testing on which they were based relied on a very small sample.

Using evidence based mainly on rock formations, skeletal remains and interpretations of indigenous mythology, it has also been asserted that an advanced Stone Age society called 'Uru' existed in Australia.[3] Claims have also been made that the Phoenicians, a seafaring empire established in the Middle East from around 1200–539BC, reached the southern land and established at least one colony here.[4] Such speculations have generally been met with scepticism, not necessarily because they seem incredible but because they lack substantive and verifiable evidence to support them. But their existence does highlight the extent to which the strange southern continent was wreathed in myth and speculation from its earliest appearances in recorded history. The tradition continues today with some even more intriguing possibilities combining history and folklore.

Consider what Leading Aircraftman Maurie Isenberg found on a remote beach in 1944. He was manning a radar post on the Wessell Islands off the Northern Territory.[5] One day he went fishing and stumbled on a cache of ancient coins. Five of the coins were copper, dating to the tenth century sultanate of Kilwa, an island near modern Tanzania in East Africa. Even more amazingly, found with these coins were four Dutch coins from the seventeenth and eighteenth centuries. Isenberg packed his treasure away and thought no more about the coins until 1979 when he took them to a museum where they were identified. As if from the script of a folktale, Isenberg also provided a map marked with an 'X' at the spot where he made his find. Then the coins were again completely forgotten for the next thirty years or so.

In 2013 a group of researchers mounted an expedition to the Wessell Islands to investigate the coins further. The Yolgnu people of the area hold oral traditions about possible contact with Indian Ocean traders and fishermen long before Europeans entered the region, probably via a trade route that operated between Kilwa, Great Zimbabwe, Arabia, Persia, India and islands in present-day Indonesia. In another echo of lost treasure lore, this story comes complete with a legend of a secret cave somewhere near the place the coins were found. It is said to contain old weapons and, of course, many more coins.[6] The 2013 expedition found no coins, but did turn up evidence of early shipwrecks and depictions of sailing ships preserved in Aboriginal rock art. Whatever the truth of these intriguing tales turns out to be, they hold tantalising possibilities for the unknown discovery of Australia. And there are many more.

The Chinese

In one highly controversial theory, it may have been the Chinese who first recorded the southern continent in 1421, but Marco Polo also wrote of a previously unknown south land in his account of his travels between 1271 and 1295. He described two uninhabited islands said to lie seven hundred and fifty miles south west of Java as

> an extensive and rich province, that forms a part of the main land, and is named Lochac. Its inhabitants are idolaters. They have a language peculiar to themselves, and are governed by their own king, who pays no tribute to any other, the situation of the country being such as to protect it from any hostile attack. Were it assailable, the Grand Khan would not have delayed to bring it under his dominion. In this country sappan or brazil wood is produced in large quantities. Gold is abundant to a degree scarcely credible; elephants are found there; and the objects of the chase, either with dogs or birds, are in plenty.[7]

The famous explorer went on to provide even more specific directions about a land of plenty named Pentam, a further five hundred miles south, 'the coast of which is wild and uncultivated, but the woods abound with sweet scented trees'. Only another thirty miles further 'you arrive at an island, in itself a kingdom, named Malaiur, which is likewise the name of its city. The people are governed by a king, and have their own peculiar language. The town is large and well built. A considerable trade is there carried on in spices and drugs, with which the place abounds.'[8]

Marco Polo is not writing of the land we now call Australia but probably of somewhere around modern Cambodia. But so little was known of geography at the time that his description stood for centuries, further contributing to the mystery of the missing southern continent and also bolstering the notion that the Chinese had earlier discovered it and inspiring a latter-day claim to that effect.

According to Gavin Menzies in his book *1421, The Year China Discovered the World*[9], several large Chinese treasure fleets set sail at that time under the command of Admiral Zheng He. One of these fleets was said to have reached the east coast of the continent and to have travelled along what is now the coast of Victoria, New South Wales and Queensland. They did not seem to have ventured ashore, at least according to the extensive, if circumstantial, array of cartographic, nautical and archival material that Menzies presents in support of his contention.

Menzies' theory that Australia (as well as America and many other places) was discovered by the Chinese has been roundly and widely discredited, dissected and effectively destroyed by a host of academics and other specialists. It appears to be a hoax, or at least a misguided accretion of pseudo-evidence, speculation and assertion. In short, it is a fairly typical product of the fantabulism that has always been associated with *Terra Australis Incognita*. Menzies' methodology and scholarship have been criticised on many grounds by historians such as Robert Finlay: 'The reasoning of 1421 is inexorably circular, its evidence spurious, its research derisory, its borrowings unacknowledged, its citations slipshod, and its assertions preposterous.' Nevertheless, Finlay did see some use for the book, conceding: 'It may have some pedagogical value in world history courses. Assigning selections from the book to high-schoolers and undergraduates, it might serve as an outstanding example of how not to (re)write world history.'[10]

But we should not entirely suspend our incredulity in relation to this theory. Better to read it as a parable, a moral tale that highlights the murky nature of Australian pre-history and its propensity to produce folkloric red herrings. There has always been unsubstantiated information and speculation masquerading as fact in relation to the island continent,[11] but some of these threads do finally lead to historically and scientifically verifiable conclusions.

Northern contacts

Certainly there were early contacts between indigenous Australian people and the fishermen and traders known as Macassans from Sulawesi and other islands now part of Indonesia. The Macassans came in *praus*, sailing craft of around 25 tons. They sought trepang, or sea cucumber, for the Chinese market and carried on extensive trade and other contacts with the Yolgnu and other indigenous people along the northern coast of Australia from at least the early eighteenth century. Archaeological evidence from Arnhem Land suggests the possibility that Macassan contact began much earlier. At a place known as Djulirri in the Wellington Range, about 20 kilometres inland, is a gallery of rock art. The gallery contains paintings of sailing ships, both European and Macassan. Radio carbon dating of beeswax images painted over the Macassan *praus* gives an age in the mid-seventeenth century, meaning that the images beneath must be even earlier.[12] While this is not definitive, it does suggest that Macassan contact might be very old indeed.

The Macassans had yet another name for what Europeans generally called the Southland—they called it *Marege*, meaning 'the wild land'. The remains of their camps and processing plants have been found in these northern coastal regions, together with artefacts, Aboriginal rock art and linguistic evidence of extensive interactions over a considerable period. During this time it seems that there was some cultural impact on Australian indigenous society and culture, with the adoption of trepanger dugout canoes and aspects of Islamic religion into ritual and custom.[13]

The oral traditions of the Yirritja moiety of the Yolgnu tell of a people called the *Baiini* (or *Bajini*) who came to the land in sailing ships. These people were light brown in colour, built houses of stone and cultivated rice. The women, noted for their great beauty, dressed in sarongs and wove brightly coloured cloth. It is said that, after settling for some considerable time, the *Baiini* returned to their homelands, far away to the west, perhaps the Celebes. Although the tradition is that the *Baiini* were Dreaming figures, it is thought that the stories represent a more recent group of settlers who arrived perhaps as early as the fifteenth century and made their homes in the Kimberley, Arnhem Land and Cape York regions. As well as their stories, the *Baiini* influence can be seen in Yirritja art and craft.[14] The trepangers were banned from colonial Australian waters in 1906, severing trade and cultural ties with the Yolgnu. It was not until a 1988 Bicentennial project when a *prau* named *Hati Marege* sailed into northern Australia that contact was re-established and ongoing joint activities mounted.[15]

The other indigenous Australians, the Torres Strait Islanders, probably settled the northern waters around 3000 years ago. They are a Melanesian, seafaring people who also hunted and cultivated their lands and were effectively a cultural bridge between what is now Papua New Guinea and the mainland inhabitants of Cape York and, perhaps, further inland. As far as we know, these contacts were primarily for trade, ceremony and occasional warfare. The first European settlement in the Torres Strait region was in 1863, though Dutch and Portuguese ships threaded their way through from at least the early seventeenth century, often seeking a passage to the Pacific Ocean.[16]

Terra Australis was still undiscovered by Europeans in the fifteenth century, though a map showing the landmass was printed in 1483. Five years later the Portuguese navigator Bartolomeu Dias (Bartholomew Diaz) rounded the Cape of Good Hope. As far as is known, he was the first person to do so. This opened the way for European navigators to explore the mysterious southern seas that lay beyond Africa. But the southern continent would not appear to explorers, even partially, for more than another 120 years. Unless the fantastic story of the voyage of the *Espoir* and its long aftermath can be believed.

The French claim

On 24 June 1503 the Norman noble and navigator Binot Paulmier de Gonneville sailed from the port of Honfleur aboard the *Espoir*. With a well-equipped ship and sixty seasoned crewmen, de Gonneville had also taken the trouble to include two Portuguese merchants among the company. They were there for trade, of course, but were also thought to possess the best intelligence about trade routes to the Indies as these had been pioneered by the Portuguese Vasco da Gama six years earlier.

The French sailed for the Cape of Good Hope, reaching its approximate latitude after five months. The ship was subsequently caught in a massive storm that blew unabated for three weeks. It was not until just before Christmas that the weather-beaten seafarers were able to take stock of their position in calmer, but unknown waters. In search of fresh water for their depleted supplies, de Gonneville followed the path of migrating seabirds south towards what he hoped would be a landing. Shortly after New Year's Day of 1504, the *Espoir* sighted land. They sailed up a large river into a lush green tropical region where they came upon a band of local inhabitants.

The French had no idea who these people were. They wore skins, woven reed garments and down cloaks. The men sported feathers in their hair, while the women wore bone and shell necklaces. Fortunately they were friendly.

De Gonneville and his men soon developed amicable relations with them, assisted by the trade goods they had brought in their ship, such as fabrics, jewellery, mirrors, knives, axes and scythes. The 'Indians', as they called these people, had never seen Europeans and were completely unfamiliar with metals, paper and most other items of European civilisation, including firearms. Their leader was a noble individual named Arosca, who ruled over a scattered kingdom of small hut villages inhabited by thirty to sixty people, all within a day or so's journey from the river. There were other tribes in the general vicinity, and Arosca and his people were in a state of more or less perpetual conflict with one of these. Arosca invited the French to join his warriors in battle with their enemies, though de Gonneville wisely declined.

The newcomers soon found that the country was not only lush, but rich in wildlife, much of it 'never before seen in all of Christendom', as the *Espoir*'s scholar, Master Nicole de Fevre, described them. And it was Christendom to which the French annexed this strange new land and its people.

After establishing a basic pidgin and sign language form of communication, de Gonneville determined to demonstrate the greatness of the Christian faith to the inhabitants of this land. He had a large cross constructed from the wooden spars of his ship, currently under repair by his men. Thirty-five feet high, this vividly painted cross was erected at Easter in a spot from where it would be visible from the sea. De Fevre had an inscription prepared for the cross, which gave the date and the names of all the *Espoir*'s crew, preceded of course by those of the pope, the king of France and de Gonneville. The ritual was witnessed by the Indians who, de Gonneville claimed, also participated enthusiastically, perhaps impressed by the celebrations that went with the erection, which included the firing of the *Espoir*'s cannon and her sailors' small arms.

After this observance of Christ's crucifixion and resurrection, the French continued repairing their ship, completing the task less than three months later. It was time to return home, bearing news of strange new lands with potentially untold riches for trade and colonisation. But Arosca wanted more than just a fond farewell. He and his people had been mightily impressed by the armaments of the French and wished to procure the technology for use in their ongoing warfare. To this end, he requested that de Gonneville take his sixteen-year-old son, Essomeric, back to France so that he could learn the secrets of this wondrous new way of killing people.

Promising to return with Essomeric in 'twenty moons' (months), de Gonneville sailed on 3 July 1504. Amid gift-giving and, according to de Gonneville, the Indians all making the sign of the cross in farewell, the *Espoir* left for home.

The journey took eleven months, during which some of the crew and Essomeric's Indian companion, Namoa, died of fever. Essomeric also fell ill and the French offered him baptism into the Christian faith, believing that if he died his soul would be saved, an offer Essomeric accepted on 14 September. At the same time, de Gonneville adopted Essomeric and gave him the name Binot Paulmier.

Miraculously, the French wrote in their journals, Essomeric recovered from the deadly fever and the *Espoir* struggled on through unknown watery wastes. After three months, they sighted land and went ashore for water and supplies, only to be attacked by 'cannibals' who clearly had previous experience of firearms. The natives feigned friendship until the sailors went ashore, attacking them as they refilled their water containers. Three of the crew died there and four wounded men escaped to the ship. One of the wounded escapees was Nicole de Fevre, who did not survive.

The *Espoir* continued her perilous voyage for some weeks, again seeking food and water ashore among hostile natives. This time, however, they were prepared for trouble and succeeded in bartering for their needs without violence. The Frenchmen and their Indian companion crossed the equator in early February 1505, reaching the Azores in early March. Here, the ship was recaulked, then sailed for Ireland.

After spending some time there, the *Espoir* made for France but on 7 May was attacked by pirate ships—one English and one French—near the Channel Islands. The *Espoir* was well equipped with arms and soldiers trained to use them. She made a spirited defence but, outnumbered, was forced to run for the nearest island coast, foundering there with the loss of another sixteen crew.

The survivors were assisted by the islanders but the *Espoir* was plundered then broken up and sunk, together with all records of her voyage, including the drawings and examples of the wildlife and natural features of the new land they had lived on for six months.

De Gonneville and the survivors managed to reach their home port of Honfleur a few weeks later. They were welcomed, but required to appear before the admiralty court two months later in order to explain the loss of their vessel. The records of this court became the only surviving account of this remarkable voyage. It remained secret, and therefore unknown, for a century or more, until an even stranger consequence occurred.

After the admiralty court proceedings, de Gonneville was faced with a dilemma. He had lost all the charts and related navigational information that could take him back to the great south land he believed he had discovered. What was to become of Essomeric? Unable to keep his promise to return Arosca's son, de Gonneville instead provided Essomeric with a substantial property and arranged his marriage to a suitable local woman. The warrior from *Terra Australis* now became a person of reasonable substance in Normandy, living until 1583. While that might have been the end of this strange story, the legend of Essomeric lived on among his descendants.

More than eighty years after Essomeric's death, the abbott Jean Paulmier, Canon of the Cathedral Church de Pierre in Lisieux, published an astonishing book titled *Memoirs Concerning the Establishment of a Christian Mission to the Third World, Otherwise Known as the Austral Lands: Southern, Antarctic and Unknown.* The author was the great-grandson of Essomeric, and claimed to be 'a Priest Who Is a Native of That Land'. In his book, Paulmier referred to the '*Relation de Gonneville*' and also to the traditions of the land handed down from his great-grandfather. He considered himself to have a hereditary right and obligation to bring about the Christianisation of his ancestral people. Such was the impact of this work that in 1666 the pope appointed Jean Paulmier as the official vicar to the Southland, giving it divine representation more than a century before the First Fleet arrived.

Recent research on the de Gonneville story, especially the alleged descendants of Essomeric, has concluded that it was probably a hoax designed to stimulate plans for French imperial expansion. If so, it was successful.[17] The story lingered for generations, inspiring continuing French interest in what might lie at the southern extremity of the globe.

Further fantabulations

Paulmier's work, eventually translated into English, stirred a broader interest in the uncharted southern continent, leading ultimately to the voyage of James Cook. While both de Gonneville's and Paulmier's claims about discovering the Southland in 1504 were dismissed by some later historians, one man, a French immigrant to Australia named Marin la Meslée (1852–93), believed that they were true. More importantly, he believed he had proved it so.

La Meslée's theory was based on the discovery of Aboriginal rock paintings and a giant carved head in the rocks of the Kimberley region of north-west Australia. These were found by the explorer George Grey (later Sir), who made an expedition through the then-unmapped Kimberley during 1838. Grey was the first European to behold some of the great treasure trove of ancient Aboriginal rock art that is found mainly in caves across a wide expanse of the north-west. According to la Meslée, one of Grey's renditions of markings on a figure, found painted in the narrow back part of a cave, was evidence of an attempt to write in Latin script. This, he claimed, reinforced de Gonneville's claim that he had sojourned on the Southland for half a year. He bolstered this with another discovery made by Grey of a large head carved in a rock. This very un-Aboriginal form of representation was, according to Grey, unlikely to have been carved with stone implements, the implication being that it had to have been scored with metal tools.

As well as these strange creations, Grey also found lush lands peopled by groups of Aborigines living in small clusters of huts rather than the more basic temporary dwellings usually thought to be erected by the indigenous people. This settlement was built along the banks of a large navigable watercourse in the vicinity of the Glenelg and Prince Regent rivers, very similar to the scene described in the *Relation de Gonneville*. La Meslée argued that these unexpected sightings, together with other scraps of linguistic and physiological evidence, showed that this part of the country was 'Arosca's Land', as discovered and settled by de Gonneville in the early sixteenth century, and so must be the home of the sundered Essomeric, a native Australian stranded at the other end of the world.

Whether de Gonneville had actually discovered and temporarily settled the Southland or not, speculations, fantasies and rumours that such a place had been secretly discovered—by the Dutch, the French, the Spanish, the Portuguese or the English— were whispered in the taverns and sea ports of the known world. Baseless though these fabrications were, they shared some common features. Wherever the Southland might be, it was certain that it would be a strange, unworldly place, inhabited by winged horses and fish. The people who lived there must be equally strange, perhaps being hermaphrodites. One especially persistent stereotype that was to have ongoing consequences for indigenous Australians was the belief that they would have the features of monkeys.

These absurdities were freely circulated through Europe. As well as accounts of real, if inconclusive, voyages such as those of Pedro Fernandez de Quiros[18], the Southland was a favoured location for early travellers' tales, fictions and satires. Jonathan Swift's *Gulliver's*

Travels, first published in 1726, appears to locate the islands of Lilliput and Blefescu in the general vicinity of Van Diemen's Land or, by some estimates, Western Australia. These fictional locations, separated only by a narrow channel, are peopled by minute beings who simply cannot get on with each other and provide foils for Swift's sharp social and political satire on the England and France of his time. Almost a quarter of a century later, *The Travels of Henry Wanton* were published by Zaccaria Seriman. These depict the natives of the Southland as high-living and dandified apes. In 1675 a French writer, Denis Vairasse, published a utopian novel titled *History of the Severites*, located in the western Southland region. This was quickly followed a year later by Gabriel de Foigny's *La Terre Australe Connue* (*The Southern Land Known*). Once again, in this fiction, the west coast was the favoured location, this time for the adventures of a castaway named Jacques Sadeur. According to Sadeur, the beings populating this place were naked hermaphrodites with small breasts growing low on their torsos. Jacques had many adventures, including flying into the sky on the back of a giant bird, called an 'Urg'.

And so it went on as writers continued the literary tradition established by Euhemeris. Speculations and fabrications continued to be written and published in significant numbers, presenting the still largely unknown Southland as a place where strange things happened and where even stranger creatures—and beings—lurked. These tantalising texts existed alongside the sometimes equally fabulous imaginings of mapmakers, contributing to the image of the Southland as a place clouded in myth and legend—if it were even there at all.

The mystery that surrounded the uncharted continent was also reflected in the various names by which it was known. As well as *Terra Australis*, and *Terra Australis Incognita*, it was also called *Boesche* (Beach)[19], 'The Antipodes' by the more geographically minded, and even the 'Great South Land of the Holy Spirit' by the Spanish.[20] There were, of course, also the many variations of 'Southland'. By the seventeenth century, it was being called 'New Holland', as well as several other names derived from contacts with Dutch navigators. When the prosaic James Cook claimed the east coast in 1770, he would just name it 'New South Wales'.

Caravelles and galleons

While the Southland would remain unmapped for a very long time, its real location, shape and size would be slowly revealed over centuries by adventuresome merchant navigators. The Portuguese voyaged to the East Indies, or the Spice Islands, as the islands that make up modern Indonesia were then known. From the 1490s they established trading routes and, in the manner of the time, sought to keep out their competitors by restricting navigational infor-mation. This historical uncertainty has led to a persistent theme in Australian maritime history that the continent was visited by Portuguese mariners as early as the 1520s, sailing as far as what is now South Australia.[21]

The most common version of this theory is that Cristóvão de Mendonça commanded a flotilla of Portuguese ships on a secret voyage to the east coast around the early 1520s. The voyage was kept quiet because the Treaty of Tordesillas, reached in 1494, made a division of the known and unknown world between Spain and Portugal, giving each the right to their own half. Naturally, this was completely disregarded by all other nations. It was even flouted by the Spanish and Portuguese themselves, who habitually trespassed on each other's generous portions. Nevertheless, the imperative for secrecy generated by such an arrangement has provided a fertile basis for conjecture by subsequent historians.

This suggestion, vigorously propounded by some and as robustly countered by others, is founded on the presence of the Portuguese in the trade and colonial machinations of the area. Given that they were the first to enter the southern realms, probably the first

Europeans to pass through the Torres Strait, and they possessed a vast fleet, it is not unfeasible that the Portuguese did come across the Southland. There is certainly a long line of argument that they did, stemming from the industrious Alexander Dalrymple in the 1780s and a number of well-informed historians since.

The evidence provided for the theory is diverse. It includes the maps of the Dieppe school of cartographers, active from the 1540s to the 1560s, possible Portuguese place names, and various artefacts and structures found in Australia, including a swivel gun unearthed on a Darwin beach in 2010. Most recently, the reported discovery in 2014 of what was said to be an image of a kangaroo in a sixteenth-century Portuguese manuscript fired up the controversy once again. These arguments are characteristically convoluted and depend on repositioning or reinterpreting old charts, some of shaky provenance, and a host of circumstantial indications. In the absence of any incontrovertible documentation, none of this evidence has been sufficiently convincing to establish a Portuguese charting or landing. In the space between history and speculation, myth arises.

The well-known story of the Mahogany Ship, said to lie somewhere beneath the sands of Armstrong Bay near Warrnambool, Victoria, goes back to at least the earliest newspaper account in 1847. The area was barely settled at that time, though was visited by whalers and sealers. It also lay on an overland droving route, so Europeans were in at least some contact with the place. It has also been suggested that the story of the Mahogany Ship derived originally from earlier wrecks—probably of whalers or sealers—in the Hopkins River area. Wherever it came from, the Mahogany Ship was seen by many people.

In 1876 a local man, John Mason, wrote a letter to the Melbourne *Argus* detailing what he saw one summer's day thirty years before, while riding from Port Fairy to Warrnambool:

My attention was attracted to the hull of a vessel embedded high and dry in the Hummocks, far above the reach of any tide. It appeared to have been that of a vessel about 100 tons burden, and from its bleached and weather-beaten appearance, must have remained there many years. The spars and deck were gone, and the hull was full of drift sand. The timber of which she was built had the appearance of cedar or mahogany. The fact of the vessel being in that position was well known to the whalers in 1846, when the first whaling station was formed in that neighbourhood, and the oldest natives, when questioned, stated their knowledge of it extended from their earliest recollection. My attention was again directed to this wreck during a conversation with Mr M'Gowan, the superintendent of the Post-office, in 1869, who, on making inquiries as to the exact locality, informed me that it was supposed to be one of a fleet of Portuguese or Spanish discovery ships, one of them having parted from the others during a storm, and was never again heard of. He referred me to a notice of a wreck having appeared in the novel *Geoffrey Hamlyn*, written by Henry Kingsley, in which it is set down as a Dutch or Spanish vessel, and forms the subject of a remark from one of the characters, a doctor, who said that the English should never sneer at those two nations—they were before you everywhere. The wreck lies about midway between Belfast and Warrnambool, and is probably by this time entirely covered with drift sand, as during a search made for it within the last few months it was not to be seen.

Whatever the origins of the tale, it has attracted extensive investigation by historians, archaeologists, treasure hunters and history enthusiasts since it was published. One of the consistent, if controversial, themes in the story has the ship as a Portuguese—sometimes Spanish—caravelle wrecked in the area some considerable time before documented European occupation. It has also been claimed by author Gavin Menzies that the Mahogany Ship is of Chinese origin and that there is a local Aboriginal legend of 'yellow men' coming ashore. The few relatively reliable eyewitness accounts of the wreck before it disappeared beneath the shifting sand dunes suggest that the ship was of an unusual design. This could mean many things, of course, but has also led to a suggestion that it might have been a roughly made craft from a documented Tasmanian convict escape attempt. Until the Mahogany Ship is rediscovered, or an authenticated document indicating contact is found, speculation will continue.

A similar tradition exists on Queensland's Stradbroke Island where the remains of a Spanish galleon are said to be disintegrating in coastal swamplands. The first documented sighting of the high-prowed timber ship dates from the 1860s. A local pilot and lighthouse keeper found the wreck at the southern end of the island and removed its anchor to use as an ornament in his home. His Aboriginal wife then told him of the local indigenous knowledge of the wreck. There were further sightings in the 1880s when the supposition that the mysterious vessel was of Spanish origin began to gain traction. This rapidly became a lost treasure tale and inspired serious searches for the galleon. One group in 1894 claimed to have found the wreck and removed a substantial load of copper fittings from it, but when they tried to find the wreck again, the intriguing structure had disappeared.

Subsequent sightings have either been due to Aboriginal people taking settlers to the site or after bushfires have revealed the smoking timbers through burnt-out vegetation. No sightings have been reported since the 1970s, though there are persistent suggestions that local people possess secret knowledge of the galleon's treasure, fuelling continued searches for the site. One researcher was contacted by an Aboriginal woman who claimed to be descended from the survivors of the wrecked galleon. A 2007 expedition unearthed a corroding coin said to date between the late 1590s and the 1690s.[22]

Mysterious human remains are another source of supposition about pre-1788 European occupation. In 2011 a human skull was found on a riverbank near Taree, New South Wales. Subsequent radio carbon dating established the remains belonged to someone of European origin who may have been born as early as 1650. When these results were reported by the Australian National University in mid-2013, researchers cautioned that the skull may have been the property of a colonial bone collector, or even a hoax. Regardless, suggestions of an earlier European presence on the east coast quickly flowed into the press and social media.[23]

Yarns from local folklore[24] tend to be ignored by academic historians, but they attract serious popular interest and activity. Their number and persistence suggest that there is an intense appeal about the possibility of Australia's pre-1788 European discovery, charting and even settlement.

The Dutch East India Company

While there is a high level of mythmaking in relation to the Dutch presence around and on the Southland, there is also a great deal of reliable historical evidence. Indeed, as with the search of the Spanish and the Portuguese for the fabled lands of gold, the down-to-earth Dutch were also inspired to some degree by the centuries of myth surrounding the uncharted continent. The seamen of the *Verenigde Oostindische Compagnie*—commonly referred to by the initials 'VOC', or called the 'Dutch East India Company'[25]— were a tough and tenacious band. Motivated by both duty to the company and the promise of untold riches as a part of any bounty to come from such perilous voyages, they struck out across the world's little-known oceans, determined to wrest their share, or more, of riches from the newly discovered world. In 1595 Cornelius de Houtman reached the 'East Indies' and three years later the Dutch East India Company was firmly established there.

The VOC was much more than a trading company. It was a mobile empire with extensive legal powers that even enabled it to try, imprison and execute those who incurred the displeasure of the

Grand Herren, or 'Seventeen Gentlemen',[26] who ran it, each representing the regional 'chambers' that made up the enterprise. The company was also able to engage in wars, issue its own currency and found colonies.

Formed in 1602, the VOC was granted a 21-year monopoly on trade and associated activities throughout Asia. Of particular interest were the riches of the Spice Islands or the East Indies, now mainly what is the Republic of Indonesia and East Timor. However, the Portuguese had control of this trade and were not inclined to hand it over. This led to several centuries of conflict between the two colonial powers throughout the region, beginning a decade or more before the foundation of the VOC. Those Dutch ships that did manage to make successful expeditions to the Spice Islands, avoiding or trouncing the Portuguese along the way, returned home with spectacularly profitable cargos of spices and other exotic goods.

Just a year after the VOC began, a permanent Dutch trade settlement was established in the west of Java, at Banten (Bantam). From 1610 to 1619 the company made its headquarters at Ambon (Amboina) but by 1611 had founded Jayakarta, soon to be known as Batavia and the origin of modern-day Jakarta. This was to become the main VOC base for the East Indies.

It was not only the Dutch and Portuguese who coveted the riches of the Spice Islands. The British formed the English East India Company in 1600 and began to send ships there, leading to further conflict. The British established trading bases of their own, sometimes in close proximity to those of the Dutch, and hostilities continued with a brief respite from 1620. This ended with a Dutch massacre of ten English hostages in Amboina three years later. After this, the British gradually changed their focus from the Spice Islands to other parts of Asia. With a few notable exceptions, the British had little further to do with the Southland until the arrival of the First Fleet in 1788.

As part of their doctrine of trade expansion, the Dutch were keen to explore near to the Spice Islands in the hope of discovering further riches. They sent ships around what is now Papua New Guinea to look for trade opportunities and to learn whatever they could from the inhabitants of the strange new lands they found. Judging from the surviving journals of these expeditions, this usually involved attempts at friendly discussion, bestowing of gifts, and the abduction or hostaging of native people with the intention of learning from them about their lands and any tradeable goods these might contain. Not unreasonably, the 'natives' often resisted this treatment and VOC colonial relations were generally characterised by violence and deceit. While the Dutch—and other colonial powers—engaged in these interactions with indigenous people of the lands they sought to plunder, they were also busily mapping the coastlines of their desire.

The first ship we know of that definitely made such a voyage was a small craft named *Duyfken*. We have only some scanty and sometimes murky details of this momentous event, mainly from a surviving map, the first entry in what would become the secret atlas of the Southland.

2

First encounters

The coming of Europeans to the unknown shores of the Southland was a momentous event. For the first recorded time in history the northern descendants of the first humans met the most southern descendants of their common ancestors. Each had been separated from the other for over fifty millennia. These encounters could only have profound consequences.

A little dove

One day between January and March 1606 on the eastern shore of what we now call the Gulf of Carpentaria, an indigenous Australian and a European laid eyes on each other for the first time in history. We will never know who that Aboriginal man was, but the European may have been Willem Jansz, master of the small Dutch vessel known as *Duyfken* ('Little Dove'). In this first contact the Europeans acted in a way that would be repeated many times over succeeding centuries—the Aboriginal man was shot dead. We cannot know the exact circumstances or details of this sadly prophetic encounter, as Jansz's original journal of his historic voyage from Batavia to the northern extremity of the

Southland has long been lost. But there are a number of references to the journal in other archival documents and in a Dutch map that records the charting of the northern coastline carried out by Jansz and his crew.

Built around 1595, the 110-ton *Duyfken* was a fast and nimble craft about 20 metres long and 6 metres broad. She was classed as a *jacht*, lightly armed with eight cannon and usually crewed by fewer than twenty sailors. Just after the Christmas of 1601, she was among a fleet of five Dutch ships which attacked and dispersed a Portuguese force six times their number at Banten (Bantam) in Java. The Dutch were now in possession of the highly desirable Spice Islands and when the *Verenigde Oostindische Compagnie* (VOC), or Dutch East India Company, was formed later that year, they already had a fleet conveniently on the spot.

Duyfken returned to the Netherlands with a rich cargo of spices in 1603 and in December that year sailed south again with another VOC fleet. After several encounters with the Portuguese, *Duyfken* reached Banten again on New Year's Eve and more fighting with the Portuguese followed. Later, in 1605, Jansz and his men were directed to voyage towards the Southland.

On 18 October 1605, John Saris, an agent of the rival British East India Company, made a careful note of the *Duyfken*'s departure and return from Banten, no doubt to furnish the intelligence of Dutch shipping movements to his mercantile masters. In the early seventeenth century, this part of the world was a busy trade territory ferried by Dutch, British and Portuguese craft, all intent on locating and exploiting whatever resources might be found in the East Indies and beyond. The potential prizes were enormous riches and competition was accordingly cut-throat.

Probably in his mid-thirties, Jansz was an experienced Indies skipper and well versed in the VOC's primary mission. His orders were to seek trading possibilities in New Guinea and any other lands to the east and south. After some months sailing around

New Guinea and the many islands in the region, Jansz landed on Southland on 26 February 1606, at what is now called the Pennefather River on the western coast of Cape York.[1]

While we do not have Jansz's own account of his voyage, further intelligence of the *Duyfken*'s doings during her eight-month absence was provided by Captain John Saris, from the information of a Tamil sailor trading through Banda. According to Saris, the 'Flemming's Pinnasse', as he called the *Duyfken*, had landed in search of natives 'to intreate of Trade' but had been greeted with armed defiance and nine of the intruders were 'killed by the Heathens' who were also, it was claimed, 'man-eaters'. Apparently, the *Duyfken* men decided that discretion was the better part of valour and, as they had seen no tradeable commodities or exploitable resources while ashore—'finding no good to be done there'—returned to the safety of their ship.[2] Whether or not all these men died during the same encounter is unclear from Saris's espionage report. It seems more likely that there were a number of confrontations in what is now Papua New Guinea, as well as others on the Southland shore. But at least one European sailor bled out his life here, and it is thought that this encounter took place on the Pennefather River, making this a significant historical site.[3]

That was not the last fatal encounter of the inaptly named 'Little Dove' and her crew with the inhabitants of the Southland. On the return voyage they landed once again, or attempted to, probably near the Wenlock River. Here, the *Duyfken* was attacked by Aborigines who speared one crewman to death. This incident was recounted in the journal of a later voyager, Jan Carstensz in the *Pera*. He had seen or been told the contents of Jansz's original report, and he would note in passing that the blacks he met were already familiar with muskets and the death they dealt.[4]

The visit of the *Duyfken*[5] had left its ineradicable mark on indigenous Australia and is still remembered in the oral traditions of the Wik people. According to these accounts, the Dutch were first sighted north of the Kirke River. They describe the wooden wind-ship—which they believed to be *Duyfken*—as 'a big mob of logs'[6] and their sailors as 'devils'.[7] The Dutch came ashore and began digging. The Aborigines wanted to know what the strangers were doing on their land. Through sign language it was understood the Dutch wanted water. They showed the Aborigines how to use the metal tools they had for this job and recruited them as labour to dig a well. They also taught them how to smoke tobacco, bake damper, make tea and shoot ducks. The Aborigines eventually decided that the strangers were *onya*, or malevolent nuisances, an impression reinforced when they either stole two women, or after having been made a gift of them—a hospitality custom at the time—detained them too long. Eventually, when the Dutch climbed back into one of the numerous wells they were digging with the help of the local people, the warriors waited until last, jumped in on top of the luckless sailors and killed them. This sparked a battle during which a number of Wik men were shot and some of the incomers speared. The Dutch retreated to their ship and sailed away, quite possibly with difficulty as they had now lost several crewmen. The Wik disposed of the Dutch bodies and, presumably, their own dead.[8]

In one version or another, this story remains in oral tradition as an historical account of the repulsion of the incursions of the *Duyfken* in 1606, which it may well be. It could also relate to the visit by Carstensz and his sailors aboard the *Pera* seventeen years later. Before that voyage, though, there would be some other momentous incidents in the early European discovery of the uncharted continent. The next of these was to remain secret to most of the world for more than 150 years.

Early voyagers

A few months after Jansz was beating *Duyfken* along the coasts of Carpentaria, a Galician mariner working for the Spanish crown accomplished another significant deed. Luis Vaez de Torres, commanding the ships *San Pedro* and *Los Trey Reyes*, made a passage between New Guinea and what is now Cape York Peninsula. At that time it was thought New Guinea and Australia were joined together and so there was no access to the Pacific Ocean. De Torres, by some careful navigation, threaded his way through the confusion of islands and reefs between Australia and New Guinea, though it took him several months. On either 2 or 3 October 1606, de Torres' passage through what is now known as Endeavour Strait would have brought him in sight of the mainland. Despite noting 'very large islands, and more to the south', de Torres does not appear to have realised that this was the long-fabled southern continent. He sailed on, claiming New Guinea for the King of Spain, then continued to Manila. From here, de Torres disappears from history, though his records of the voyage were secreted carefully away until eventually uncovered to play a part in the revelation of the Southland.

As Spain was one of the competitors in the grand game of trade and colonisation that the known world was playing, it had a strong motive for not making de Torres' achievement widely known. His discovery of the passage between New Guinea and Australia did not become general knowledge until Captain James Cook sailed through the same passage. Alexander Dalrymple, the eminent Admiralty hydrographer, had initiated Cook's expedition largely in response to his own unearthing of de Torres' hitherto unknown voyage. Some time in the early to mid 1760s, Dalrymple found de Torres' account of his voyage in Spanish archives captured in the Philippines several years earlier. He finally published his researches and speculations in 1770, the year Captain James Cook sailed through the Torres Strait after charting and claiming the entire eastern seaboard for the British crown.[9]

Today, courtesy of Dalrymple, the passage bears the name of its original European discoverer, as do the islands that are home to Australia's other indigenous people, the Torres Strait Islanders. De Torres did make violent contact with the 'very corpulent' peoples of the region: 'Moors', as he called them in the language of the day. He fought with them and even managed to abduct 'twenty persons of different nations' from the islands. But he seems not to have touched upon the mainland, despite sighting the hills of Cape York. For the Spanish, this enigmatic landmass remained the Great South Land of the Holy Spirit and still unknown.

But it was no longer completely unknown to the Dutch—these enterprising adventurers had found a new route to the riches they believed lay waiting for them. In 1610 to 1611 Hendrik Brouwer discovered a new—and fast—way to reach the Spice Islands. Until then, the coast-hugging routes taken by the Arabs and the Portuguese followed the east coast of Africa from the Cape of Good Hope and sailed to Java across the Indian Ocean, sometimes via India. Instead, Brouwer sailed 4000 miles southwards straight into the unknown ocean. Powered by the westerly winds known as the 'Roaring Forties', he then swung east and headed for the Sunda Strait with a direct run into the main port of Batavia (modern Jakarta) on the island of Java.[10] Brouwer's route was twice as fast, and took only six months, not the usual twelve; the shorter passage also killed far fewer of the crew from scurvy, plague and other maladies common on long sea voyages.

Within a few years VOC ships were regularly plying this route, bringing materials and vast amounts of money to support the company's trading operations. Brouwer's outstanding feat of navigation gave the VOC a major advantage over their competitors and so, from 1617, all company ships were required to sail this way rather than any of the other Dutch routes to Java. The new course took the VOC ships well towards the western coast of the Southland. With the relatively basic navigational methods and instruments of the day, it was only a matter of time before a navigator or master would miscalculate the complexities of wind, wave and longitude, leading to unscheduled contact with the continent. Some of those contacts were straightforward landings on unknown shores. Others were catastrophic. But all would have consequences up to the present day.

The first known contact on the western shores was in many ways almost humdrum, though as far as we know, it was the first time a European walked on that side of the continent. It was also the first authenticated example of a structure erected on the Southland as a deliberate record left behind for later mariners.

Dirk Hartog was born into a family of Dutch seafarers in 1580, commanding his first ship at the age of thirty. Later he purchased a vessel of his own and began a successful series of trading voyages around the Baltic and Mediterranean seas. He joined the VOC in 1615, shipping out to the Indies as master of the *Eendracht* early the next year. After a difficult voyage to the Cape of Good Hope, Hartog followed the Roaring Forties across the Indian Ocean. On 25 October 1616, he sighted land between 22 and 26 degrees latitude south by the navigational reckoning of the time (actually 25 degrees south), anchoring near an island in an expansive sound. Naming the island and the waters around it after himself—and the mainland beyond after his ship—Hartog then had a pewter plate flattened and inscribed with a brief message:

> *On the 25th of October, 1616, arrived here the ship Endraght, of Amsterdam; the first merchant, Gilles Mibais Van Luyck; Captain Dirck Hartog, of Amsterdam; the 27th ditto set sail for Bantam; undermerchant, Jan Stoyn; upper steersman, Pieter Dockes, from Bil. Anno 1616.*

The plate was nailed to a wooden post and left on the island now bearing his name.

After two days of exploring, Hartog and his crew found little to interest them or their masters and made no contact with the indigenous inhabitants. They continued on to Banten, charting the coast along the way and arriving five months late with little to show for a very lengthy voyage.

A year later, not surprisingly perhaps, Hartog left the VOC and resumed trading for himself in the Baltic. He died in 1621 but the pewter plate he caused to be made and stood upright at the end of the known world is his enduring legacy.

The following year, another navigator made his second contact with the southern continent. This man was returning aboard the VOC ship *Mauritius*, as recorded in his letter: 'On the 31st of July we discovered an island and landed on the same, where we found the marks of human footsteps: on the west side it extends N.N.E. and S.S.W.; it measures 15 miles in length, and its northern extremity is in 22 deg. S. lat. It bears S.S.E. and N.N.W. from the south point of Sunda at 240 miles distance.'[11]

So wrote Willem Jansz as he once again walked on the Southland, either at Exmouth Gulf or, as more recent research suggests, at Yardie Creek on the Northwest Cape peninsula.[12]

Jansz was considerably elevated in status since his previous visit as master of the tiny *Duyfken*. He was now a chief merchant and stayed only long enough to name a river after himself (probably now the Ashburton River). He apparently had no contact with the local inhabitants whose presence he simply noted in his journal. It seems likely that he became yet more eminent in his subsequent career, probably being appointed Governor of Banda in 1623 and serving in that capacity until his retirement six years later.

Neither Jansz nor the master of the VOC ship *Zeewolf*, which also sighted the Southland north of Exmouth in 1618, had very much of consequence to report. The following year, though, Frederick de Houtman, out from Cape Town in the *Dordrecht*, encountered land at the most southerly point then recorded. He sailed north along the western shores from somewhere around present-day Perth. He and the ship accompanying him, the *Amsterdam*, almost ended up on a group of shoals and islands extending far off the coast. After naming these the Houtman Abrolhos, a place that would feature prominently in later shipwreck sagas, the navigators passed the site of Hartog's earlier landfall[13] and continued uneventfully to Batavia.

Cruising back home was not to be the case with the next group of Europeans to find themselves on some of the Southland's many treacherous reefs and bare islands.

The lost reef

It was an hour or more before midnight on 25 May 1622. The weather was fair and the sea smooth. In the dark emptiness of the Indian Ocean, the English East India Company ship *Tryall* ploughed confidently north-east for the western shores of Java. She was on her maiden voyage, leaving Plymouth on 4 September 1621, bound for Batavia via the Cape of Good Hope. Under the command of Captain John Brookes (sometimes Brooke), she was following in the wake of Captain Humfry Fitzherbert's voyage of a few years earlier in which Fitzherbert had pioneered the English use of Brouwer's new route to the Indies. Brookes had never sailed to Batavia, nor had any of his officers. He tried to recruit sailors with Spice Islands experience during his stopover in Cape Town but, sensibly, none wished to join him, so he relied on his copy of Fitzherbert's journal for a safe voyage. Confident there was no danger, Brookes had failed to post a lookout.

Suddenly, in what appeared to be mid-ocean with 'neyther beach, land, rocks, change of watter nor signe of danger'[14], the wooden ship splintered into partly submerged rocks. Brookes and many of his crew were 'in such a mayze' that their ship had run aground, but the heaving of a sounding lead showed they were in only three fathoms of water. They were, in fact, on the western coast of the Southland.

The master of the stricken vessel cried to his men to tack to the west—'they did ther beste, but ye rock being sharpe ye ship was presentlie full of water'. Confirming that the *Tryall* was firmly snared on jagged rocks with no chance of refloating, the crew readied the longboat and the skiff. With the wind increasing and heavy seas smashing over and into the stricken *Tryall,* it took them hours to load the boats with as many supplies as they could. The two boats finally got off the wreck about four in the morning, rowing desperately for 'a little low Iland . . . seven leags to ye SE warde of ye place where ye ship was Cast awae', and where she was now beginning to disintegrate in the pounding waves. Barely half-an-hour after the boats left her, the bow of the *Tryall* broke up. Ninety-three—perhaps more[15]—of her crew were abandoned to the ocean and only forty-six sailors in the boats survived the wrecking. Now they were stranded off an unknown coast with a few barrels of water, some of alcohol and about 8 pounds of bread between them.

Brookes, together with his 'boye' and nine crewmen, was in a skiff, possibly carrying some of the ship's silver cargo. Thirty-six others, including a man named Thomas Bright, who would play a part in revealing the cause of the wreck, found themselves crammed into the remaining longboat. The boats made their way separately to Batavia. One man died in the skiff, which arrived at its destination on 25 June. The longboat landed on the Montebello Islands in search of water and reached safety a few days after the captain's skiff with all accounted for. No one knows the fate of the ninety or so left behind.

Although the *Tryall* survivors mostly made it to safety, that was not the end of the saga. For centuries after the disaster, the 'Tryall Rocks', as they became known, disappeared. Mariners searched for them in vain, keen to accurately locate the dangerous shoals for the safety of future shipping. But they could not be found.

Ships of the Dutch East India Company had already come perilously close to foundering in the general area of the Tryall Rocks. There was considerable concern by the Dutch, as well as the English, to locate and chart this danger. Various voyagers were tasked to look for the rocks. But despite being marked on Dutch and English charts for centuries, the elusive obstacles were never seen again. When Matthew Flinders could not locate the obtrudances during his much later epic voyage around Australia, the British admiralty decided that they did not exist.

But in 1818 the brig *Greyhound* encountered a group of small islands that became known as Ritchie's Rocks, after the ship's captain. These were, of course, the missing Tryall Rocks, though it was not until 1840 that the rocks were accurately charted in their true location between the Montebello Islands and Barrow Island. And it would not be until 1934 that some determined historical investigations confirmed that Ritchie's Rocks were indeed the Tryall Rocks.[16]

Why did it take almost 300 years to locate a significant danger to navigation off the Western Australian coast? The answer to the mystery lies in the character and behaviour of the *Tryall*'s captain, John Brookes.

The loss of a brand new vessel was a major financial blow to the English East India Company. Brookes was in deep trouble as the company wanted to know who or what was to blame for their loss. He was required to present his charts and documents and to make a full report. These concentrated on the technical and navigational details of the *Tryall*'s voyage and the subsequent survival passage to Batavia. (No one was very concerned about the ninety-or-so souls who had, probably, perished on the wreck.[17]) Questions were raised: Was Brookes following the course laid down by Fitzherbert? Or had he recklessly endangered his ship and crew by taking some adventurous course? Perhaps he was merely, if murderously, incompetent?

Knowing that he was damned by whatever answer was forthcoming, Brookes simply falsified his position. He claimed to have faithfully followed Fitzherbert's course by sailing north-easterly, so implying that the earlier navigator had only narrowly missed the rocks that sank the *Tryall*. It was, according to him, just bad luck.

At the time, it seems that none of the survivors contradicted this fiction so Brookes was exonerated and given another command. But in an extant letter from the *Tryall*'s first mate, Thomas Bright, the survivor is clear that the wreck was due to Brookes' negligence in not posting a watch that night. Worse, Bright also claims that in the desperate hours of escape from the disintegrating hulk, Brookes threw overboard any papers that would incriminate him or otherwise contradict his story. He also accused the captain of stealing and, worst of all in such extreme circumstances, of betraying his men, 'like a Judasse'. According to Bright, although Brookes promised the sailors loading the escape boats that he would take them with him, he waited for a moment when they were distracted and launched the skiff with only nine men 'and his boye', abandoning the rest and making for the Sunda Strait without waiting to see 'the lamentable end of ship the tyme shee splitt'.

The consequence of Brookes' perfidy was the long failure to accurately locate Tryall Rocks. The troublesome navigator was subsequently sent on an exploratory voyage to Sumatra and then given command of the worm-eaten *Moon*. He sailed her back to England but lost her and her valuable cargo of spices almost within sight of Dover—perhaps on purpose, as originally charged by the company. After years of legal disputation, including appeals to the House of Commons by Brookes and to the House of Lords by the English East India Company, the mariner was bankrupted. He submitted a petition craving the company's pardon in return for their dropping proceedings and was released from the company and the charges in August 1626, passing into the oblivion of history's frauds and failures.

The wreckage of the *Tryall* remained hidden, battered by sea and wind for another 300 years. Then, in 1969, a group of skin-divers from Perth found cannon, anchors and other artefacts. One member of the group had previously been involved with excavations on the *Zuytdorp* and *Vergulde Draeck* wreck sites. He was accused of conducting illegal dives on the wreck, causing considerable damage through the use of gelignite and removing several artefacts including a bronze gun. This colourful character, Alan Robinson, was arrested and although acquitted of the charges, subsequently became a notorious local media celebrity dubbed 'the gelignite buccaneer'. After later claims of Spanish, Chinese and Phoenician visitors to the Southland, Robinson eventually hanged himself in prison while awaiting the verdict on a murder charge. But his treasure hunting called into question the power of the Western Australian shipwreck protection legislation and this was subsequently strengthened through Commonwealth regulation.

Later expeditions were mounted by members of the Western Australian Maritime Museum to confirm the exact identity of the wreck. The evidence was ambivalent, but it is generally accepted today that the wreckage is that of John Brookes' ill-fated command. Expeditions and surveys have discovered cannon, anchors, lead shot and sheeting, as well as granite ballast. The *Tryall*'s inglorious end was an early episode in the long story of finding the Southland and of rendering its mysteries and treacheries on parchment, vellum and paper.

The secret atlas

The most valued possessions of the early navigators were their charts. Even more than their crude navigational instruments, well-drawn representation of the location and maritime conditions of those places to and from which they travelled were indispensable tools of the trade. They were also carefully safeguarded intellectual property of the governments and private concerns involved in colonising the far corners of the globe. It was said that the Portuguese forbade the export of charts of southern waters on pain of death.[18] The French captain Gédéon Nicolas de Voutron made the same claim against the Dutch in 1699: 'The Dutch fear that another nation will take them [the southern lands] over …

they have forbidden their pilots on pain of death to make maps of them, or to tell foreigners about them.'[19]

The knowledge coded into these documents was the basis for significant investments of wealth, manpower and other resources. All navigators were therefore charged with charting their discoveries and returning that knowledge to their masters. The VOC was especially adept at this aspect of the business, and at keeping their knowledge confidential, but they were not alone. The Portuguese, Spanish, French and British also maintained extensive archives of navigational and geographic information in charts that were constantly being drawn and redrawn into ever more detailed representations of the known and the unknown world as new details came to hand from the logs and journals of returning voyagers.

This 'secret atlas'[20] still exists but can now only be pieced together by reference to a large number of charts held in libraries, archives and private collections around the world. What were once the workaday tools of navigators, explorers and their masters are now valuable works of art, traded between museums, archives, libraries and wealthy private collectors. Some have been lost, some are inaccurate, others incomprehensible. A few are almost certainly fakes. But through them it is possible to trace the slow yet persistent revelation of the true size, shape and location of the Southland.

From antiquity, cartographers of the Greek and Islamic cultures had been drawing maps of the world that included some reference to a mysterious southern continent. A map made by Muhammad ibn Musa al-Khwarizmi in 820AD is said to include the Sea of Java, Cape York Peninsula, the Gulf of Carpentaria and Arnhem Land, details that also appear in a later work by Abu Isak Al-Farisi Istakhari dated at 934AD. If these maps are indeed of the northern coast of Australia, obtained by unidentified ancient voyagers, then the knowledge was either kept secret from Christendom or was lost.

A map made in 1547 by Nicolas Vallard is sometimes said to be the first partial representation of a sizeable section of the eastern Australian coastline. Vallard followed what is known as the 'Dieppe School' of French mapmaking, a movement strongly influenced by Portuguese discoveries. If, as argued by some, the Portuguese did reach the Southland as early as claimed, Vallard's map could be the result of such a voyage. But historians are generally sceptical on Portuguese claims and if the depictions of the peoples of the land included with the map are even faintly based on authentic accounts, they suggest south Asia and perhaps New Guinea rather than Australia.

In 1570 a map by Abraham Ortelius (1527–98) was published his *Theatrum Orbis Terrarum*, or 'Theatre of the World', which depicted *Terra Australis Nondum Cognita* as a gigantic continent that occupied almost the entire lower third of the globe. It showed barely any detailed geographical features and ran from New Guinea, across the then-unexplored Pacific Ocean, to South America. This expansive portrayal seems to have been derived from information brought back to Europe by early sixteenth-century travellers, such as Marco Polo, and harked back to ideas about the Southland held since antiquity.

The players in this great game employed censorship to keep their sailing secrets safe from rivals. A map prepared for the 1598 publication of an account of Cornelis de Houtman's discovery of a route to the Spice Islands was withheld by order of the authorities because it carried valuable commercial information about Java and Sumatra. It is also thought to mention the *Duyfken*, eight or nine years before her historic voyage to northern Australia.[21]

By the time VOC ships began to appear in the Spice Islands, it was widely recognised that if there was a landmass in the Antipodes, it was not as expansive as Ortelius had depicted just a quarter of a century earlier. These regions were reasonably well known by then. The real mystery was what lay to the south. If a bold captain navigated his ship along the shores of 'Nova Guinea', would he discover a passage through to the Pacific Ocean, founder upon the Southland itself, or face unknowable terrors of some fatal kind?

According to standard VOC orders, Willem Jansz charted the shores along which he sailed for some 320 kilometres in 1606. His voyage produced the first known European representation of the southern continent, as opposed to the speculations and fantasies that had been the standard depiction since antiquity. The chart contributed to Hessel Gerritsz's famous 1622 map of the Pacific Ocean, the first to include a view of the Southland by someone who had actually been there. Gerritsz was the first official VOC cartographer. Together with a host of helpers, his job was to bring together the drawings and notes of VOC captains into usable charts to further the company's trade. Charts, logs and related documents produced on all VOC voyages were gathered together in the East India House in Amsterdam. Here, they were organised, filed and pored over by mapmakers seeking the latest knowledge of the many regions in which the company had interests. When a voyage was planned, a VOC ship was provided with thirty to fifty charts, globes and usually detailed navigation instructions. These maps and the information they encoded were what we would today call the 'core intellectual property' of the VOC and their 'commercial-in-confidence' status was carefully protected.

Before the mast, behind the mast

All these documented contacts with the Southland, and possibly some or many of which we know nothing, contributed to the gradual revelation of its contours, conundrums and secrets. Despite the puzzlements of indigenous ways, we read more about their lifestyle than those of the European sailors who first crewed their vessels of trade and discovery to alien shores. The bare names of ships, their captains and of places on maps conceal the reality of daily life aboard a VOC sailing craft. The command structure and the conditions in which crew and officers lived—or not—for many months were part of a carefully crafted mechanism designed to move men and materials from one end of the globe to the other and, hopefully, back again. This machine was expected to bring the riches of the Antipodes back to Europe via Amsterdam, filling the already stuffed coffers of the company ever higher and continually returning stratospheric dividends to shareholders. But ideal though the design of the machine might be, it was still run by humans with their many needs, prejudices and desires. On a VOC sailing ship, these played out in a theatre determined by one's position before or behind the mast.

The hierarchy of Dutch vessels was designed to bring the trading interests and maritime necessities into a single unit. Until 1742 the highest authority on a VOC ship was not the master or captain, but the *opperkoopman* (senior- or upper-merchant), sometimes referred to as the 'super-cargo'. This person was usually a senior merchant within the VOC. Another merchant assisted the upper-merchant, with responsibilities for recording business conducted on the ship or off it. This individual was also considered a major officer. The officers had cabins 'behind the mast', along with the ship's surgeon, reverend and any official guests or paying customers.

A VOC captain was supposedly skilled in the highest arts of the sea and the ways to navigate it. Many were. But some were seemingly unable to make sensible decisions. Equally skilled, sometimes more so, in seafaring was the upper-steersman or first mate and, depending on the size of the ship, perhaps a second or even a third steersman. A sensible master would consult with one or more of these colleagues before taking serious sailing decisions. Some of the notable VOC shipwrecks were a consequence of a failure to do so or of the master simply ignoring the sound advice he had received.

The chief merchant, assistant merchant, master, upper-steersman and *hoogbootsman* (in charge of the sailors' labour and therefore a petty officer) constituted the ship's council. When important decisions were needed, the council met and discussed options or conducted disciplinary proceedings if required. Towards the end of the seventeenth century, merchants less frequently travelled with VOC ships and were replaced on the council by another officer. When soldiers were tried, the highest ranking military man took the place of the upper-steersman and the *hoogbootsman*. Discipline was rigid and punishments, dictated by the company, were brutal. Mutiny, murder and sodomy were punishable by death, sometimes by the method of marooning on a deserted island or distant shore. Other punishments ranged from large fines through incarceration, flogging, branding, running the gauntlet and keel-hauling, during which the victim was dragged beneath the barnacle-encrusted ship's keel, an agonising trauma that could easily end in death. Such punishments were carried out by the provost, an official with responsibility for order and, when required, torture. The provost was often assisted by the ship's quartermaster, the two forming an effective disciplinary unit that frequently oppressed the common sailors, as might the assistant merchant or the *bottelier* in charge of food and water.

The captain was bound by the decisions of the ship's council, at least in theory. Captains were known to defy the decisions of the council and in an emergency would often exercise ultimate authority. An incident during an attack on a VOC ship in 1622 resulted in the captain and senior merchant issuing the sailors with contradictory orders. The crew did as the captain told them—fortunately, as they survived. The captain also determined almost every other aspect of the sailors' daily lives, including rations and entertainments.

Before the mast, in the least comfortable part of the ship, was the crew's domain, and that of the soldiers and petty officers.

Stationed aboard ships of sufficient size was usually a detachment of VOC soldiers under the joint command of the upper-merchant and the master. A group of sixty or more soldiers was usually commanded by a sergeant, while smaller groups were in the charge of a corporal.

Sailors lived and laboured largely separate from soldiers, who did not work on board, one cause of the strong resentment between the two groups. This tension was often reinforced through ethnic and religious conflicts, especially between Lutherans, Calvinists and Roman Catholics. The only form of religious observance approved by the VOC was Calvinism. Others were tolerated but religious disputes were subject to harsh penalties, perhaps a reason why they were relatively few.

Aboard ship, sailors belonged to small groups of six or seven men called *baks*. Members ate at their own table and had a *bakmeester* to allocate supplies. Breakfast could be porridge and prunes. Lunch often consisted of peas, beans, salt meat, fish and bread. Dinner could be whatever was left. These basics were supplemented with half a pound of butter and 5 pounds of bread or the hard, dry lump of flour and water known as ship's biscuit when the bread ran out. Water and beer were provided each day, though after a while would be laden with insects and worms that had to be strained out through a man's teeth. While it was available, officers were served with fresh meats and vegetables. As fresh food ran out, even with the supplement of the vegetable gardens kept aboard many ships, scurvy and related diseases flourished.

Ship's boys performed menial duties for the *bak*, such as cleaning up after meals, though were apparently not usually part of a *bak* due to their age and inexperience. Sailors were organised into watches of seven, known as 'quarters'. In these groupings they worked shifts of four hours on and four hours off, ate and slept together, and often operated together as a unit when ashore.

When the master allowed it, sailors entertained themselves through music making, gambling (despite its illegality), horseplay, board games such as checkers (draughts), sometimes chess and smoking tobacco. The very few accounts of shipboard life at this time suggest that it included extensive black markets in food and other items, even books, along with theft from sailors and any passengers, sometimes of a serious and organised kind. Soldiers and sailors were allowed to take a single chest of exotic eastern goods on the return trip to the Netherlands, providing further opportunities for small-scale trade and barter. It seems that these restrictions were regularly flouted.

VOC ships are estimated to have formed between 30 and 60 per cent of their crews from 'nationalities' other than Dutch, the higher figures especially around the mid-1600s and again after 1740. Most of the surprisingly few mutinies aboard VOC vessels were carried out by men of non-Dutch extraction.[22]

A retourschip, then, was often little more than a floating mob, with assault, theft, bullying, extortion and even rape not unusual. While the voyage was going reasonably well, order was maintained by the officers and rigid discipline. If things went badly, muttering soon arose and could lead to tense, sometimes violent, confrontations between the crew and their officers. One reason why there were not more mutinies may have been that crews became too depleted or ill to take action, much as some might have wished they could. But if the command structure did break down, officers were well outnumbered by the heaving mass of maritime labourers before the mast.

The year 1622 had been a busy one along the East Indies trade routes. Brookes lost his command and abandoned many of his men to their castaway fate. In June, the VOC's *Wapen van Hoorn*

grounded off the westernmost point of the Southland. She was luckier, and probably more cautious, than the English ship and the crew managed to get her off the reef relatively undamaged.

Another VOC vessel encountered the Southland in happier circumstances. We do not know who commanded her, but the *Leeuwin* sighted the south-west of the continent at what is now Cape Leeuwin. Her anonymous master charted this southernmost sighting of 'low like drowned land', providing another leaf in the secret atlas. The *Leeuwin's* information would feature in Hessel Gerritsz's map published only a few years later. This map, known as *Caert van't Landt van d'Eendracht,* is now part of the collection of the State Library of New South Wales. The map incorporates discoveries by a number of VOC ships, including *Mauritius* and Dirk Hartog's *Eendracht.* Cartographers and Dutch mariners now had sketchy details of Cape York, the Gulf of Carpentaria and much of the western coast. They even had some knowledge of the southern coast and the waters we know as the Great Australian Bight.

In 1623 two small VOC craft out of Batavia followed in the *Duyfken's* wake—and beyond. They would extend the knowledge of the northernmost reaches of the continent and make further contact with the mysterious people of the Southland.

3

'More like monsters'

The mind of the seventeenth-century sailor was conditioned by centuries of ignorance and wild fantasy. To them, the indigenous inhabitants of the new worlds they sought to exploit could only be 'savages' and 'monsters'. All the preparations and activities of the discoverers were founded on these mistaken presumptions.

News of the *Tryall* wreck and details of her last location were known to the VOC and the danger to their ships along the treacherous Southland coasts was clear. In 1622, the Council of the Indies, the ruling body of the Dutch trading operations in this part of the globe, prepared an expedition 'to discover and survey all capes, forelands, bays, lands, islands, rocks, reefs, sandbanks, deeps, shallows, roadsteads, winds, currents and whatever else appertains to the same, so that they may be charted and noted, with their true latitudes, longitudes, bearings and conditions'.

The detailed sailing instructions for the ships that eventually carried out this momentous voyage also directed the sailors to find out all they could about the inhabitants, if any, 'and what sort of people and country there are'. The company was especially interested in any resources that might be found 'more especially what minerals they have, such as gold, silver, tin, iron, lead and copper, as well as precious stones and pearls, and what vegetables, animals and fruits these lands afford'. They were also to name their discoveries after Dutch towns, 'or any other dignified names', and to build stone columns in these places on which were to be inscribed the date and other details about 'when such possession has been taken on behalf of the States General'. Covenants were to be made with the rulers of any 'other parties' encountered, bringing them under the 'protection' of the Netherlands.

All these details, and any others, were to be carefully marked on charts. Expeditioners were reminded that all these materials belonged to the company: 'None of you shall be allowed to secrete, or by underhand means to retain any written documents, journals, drawings or observations touching the expedition but every one of you shall be bound on his return here faithfully to deliver up the same without exception.' They were provided with goods to trade—'for an experiment'—including ironware, cloth, as well as 'samples of gold, silver, copper, iron, lead and pearls, that you may inquire whether these articles are known to the inhabitants and might be obtained there in any reasonable quantity'. They also needed to be on the lookout for spices and sandalwood, all highly desirable goods, as well as for potential harbours to assist possible colonisation. They were to take care of themselves and also of any natives who approached them from the shore. Overall, the orders unnecessarily entreated, 'In a word, let nothing pass you unobserved, and whatever you find bring us a full and particular report of it, by which you will do the States of the United Netherlands service and lay up special honour for yourselves.'

And there was one further important task. Wherever the sailors came across people, they should 'hold of some adults, or, still better, young lads or girls, to the end that they should be brought up here, and later, when opportunity offers, be broken in at the said quarters'. What being 'broken in' might entail was not specified but was apparently well enough understood. The VOC was just as interested in the skin trade as in any other form of exchange, peaceable or not.[1]

The man selected to perform these many tasks was Jan Carstensz (Carstenszoon), the upper-merchant of the *Pera* and overall commander[2] of the entire expedition, which included the *Aernem*. Dirk Meliszoon was master of *Pera*, and her under-steersman, or second mate, was Willem Joosten Van Coolsteerdt. Both craft were described as *jacht*s and each carried approximately fifteen crewmen who, as well as sailing the vessels, acted variously as cooks, carpenters, armed marines, doctor, traders and, on occasion, abductors. There was also a '*jurabass*', a native man from Aru with knowledge of local languages, customs and places.[3] While the VOC orders referred to the great cost burden the company was shouldering in mounting this expedition, they were clearly doing it on the cheap, taking full advantage of what we would now call the multitasking abilities of its employees. These small vessels and perhaps thirty or more[4] mariners left Amboina[5] on 21 January 1623.

The claiming of Carpentaria

Carstensz and his crew sailed in accordance with their instructions: firstly to the Dutch-controlled island of Banda, where they took aboard a stonemason, a carpenter and a surgeon, substituting these for three of the original crew who were left ashore. They then voyaged to various islands, including Oeij and Aru, along the southern coast of what is now Papua New Guinea, parleying and trading with the native villages in the manner of the time. This involved an elaborate system of mutual hostages as a symbol of good faith on both sides. With the sometimes-erratic assistance of their native interpreter and cultural go-between, Carstensz successfully negotiated the acquiescence of several villages to 'the Prince's flag' and the protections and privileges it allegedly conferred. Perhaps lulled into a false sense of security by this successful pre-colonisation, on 11 February the master of the *Aernem* made a fatal error.

The events were recounted in Carstensz's journal: 'The skipper of the yacht Aernem, Dirck Melisz(oon), without knowledge of myself, of the supercargo [upper merchant] or steersman of the said yacht, unadvisedly went ashore to the open beach in the pinnace, taking with him 15 persons, both officers and common sailors, and no more than four muskets, for the purpose of fishing with a seine-net.'

The landing was poorly managed and the men were attacked by a large group of natives. Carstensz reported that:

> [The natives] first seized and tore to pieces an assistant, named Jan Willemsz(oon) Van den Briel who happened to be unarmed, after which they slew with arrows, callaways [spears] and with the oars which they had snatched from the pinnace, no less than nine of our men, who were unable to defend themselves, at the same time wounding the remaining seven (among them the skipper, who was the first to take to his heels); these last seven men at last returned on board in very sorry plight with the pinnace and one oar.[6]

Melisz died in agony the following day. The under-steersman, Willem Joosten Van Coolsteerdt, would later be appointed skipper of the *Aernem* and what was left of her crew.

After many days sailing, stormy weather and a shattered fore-topmast on the *Aernem*—never a good sailing craft—the two ships came to Ceram. The island had pleasant valleys and abundant fresh water but, Carstensz wrote, 'The natives whom we found to be savages and man-eaters, refused to hold parley with us, and fell upon our men who suffered grievous damage.' He described the natives as 'tall black men with curly heads of hair and two large holes through their noses, stark naked, not covering even their privities; their arms are arrows, bows, assagays, callaways and the like'.

Following this incident the ships rode out the next night and morning of 'dirty weather and a very high sea', and heavy rain that compelled them to remain at anchor. The *Pera*'s anchor cable broke and she drifted away from the *Aernem*, losing all sight of the other ship by the morning of 28 February. A few days later they found the *Aernem* again. She had suffered storm damage and water had spoiled much of their rice, powder and matches. Anchoring on the morning of 7 March, Carstensz went ashore with two well-manned and armed pinnaces:

> Because on the 6th aforesaid we had seen 4 or 5 canoes making from the land for the yachts; when we got near the land we saw a small canoe with three blacks; when we rowed towards them, they went back to the land and put one of the three ashore, as we supposed, in order to give warning for the natives there to come in great numbers and seize and capture our pinnaces; for as soon as we made towards them, they tried to draw us on, slowly paddling on towards the land.

The *jurabass* then swam to the natives with an offering of trade beads, but they were not interested. As the pinnaces pulled back to the relative safety of the ship, the canoes followed them:

> And when we showed them beads and iron objects, they cautiously came near one of our pinnaces; one of the sailors in the pinnace inadvertently touching the canoe with one of his oars, the blacks forthwith began to attack our men, and threw several callaways into the pinnace, without, however, doing any damage owing to the caution used by the men in her; in order to frighten them the corporal fired a musket, which hit them both, so that they died on the spot.[7]

The Dutch rowed back to the ships and remained at anchor in a strong gale overnight before sailing on 9 March, heading north-north-west, and were again attacked ineffectually by seven or eight native canoes. Next day they anchored about two kilometres off a 'low-lying and half-submerged' coast. Here, Carstensz observed:

> The natives are coal-black like the Caffres; they go about stark naked, carrying their privities in a small conch-shell, tied to the body with a bit of string; they have two holes in the midst of the nose, with fangs of hogs or swordfishes through them, protruding at least three fingers' breadths on either side, so that in appearance they are more like monsters than human beings; they seem to be evil-natured and malignant.

Carstensz also noted that they were skilful users of their weapons, which included bows and arrows.[8]

The crew quickly left this barren landscape, which was described as being 'inhabited by savages', with fish that were 'unnatural monsters' and birds 'as wild and shy as the men'. They headed south-south-west and, two days later, on 12 March, Carstensz and two pinnaces of well-armed sailors rowed ashore again, having to wade through waist-deep mud to reach the beach. They followed footprints into the 'wood' (bush) and found around twenty small grass huts: 'the said huts being so small and cramped that a man could hardly get into them on all fours, from which we could suffi-ciently conclude that the natives here must be of small stature, poor and wretched.' On venturing further into the wood, they were ambushed 'with great fury and loud shouts', during which a carpenter and his assistant were wounded:

> We were all of us hard pressed, upon which we fired three or four muskets at them killing one of the blacks stone-dead, which utterly took away their courage; they dragged the dead man into the wood, and we, being so far from the pinnaces and having a very difficult path to go in order to get back to them, resolved to return and row back to the yachts.

These violent events were all in a day's work for the men of the *Aernem* and *Pera*. After recording the attack, Carstensz simply continues his journal, noting the location of a large sandbank and a cape of land, 'about 70 miles east of Aru', which he named 'de Valsch Caep'. However, he did not fail to comment that the natives of this area were 'quite black and naked without any covering to hide their privy parts; their hair curly in the manner of the Papues'. He observed that they wore 'certain fish-bones through the nose, and through their ears, pieces of tree-bark, a span in length'—and again he drew the conclusion that 'they look more like monsters than like human beings'.

On 22 March, during an attempted landing on a small island infested with bats, the two vessels were involved in an accident of wind and current—'causing grievous damage to both the ships; *Pera* lost its gallion equipment and several guns and *Aernem* lost its rudder'. Several days were spent building a makeshift rudder and adjusting the masts and rigging of *Pera* to furnish enough wood for the task. They named the island *Vleermuys-Eylant* (Bats' Island) and noted signs of previous human visits to the fertile and fruitful place.

The ships were able to sail again on 25 March and the next day were approached by four canoes, each with around twenty-five natives. Carstensz wrote: '[They] called out and made signs for us to come ashore; we then threw out to them some small pieces of iron and strings of beads, at which they showed great satisfaction; they paid little or no attention to the gold, silver, copper, nutmegs and cloves which we showed them, though they were quite ready to accept these articles as presents.'

The natives were tall and well built, naked and paddling large canoes able to carry up to twenty men—'some of them have two, others three holes through the nose, in which they wear fangs or teeth of hogs or swordfishes.' Always with an eye to trading possibilities, Carstensz noted: 'They wear no rings of gold, silver, copper,

49

tin, or iron on their persons, but adorn themselves with rings made of tortoiseshell or terturago, from which it may be inferred that their land yields no metals or wood of any value.'

Among the group were a few men wearing strings of human teeth around their necks 'and excelling all the others in ugliness'. They carried 'on the left arm a hammer with a wooden handle and at one end a black conch-shell, the size of a man's fist, the other end by which they hold it, being fitted with a three-sided bone, not unlike a piece of stag's horn'. Carstensz thought that 'those who carry the hammers aforesaid would seem to be noblemen or valiant soldiers' and opined that these people were 'cunning and suspicious, and no stratagems on our part availed to draw them near enough to us to enable us to catch one or two with nooses which we had prepared for the purpose'.

The sailors tried to barter beads and pieces of iron for one of the hammers but were refused. Instead, the natives indicated they would trade for one of the ship's boys 'whom they seemed to have a great mind to'. It seems that all sides had interest in the skin trade. The natives kept holding up what Carstensz took to be human thigh bones, though for what purpose none could fathom, or perhaps preferred not to. They then gestured for the Dutch to cast them a line by which they would tow their boat to shore. This proved to be too difficult and the natives paddled back to land in a great hurry.[9]

More local people were approached on 18 April near what is now the Edward River on the western shore of Cape York Peninsula. Carstensz described them as 'coal-black, with lean bodies and stark naked, having twisted baskets or nets round their heads; in hair and figure they are like the blacks of the Coromandel coast, but they seem to be less cunning, bold and evil-natured than the blacks at the western extremity of Nova Guinea'. The weapons of these people were 'assagays, shields, clubs and sticks about half a fathom in length'; no bows and arrows were noted. They were shown the trade trinkets of the Dutch and 'wanted to have all they saw', taking the iron and beads they were offered. Nor were they frightened of the newcomers, being 'so forward and so bold that they grasped the muskets of our men'.

But this more promising start was soon destroyed when a sailor caught hold of a native for transportation back to Amboina, as Carstensz had been instructed by the VOC. 'The blacks who remained on the beach, set up dreadful howls and made violent gestures, but the others who kept concealed in the wood remained there.'

On the same day, the *jurabass* from Aru died. He had been in great pain for two days. The surgeon cut the man open and found 'that he had much clotted blood around his heart, which apparently caused his death'. We are never told the man's name.

Next day the Dutch were ashore cutting firewood when they were surprised by a group of two hundred or so Aborigines, not unreasonably intent on having their stolen kinsman returned. This time, after the sailors fired two shots, they became afraid of the muskets and disappeared into the bush, with 'one of their number having been hit and having fallen'. According to Carstensz, 'Our men then proceeded somewhat farther up the country, where they found several weapons, of which they took some along with them by way of curiosities. During their march they observed in various places great quantities of divers human bones, from which it may be safely concluded that the blacks along the coast of Nova Guinea are man-eaters who do not spare each other when driven by hunger.'

Carstensz, apparently thinking he was still in New Guinea, remained concerned with abducting some natives. He reported that, at a meeting of the ship's council:

It was furthermore proposed by me and ultimately approved of by the council, to give 10 pieces of eight to the boatmen for every black they shall get hold of on shore, and carry off to the yachts, to the end that the men may use greater care and diligence in this matter, and Our Masters may reap benefit from the capture of the blacks, which may afterwards redound to certain advantage.

A day or two later, on 25 April, the skipper of the *Pera* and two rowboats of well-armed sailors went ashore. They found seven small huts made of dry hay and a group of natives who refused to have anything to do with them. In the afternoon, Carstensz explored a salt river he named the 'Staten' (or Staaten). They found only boggy ground and many 'footprints of men and of large dogs, running from the south to the north'. The decision was now taken to return to Amboina. They nailed a wooden tablet to a tree marking the extent of their voyage; the inscription, which was in Dutch, stated:

AD 1623 on the 24th of April[10] there arrived here
two yachts dispatched by their High Mightinesses the
States-General.

It seems that the mightiness of their masters was more important than the names of their ships, or even of their captains.

Now Carstensz was forced to make mention of a problem that lurks in the sub-text of his journal. After the death of the original skipper of the *Aernem,* the younger Willem Joosten Van Coolsteerdt had been promoted to the position. The rigours of the voyage and perhaps the demands of Carstensz seem to have been increasingly vexing to Van Coolsteerdt and his superior now included a severe note that did not bode well for the remainder of the expedition:

NOTE that the yacht Aernem, owing to bad sailing, and to the small liking and desire which the skipper and the steersman have shown towards the voyage, has on various occasions and at different times been the cause of serious delay, seeing that the Pera (which had sprung a bad leak and had to be kept above water by more than 8000 strokes of the pump every 24 hours) was every day obliged to seek and follow the Aernem for one, two or even more miles to leeward.

The trouble implied by the capitalised 'NOTE' came to a head the following night when they anchored:

We hung out a lantern, that the Aernem might keep clear of us in dropping anchor; but this proved to be useless, for on purpose and with malice prepense she cut away from us against her instructions and our resolution, and seems to have set her course for Aru (to have a good time of it there), but we shall learn in time whether she has managed to reach it.

However, as Carstensz would subsequently learn, *Aernem* did not sail for the island of Aru for 'a good time', but was instead blown westwards across the gulf on whose far shores the tiny ship and her mutinous crew would make significant discoveries of their own.

Meanwhile, the *Pera* continued searching for fresh water, the supplies of which were dangerously low. Occasionally the mariners ventured further inland. On 3 May Carstensz went ashore with ten musketeers and found a dry, flat and barren land with no fruit-bearing trees 'nor anything that man could make use of'. He and his men concluded: 'In our judgment this is the most arid and barren region that could be found anywhere on the earth; the inhabitants, too, are the most wretched and poorest creatures that I have ever seen in my age or time.' (William Dampier would make an almost identical observation more than sixty years later on the north-west coast.)

The desertion of *Aernem*, the stresses of the voyage and the absence of tradeable commodities echo clearly through Carstensz's frustrated journal entries. But he sailed on and in the morning of 4 May, with a good east-north-east wind, sighted a river and named it the 'Vereenichde' (probably the Mitchell River).

Carstensz kept to a north-north-east course and at noon the next day he cast anchor and went ashore in the pinnace with a group of armed men. Straightaway they were attacked by the inhabitants, but beat them off. The Dutch then went inland and 'found divers of their weapons, such as assagays and callaways, leaning against the trees'. Carstensz reported, 'We took care not to damage these weapons, but tied pieces of iron and strings of beads to some of them, in order to attract the blacks, who, however, seemed quite indifferent to these things, and repeatedly held up their shields with great boldness and threw them at the muskets.' He concluded his account of this incident with a familiar trope: 'These men are, like all the others we have lately seen, of tall stature and very lean to look at, but malignant and evil-natured.'

A few days later, on the morning of 7 May, there was another encounter. Word of the *Pera*'s journey along the coast was clearly being transmitted from group to group and the indigenous people were readying themselves to repel the invaders. The skipper went ashore with orders to avoid trouble and try to trade with the locals; if possible, it would also be good if he could abduct one or two of them. The men returned at noon with news that their landing had been opposed by a hundred or more naked natives with faces painted red and wearing feathers through the lower part of the nose. They were fired upon and retreated into bushes from where they continued to menace the intruders.

Still determined to capture the human flesh demanded by his VOC masters, Carstensz made another attempt on 8 May at a river he named the 'Coen' (now Pennefather River) after the ruthless governor-general then in command of the Indies:

I went ashore myself with 10 musketeers; we saw numerous footprints of men and dogs (running from south to north); we accordingly spent some time there, following the footprints aforesaid to a river, where we gathered excellent vegetables or pot-herbs; when we had got into the pinnace again, the blacks emerged with their arms from the wood at two different points; by showing them bits of iron and strings of beads we kept them on the beach, until we had come near them.

One of these men was incautious enough to put down his weapon. The skipper grabbed him around the waist while the quartermaster looped a noose around his neck, dragging him down the beach to their boat. The natives tried to rescue their man and the Dutch had to shoot one of them, causing a retreat. Carstensz wrote, somewhat disingenuously, 'We cannot, however, give any account of their customs and ceremonies, nor did we learn anything about the thickness of the population, since we had few or no opportunities for inquiring into these matters; meanwhile I hope that with God's help Your Worships will in time get information touching these points from the black we have captured, to whose utterances I would beg leave to refer you.'

The journal makes no further mention of the captured native. He was one of two Carstensz did manage to abduct and carry back to Amboina, where one of the unfortunate men later died. The other was taken to Batavia, fate unknown. Carstensz could at least report success in this one of his many assigned tasks. No doubt thinking of the reception that might be awaiting him in Batavia from the notoriously hard masters of the VOC, Carstensz capitalised the heading of another aside in his journal:

NOTE that in all places where we landed, we have treated the blacks or savages with especial kindness, offering them pieces of iron, strings of beads and pieces of cloth, hoping by so doing to get their friendship and be allowed to penetrate to some considerable distance land inward, that we might be able to give a full account and description of the same; but in spite of all our kindness and our fair semblance the blacks received us as enemies everywhere, so that in most places our landings were attended with great peril; on this account, and for various other reasons afterwards to be mentioned, we have not been able to learn anything about the population of Nova Guinea, and the nature of its inhabitants and its soil; nor did we get any information touching its towns and villages, about the division of the land, the religion of the natives, their policy, wars, rivers, vessels, or fisheries; what commodities they have, what manufactures, what minerals whether gold, silver, tin, iron, lead, copper or quicksilver.

The skipper went on to provide a catalogue of excuses for his failures, perhaps seeking to mitigate them by grouping them together into what was masquerading as a marginal note:

In the first place, in making further landings we should have been troubled by the rainy season, which might have seriously interfered with the use of our muskets, whereas it does no harm to the weapons of the savages; secondly, we should first have been obliged to seek practicable paths or roads of which we knew nothing; thirdly, we might easily have been surrounded by the crowds of blacks, and been cut off from the boats, which would entail serious peril to the sailors with whom we always effected the landings, and who are imperfectly versed in the use of muskets; if on the contrary we had had well-drilled and experienced soldiers (the men best fitted to undertake such expeditions), we might have done a good deal of useful work; still, in spite of all these difficulties and obstacles, we have shunned neither hard work, trouble, nor peril, to make a thorough examination of everything with the means at our disposal, and to do whatever our good name and our honour demanded.

The *Pera* continued her voyage home, having further encounters with the indigenous inhabitants of the Southland along the way. On 10 May they went ashore again, attempting to trade and parley with a group of armed locals, but they were not interested. Next day they revisited the footsteps of Willem Jansz, though with no fatal consequences, naming another river in the process: 'In the afternoon we sailed past a large river (which the men of the Duifken went up with a boat in 1606, and where one of them was killed by the arrows of the blacks); to this river, which is in 11° 48' Lat., we have given the name of revier de Carpentier in the new chart.'[11]

Yet another violent first contact took place the following day. The sailors went ashore to find around two hundred natives assembled in a threatening manner and unwilling to be pacified by gifts. The Dutch fired warning shots, wounding one of the men in the chest. The natives retreated behind the dunes, leaving the interlopers to search 'their wretched huts on the beach' where 'we found nothing but a square-cut assagay, two or three small pebbles, and some human bones, which they use in constructing their weapons and scraping the same'. The injured native was carried to the pinnace but died as they rowed back to their ship. He was carrying some resin and 'a piece of metal, which the wounded man had in his net, and which he had most probably got from the men of the Duyfken'.

A few days later Carstensz penned another reference to the earlier voyage of the *Duyfken*: 'So far we have but two times seen black men or savages, who received us much more hostilely than those more to southward; they are also acquainted with muskets, of which they would seem to have experienced the fatal effect when in 1606 the men of the Duyffken [*sic*] made a landing here.' Colonisation had commenced.

The *Pera* tracked back along the New Guinea coast, parleying and trading along the way, setting up wooden pillars to proclaim native loyalty to the prince and, finally, anchoring at Amboina on 8 June:

> Thereby bringing the voyage to a safe conclusion (by the mercy and safekeeping of the Lord) may He vouchsafe to grant prosperity and success in all their good undertakings to the High Mightinesses the States-General, to his Excellency

the Prince of Orange etc., to the Lords Managers of the United East India Company and to the Worshipful Lord General and his Governors.

Remaining for ever

Their High Mightinesses' etc. obedient and affectionate servant

(signed)
JAN CARSTENSZOON

Some months before, *Pera* and *Aernem* had parted company for the last time. *Aernem* had been a laggard companion, causing Carstensz to wait or double back in search of her time after time. There was also a serious morale problem aboard the slower boat that probably decided its young master to break away from *Pera*. The *Aernem* sailed west under the command of the adventurous Van Coolsteerdt, discovering and charting the western shore of the Gulf, north-eastern Arnhem Land, the Wessell Islands and perhaps even Groote Eylandt. The journal of this wildcat expedition is lost, but charts made by the men of *Aernem* (now preserved in the National Library of Australia) began to reveal the shape of Cape York and beyond, adding another small but important page in the secret atlas.

The mid 1620s were busy years for VOC shipping around the Southland. Klaas Hermanszoon in the *Leiden* charted the coast around Shark Bay.[12] A child born aboard his ship at that time is probably the first European to be born in the Southland. The parents celebrated this in naming the baby Seebaer van Niemelant, meaning 'sea-born of the new land'. There were further sightings of the continent, together with naming of observed natural features and regions, and in 1624, the *Tortelduyff* came in sight of and named Turtledove Shoal to the south of the Houtman Abrolhos. Two years later Daniel Janssen Cock in the *Leiden* traced the coast from the Zuytdorp Cliffs to Dirk Hartog Island. And in 1627 the VOC ship *Gulden Zeepaard* made it to the south coast of Western Australia and into the Great Australian Bight under the command of Francois Thijssen and the eminent Pieter Nuyts. That area of the continent was subsequently known for a long time as 'Nuytsland'. The following year David Pieterszoon de Vries in the *Wapen van Hoorn* came into Shark Bay, apparently without landing, while the *Vianen* went aground somewhere near present-day Port Hedland, managing to save herself only by offloading the valuable cargo of pepper and copper. The region was called 'De Witt's Land', though the master of *Vianen* thought it 'a foul and barren shore, green fields, and very wild, black, barbarous inhabitants'.

The results of these sightings, chartings and occasional encounters with the Southland began to appear in the maps of the period. In 1630 the Dutch cartographer and engraver Hendrik Hondius prepared a splendid map of the world (including a picture of himself in one corner). It included the discoveries of Hartog, Cornelis de Houtman and Carstensz and is thought to be the first generally available map to depict existing Dutch information about *Terra Australis*.

But while the Dutch and those who followed them were coming to know the Southland and to gradually inscribe its enigmas on their maps and charts, they were not so successful in their relations with those already there. The seemingly arbitrary and random first encounters of Aboriginals and Europeans were puzzling. It seemed to the Dutch that the same groups of natives could be welcoming, or at least tolerant, of strangers when they first arrived, yet the following day might turn upon them for reasons not apparent to the newcomers. Affrighted, the Dutch did what they were instructed to do by their superiors in the VOC and what their instincts would have dictated—they fired their guns.

Some researchers have sought to look more deeply into these apparent ambivalences and have found possible answers in the cultural gulf between the old world and the new.[13] In many indigenous cultures, it was the practice to demand a gift from any newcomers as a sign of good intentions. While the Dutch were certainly keen to trade, much of what they had to trade with—especially precious metals, jewels and cloth—was of little interest to Aboriginal people. In any case, these or any other items were supposed to be freely given rather than being part of a commercial transaction, which, of course, was the main VOC priority.

On other occasions, VOC journals report an apparent indifference to the Dutch presence, almost as if they were not there at all. Again, such behaviour towards newcomers has been noted as Aboriginal custom in many parts of the country and part of an elaborate ritual of arriving, greeting, checking out and ultimate approval to pass into or through the country of another group. The ritual requires a mutual ignoring of local and newcomer until such times as an understanding has been established. This procedure takes some time and, of course, was totally unknown to the Dutch.

These encounters were further confused by sensory perceptions and mis-perceptions. Even such basic matters as smell, touch, sight and sound could confound Aborigines and navigators alike. Especially in the later phases of contact, the French and British usually expected the locals to be immensely impressed with their bodies, clothing, manners, food and music. When the Aborigines displayed little interest, even disdain and amused contempt for the actions and attributes of the newcomers, the explorers were often affronted.[14]

Complicating the situation even more was the belief among many indigenous groups that the white people suddenly appearing from an unknown technology floating on the ocean were the returning spirits of their dead ancestors. While this aspect of indigenous belief has sometimes been overemphasised in first-contact explanations, it was certainly a feature of the Cape York indigenous groups. Their first response seems generally to have been to appease the perplexingly returning spirits. When those spirits misinterpreted the nature of such actions and reacted with violence or simply with ignorant affront, the basis was laid for the depressing history of colonial and post-colonial relations.

Just a few years after *Pera* and *Aernem* were working their quarrelsome way along the north-east coast, another VOC ship came to a disastrous end on the rugged western coast. She was called the *Batavia*, a name known in history as the world's most blood-drenched shipwreck. As well as the chilling story of the survivors and their fate, the wrecking of the *Batavia* delivered the first known European settlers to the shores of the Southland.

4

Blood islands

The trouble began long before *Batavia* smashed into the South-land on her maiden voyage from Amsterdam. Bubbling aboard Francisco Pelsaert's ship was a dark brew of lust, greed and mutiny. The man at the centre of the plot to take the ship into the business of piracy was the under-merchant Jeronimus Cornelisz, a disgraced apothecary with grievances on his mind and heresy in his heart. His enormities, and those of many who became his followers, would land the first European settlers on *Terra Australis* a century and a half before the First Fleet. But Cornelisz would also recruit a powerful figure to his mutinous cause, the captain Ariaen Jacobsz. The consequences of these personalities and their relationships would be played out on a few coral reefs and a river mouth along the western coast of Southland.

The wrecking
On 4 June 1629 the VOC ship *Batavia* had been at sea for seven months, with a short break at Cape Town. She was within a month of her namesake port in Java and, with a couple of exceptions, had made an unremarkable passage to the East Indies. Ten men had

died from disease, but this was a relatively low mortality rate for VOC ships on the Spice Islands run. The moon was bright and the winter wind strong. Around 3 a.m., the lookout reported surf spray. The ship was nowhere near any charted reefs as the skipper well knew. He told the lookout that what he thought he could see was only a trick of the moonlight. There was no need to slacken sail.

A few minutes later *Batavia* ploughed into a jagged reef at full speed. So great was the impact that the stricken vessel ground right up onto the corals like a monster heaving itself up from the deep. The approximately 330 men, women and boys aboard[1] were immediately struggling for their lives. Sailors rushed aloft to furl the acres of sail being lashed by a howling wind. Below decks everything moveable was hauled up and thrown overboard in an attempt to lighten the ship. Anchors were run out in hopes *Batavia* could be refloated on a high tide. But as the wind and rain lashed the terrified sailors, soldiers, tradesmen and passengers, Jacobsz realised that it was already high tide and there was barely any water beneath his shattered command.

As the sea receded, the mainmast began to vibrate, threatening to hammer through the ship's keel. Jacobsz ordered his sailors to cut the mast down. Instead of falling into the raging waters, it crashed straight down onto the *Batavia*. The ship was doomed and those aboard her were bound for unprecedented misery on a few outcrops of coral.

When the sun came up, the survivors had their first view of the desolate place onto which they were now cast away. A confusion of small, flat islets and coral cays was all that could be seen. The ship's boats went out to search for habitable areas and found a few likely spots that would have to suffice.

The upper-merchant and superior officer, Francisco Pelsaert[2], decided that it was more important to land his people than to save the 250,000 guilders of cash and almost as much again in jewellery and other goods, the value of which would be around twenty million dollars today. But before the boats could be gotten away, *Batavia* split and began filling rapidly with water. There was a stampede for the boats. Twelve or so dived into the sea but were immediately drowned. By nightfall they were still ferrying survivors, the few remaining supplies and some of the valuables ashore. The chests of company treasure remained on the main deck of the disintegrating hulk.

That night, about 120 people were still aboard the ship, with the rest stranded on the small coral island in the reef where the boats had taken them. Those on *Batavia* broke into the alcohol still aboard and went on a rampage of theft and violence. Later they stove open some of the treasure chest, flinging guilders at each other as if they were worthless pebbles. Next day, around sixty were brought off the ship but bad weather made it impossible to rescue more.

The survivors on the reef separated onto two islands. Salvaged supplies were already running dangerously low and fresh water was desperately needed.

The captain Jacobsz and upper-merchant Pelsaert then decided to take the ship's longboat to search for water on other islands. They found none, but were later joined by another group of ten sailors in the ship's two-masted yawl who were also searching for water. This group, commanded by the third steersman, asked Pelsaert to allow them to join him in the longboat as 'there was no one who wanted to sail back with the yawl to the other island or to the wreck'.

Now all the senior officers, together with forty-three others, including two women and a baby, were in the longboat, separated from almost 200 people left on the reef and another seventy still aboard *Batavia*. As the stricken survivors began to work out what to do in the absence of their commanding officers, Pelsaert and Jacobsz and some of the best mariners in the *Batavia* crew, now including all three steersmen, sailed and rowed their longboat along the unknown shore. The sturdy and seaworthy 30-foot-long craft had been reinforced against the waves with another 2 feet of planking above the gunwales, but she was overloaded by about sixteen bodies. No one aboard had any idea where they were or where they might find drinking water. Attempts to land were frustrated by forbidding cliffs and storms that forced them to throw most of their supplies into the ocean to preserve the boat.

They finally put some men onto the mainland on 14 June after seeing smoke rising, but they found no water. However, the next day they were able to land the boat and found drinkable rainwater near an abandoned Aboriginal campsite. It was enough to keep them all alive for perhaps another week. But they had now travelled more than 360 miles (about 800 kilometres) from the wreck and decided it was too far and too dangerous to return.

The upper-merchant and the skipper made the decision to keep sailing north after asking all aboard to provide a signed oath of agreement with such a grave action:

> Since on all the islands or reefs round about our foundered ship Batavia, there is no water to be found, in order to feed and keep the saved people alive, therefore the Commander has earnestly besought us and proposed that we should sail to the mainland in order to see if God will grant that we find water there, to assist the people with as many trips from there until we can be certain that they will be able to remain alive for some considerable time, and meanwhile command someone to bring our sad happenings to the Hon. Lord General, to which we the undersigned have consented now that the need has been placed before us of how greatly important it is to be responsible before God and the high authorities. Have agreed and resolved to do our utmost duty (*devoir*) in order to help our poor companions in their distress. In token of the truth have signed with our own hand and have sworn to it in the presence of all people, this 8th June 1629.[3]

Pelsaert and his companions were lucky. Conditions allowed the longboat to make excellent speed through the empty seas between them and Java, a distance of over 1600 kilometres. But they still suffered from hunger and thirst. Land was sighted on 27 June, just as the drinkable water was about to run out. The longboat reached Batavia a few days later with all forty-eight of its passengers still alive.

Although the settlement was in the midst of a war with the Sultan of Mataram and reduced mainly to its central fortress, the council under the feared Governor-General Coen ordered Pelsaert to return to the wreck 'since it was apparent that it was possible that some of the people and also some of the goods might be saved and salvaged'.

The recently arrived jacht *Sardam* was quickly supplied for the trip to the Barolos, together with a group of six Dutch and Guajaratii divers from western India. Pelsaert was ordered to take all the time he needed to recover the sunken cargo, but was left in no doubt that he must 'salvage the cash, which is an obligation to the Company and on which your honour depends'.

Before leaving, Pelsaert informed the council of the treachery of Jacobsz and the steersman Jan Evertsz who were both arrested and thrown into the dungeons of the Castle Batavia. Under torture, Evertsz confessed and was hanged for his part in the shipboard assault of a 27-year-old passenger named Lucretia Jansdochter. Usually called 'Creesje Jans', she was sailing to join her husband, a VOC employee in the Indies. Jacobsz was charged with his role in the attack and the wider mutiny plot, as well as 'allowing himself to be blown away by pure neglect'. He was left to rot in the dungeons while the governor-general and council considered the situation.

Pelsaert sailed for *Batavia*'s wreck on 15 July. With a stream-lined crew to allow room for the survivors, if any, he aimed to reach his destination within a month. Bad weather and only a hazy reckoning of the wreck's position meant that they did not find the islands until mid-September. The survivors had now spent almost four months on the barren coral cays. During that period, misery and oppression had been the lot of many survivors, and grisly ends had come to the rest.

Lord of the coral

Nearly 300 sailors, soldiers, artisans and passengers survived the initial grounding of *Batavia*. About twenty were women, some with babies born during the voyage. There were many young cabin boys and the large family of Gijsbert Bastiaensz, the *predikant* or minister, and his wife. The main authority figures were a handful of experienced officers who, following VOC procedure, formed a council to control a volatile and dangerous situation.

The survivors were scattered in groups across two islands and those still aboard *Batavia*. There were few supplies on the islands and little water. Those on the islands began dying before the end of the first week. A line was eventually fixed between the wreck and the islands by the bravery of a female servant, but the *Batavia* broke apart before this could be of much practical use. Most of the seventy left aboard were drowned. Twenty-four got themselves more or less safely to shore. Two days later the last man from the disintegrating hulk drifted ashore. He was in a bad way but with what minimal care could be given, returned to health. His name was Jeronimus Cornelisz.

As the assistant or under-merchant, Cornelisz was the senior ranking officer remaining after Pelsaert and Jacobsz's departure more than a week earlier. He was soon elected to the *raad*, or council, assuming his primary share of responsibility for the lives and deaths of the 208 shipwrecked souls. Before long, though, he appointed himself the lord of everything upon those forsaken islets.

There was much to be done. Cornelisz was at first efficient and effective in organising foraging parties, boatbuilding and generally managing what few resources were conveniently washing ashore from the broken *Batavia* and the natural bounty of the reef, including seals, fish and birds. But it was not long before word of the mutiny he had been planning aboard the ship became public. Fearing eventual punishment when, and if, a rescue ship returned them to Batavia, Cornelisz decided to re-ignite the original plot with the help of the dozen or so accomplices he had recruited earlier who were also stranded with him. Most of these men were young, with military experience.

Late in June, Cornelisz began corralling all the available arms and stopping work on the building of a vessel that might take survivors off the islands. Groups were sent to four other islands, ostensibly to find food and water but in reality to sequester them from the main camp in the hope that they would die of starvation and thirst. Cornelisz had carefully selected those who were thereby banished. They were those most likely to be loyal to the VOC and so the biggest threat to his plot. He had reduced the numbers on the island they now called 'Batavia's Graveyard' to no more than 140. He planned to control this group until the hoped-for rescue ship arrived. He and his cronies would then attack and take the ship, sailing away to a profitable career of piracy, leaving everyone else to die miserably.

At the beginning of July, two men were accused of pilfering supplies. The council met and Cornelisz demanded both men be executed. The council agreed to only one execution and so the next day Cornelisz dissolved it, replacing the members with his hand-picked mutineers. He was now in complete control. One of the unfortunate ex-council men was murdered by the mutineers straightaway. Two others accused of trying to escape in homemade boats were butchered the same day. Jeronimus Cornelisz had founded his empire of death.

Over the following weeks, most of the survivors were murdered. The first killings had a superficial air of legality, as they were supposedly the result of deliberations and decisions of the council. But it would not be long before people were being hacked, stabbed, strangled and bashed to death on the whim of Cornelisz, mainly by a small group of henchmen loyal to him.

The under-merchant now assumed the affectations and accou-trements of supreme command. He dressed in the elegant and expensive robes of Pelsaert, salvaged from the *Batavia* and stored, along with jewellery, cash and other valuables in Cornelisz's tent. He strutted around his coral kingdom in ridiculous finery, as did his men, who slaughtered anyone they did not like the look of or who offended them in even the smallest way. None were safe. Pregnant mothers, male and female children, ship's boys, sometimes as young as ten and rarely much older. At one point, Cornelisz became so annoyed with the crying of a sick baby that he tried to poison it. He succeeded only in making the child wail even more, his apothecary skills apparently having left him. The sick, the lame, the old, the barely born—no one was too harmless for the deranged attentions of Cornelisz and his henchmen. Even the family of a minister.

Gijsbert Bastiaensz was a minister of the Reformed Church. He shipped aboard *Batavia* to take up an ecclesiastical appointment in the East Indies. Travelling with him were his entire family of wife, three daughters and four sons. As a man of God, Bastiaensz had considerable influence with believers such as most of the survivors, with the exception of Cornelisz. Bastiaensz was also a person of standing within the society of the period. This probably saved him and his family from the early slayings. But as Cornelisz and his accomplices relentlessly reduced the number of mouths needing to be fed and potential challenges to their oppression, even the minister's family became targets. On the night of 21 July, seven of the mutineers took their knives and hatchets to the sailcloth tent which the Bastiaensz family occupied. They set upon the mother and six children of the family, hacking, stabbing and bludgeoning them all to death. Then the gang continued its murderous spree, slaying more unfortunate survivors before dawn.

The Bastiaensz family now numbered only two, the minister himself and his second-eldest daughter, the 21-year-old Judick. The murderers forbade the grieving widower to weep, threatening him with death if he did so. He was then set to work looking after the small boats and rafts in constant fear for his own life.

Despite the large number of believers among the survivors, Bastiaensz was only given permission to preach from time to time. To the mutineers, Cornelisz extolled his own heretical gospel, the beliefs that allowed him to assume the power of life and death. These stemmed from the extreme fringes of the Protestant Reformation, and perhaps ultimately limited to a radical early Christian sect known as 'Adamites' who believed in what we now call 'free love', common property and a virulent form of antinomianism, sometimes referred to as Spiritual Libertinism. The basic tenet of this interpretation of the scriptures was that as God and man were one, anything that man did must be godly, even murder. For this to be valid and holy, an individual needed to be at one with God, in a state of divine grace. Cornelisz, the failed apothecary and under-merchant, believed himself to be such an elect person.

Where had he derived these extreme views? Cornelisz grew up in a part of the country where the teachings of a radical version of Anabaptism survived. Later, in Amsterdam, he had also come into contact with the views of the artist known as 'Torrentius', or Johannes van der Beeck, a notoriously indulgent and loud-mouthed non-conformist who inevitably suffered denouncement, torture and imprisonment by the Calvinist authorities for the outlandish views he was foolish enough to loudly proclaim while in his cups, a frequent occurrence.[4] In another individual and at another time and place, such heresies, if kept discrete, would probably have led to nothing untoward. But in the circumstances of the *Batavia*'s wrecking and in the personality of the psychopath Jeronimus Cornelisz, they attained their most dreadful manifestation.

After the mass murder of the Bastiaensz family, the killings continued, even escalated, as the mutineers began to slaughter their fellow survivors for sport. By the end of July there was no further pretence at legality. Tradesmen considered lazy were dispatched without a second thought. The only person with any medical knowledge, the ship's surgeon, was violently hacked and stabbed to death. Other survivors not connected with the original mutiny plot were forced to murder to prove their loyalty. Most did this reluctantly, though one deranged youth begged to be allowed to kill. His name was Jan Pelgrom, destined for a momentous fate. As well as forcing others to murder, Cornelisz and his henchmen drew up two deeds of loyalty and compelled many of the survivors to sign their oaths upon it.

Most of the seven women left alive were forced into 'common service' at the whim of the mutineers. One of these was the desirable Creesje Jans. She had been the subject of a gang attack aboard the *Batavia* related to the mutiny and was now required to cohabit with Cornelisz. The minister's only surviving daughter was then made to 'marry' one of the mutineers, an unwelcome relationship though one that probably saved her life as the arrangement offered her some protection.

By mid-August Cornelisz and his murderous accomplices had ended the lives of perhaps 115 men, women and children, possibly more. Those left now had plenty of food and water and there was not much more to do than to think about rescue. Some hoped, some feared. The possibility of a ship turning up to save the survivors was a problem for the mutineers. It would mean the discovery of their plot and crimes with certain torture and execution. Unless, of course, any rescue ship could be seized. This became the plan, but it had one major flaw.

On an island to the north, an abandoned group had survived Cornelisz's plan for them to die of thirst and starvation. This island, the seas around it and another connected to it by an ocean causeway turned out to have ample supplies of fresh water and wildlife. The men who had inadvertently settled it had found a natural leader in the form of the soldier Wiebbe Hayes. Beginning with a small group of survivors, numbers on the island had increased as others fled from the murderous insanity on Batavia's Graveyard. The grim news they brought with them, which included another massacre on one of the islands, forewarned Hayes and his men who set about further reinforcing their naturally strategic position on a small eminence with piles of sharp coral boulders, sharpened sticks and other improvised weapons. Cornelisz had deliberately not armed them, but now their numbers and their position were strong against a rapidly dwindling number of potential attackers under the madman's erratic command.

The inevitable confrontation began with Cornelisz trying to foment disaffection among the 'defenders', as those on Hayes' island became known. He wrote an oily letter to the half dozen Frenchmen among the defenders alleging a plot by Hayes and his other men to betray them. The French should, Cornelisz suggested, attack the Hayes faction and hand them over to him. The French would then be treated as the 'greatest and truest brothers and friends'. A young VOC cadet was chosen to get this message across the reefs to the French. When he managed to contact them, the French read the letter, recognised the lies that it contained and seized the cadet. They took him to Hayes who had him imprisoned.

By this time there were forty-six men and a boy on Hayes' island, including some trained soldiers like himself. The mutineers then launched their first assault on Hayes at the end of July and were easily repelled, despite their superior weaponry. They came again in greater force on 5 August, but the long and slippery stretch of open sand between the beach and the defenders' position again saw their retreat. Realising that the odds were moving against him, Cornelisz decided to try his specialty of trickery and deceit. He proposed a meeting and exchange of goods and supplies on neutral ground. This would allow his men to get close to the defenders without the need to cross the open ground. They would then talk with them and encourage disaffection. At some point, the pretence of parley would be lifted and the mutineers would attack and kill the defenders.

The absurdity of this plan suggests the state of Cornelisz's mind. But after Bastiaensz had been sent to deliver the proposal, Hayes agreed and the parley took place on 2 September. Cornelisz and a small party of mutineers came across the open mudflats. They began conversing with the defenders and exchanging wine and clothing from the *Batavia* for the fresh water and meat so abundant on Hayes' island. The defenders were well aware of what was going on and simply fell on Cornelisz and his accomplices before they could attack them. Cornelisz was captured and all but one of the mutineers slain. He escaped to rejoin the remaining forty-six hungry and thirsty mutineers and other survivors back on Batavia's Graveyard.

In the absence of the captured Cornelisz, a new regime was instituted on the mutineers' island. The murders stopped, though the women were still forced to serve the carnal needs of the men. Another oath of allegiance was drawn up and a new council elected.

On the morning of 17 September, the mutineers again attacked the defenders on their island. This time, the mutineers had the advantage of two muskets, which they used to pick off the defenders. The battle dragged on through the morning. The flow of fighting was more or less equal, though the superior firepower of the mutineers gave them the long-term advantage. But then, around eleven in the morning, the *Sardam* appeared.

Both sides raced to reach Pelsaert's rescue ship first. Victory by one force would determine the fate of the other. The boat carrying Hayes reached the *Sardam* just before that of the mutineers. He had just enough time to spill out his story before the heavily armed mutineers came alongside, as Pelsaert noted, 'dressed mostly in red *laken* [cloth], trimmed with golden *passementen* [lace]'. Observing the contrast in the clothing of the mutineers and Hayes' ragtag men, Pelsaert made the right decision. He commanded the mutineers to put down their weapons and ordered the pikemen aboard the *Sardam* to reinforce his orders. At first the mutineers said they would only drop their weapons when allowed aboard the *Sardam*, but faced with overwhelming force, they soon realised their reign was over. They gave up their weapons and were bound up as they boarded, one by one. The mutiny and murders were over. The retribution began.

Retribution

Pelsaert started questioning the mutineers immediately. One of the early members of the plot aboard *Batavia* and a prominent slayer on the reef confessed all he knew straightaway. This gave Pelsaert a good basis to proceed with his investigation of the terrible months on the reef. The full details of the mutiny plot, and of Cornelisz's role, were laid out, confirming the suspicions Pelsaert had long held. The fallen lord of Batavia's Graveyard was brought from the hole where he had been confined on Hayes' island. According to one account, the under-merchant had been made to pluck the birds the defenders caught to feed themselves. The remnants of his once-fine gown—actually Pelsaert's—were smeared in mutton-bird bird excrement and feathers. Predictably, Cornelisz tried to defend himself and to wheedle his way out of the appalling allegations made against him. He was detained pending further investigation.

Pelsaert then assembled a Broad Council to administer the law, obliged as he was to dispense justice immediately. The mutineers were led one by one before this group to confess their crimes. The first brought to account was Jeronimus Cornelisz. He denied his guilt but after a few days' interrogation and several inflictions of water torture he confessed. He would later recant, a tactic designed to slow down the proceedings against him.

This only succeeded for a short time after which Cornelisz signed his confession. The rest of his henchmen were quickly dealt with in the investigations, assisted by Cornelisz's complete betrayal of them to the council. All the appalling details of their callous crimes were laid bare and recorded.

On 28 September, everyone on the reef was gathered together to hear the verdicts. The council found Cornelisz 'denuded of humanity' and 'In order to turn us from the wrath of God and to cleanse the name of Christianity of such an unheard villain' sentenced him to the gallows. Before execution both his hands were to be removed. As was also customary in VOC capital cases, all his belongings were forfeit to the company, effectively a punishment of his innocent widow.

The council made many findings. Some mutineers were spared immediate retribution for one reason or another. They were to be taken back to Batavia where they would be further investigated and probably tortured by the governor-general and Council of the Indies. One or two seem to have slipped through the process and escaped condemnation and subsequent prosecution. In the end, eight of the mutineers were condemned to die on the gallows being constructed on one of the nearby islands.

Cornelisz's first ploy to delay the inevitable was to request that he be baptised, possibly an indication that his radical religious background had excluded the usual childhood entry into the church. As they waited, Cornelisz became increasingly deranged, cursing and raving that God would perform a miracle so that he should not be hanged. He attempted suicide with poison he had somehow managed to have smuggled into his prison. But he was no more successful in killing himself than in poisoning babies. He became violently and unpleasantly ill, but eventually recovered sufficiently to meet his fate.

Refusing God to the end, Cornelisz was dragged to his execution on 2 October, together with the worst mutineers. He was confronted by the woman he had forced to live with him and appeared to be briefly contrite before Creesje Jans' accusations. But then his condemned accomplices began hissing and shouting their demand for him to hang first so they could see with their own eyes the death of 'the seducer of men'⁵. In accordance with the sentence of the council, both Cornelisz's hands were hacked off and, according to Pelsaert's journal, as he was forced to take the scaffold some of the condemned mutineers began to shout 'revenge' at their once-proud leader. He screamed back at them and at the council as well as all those assembled to witness his end.

One of these was Gijsbert Bastiaensz who, as a man of God, had the task of conducting the condemned man to the scaffold. Cornelisz refused to speak to him or to admit that he had done anything wrong. Bastiaensz later wrote that 'The justice and vengeance of God has been made manifest in him.' Another witness at the execution later wrote that Cornelisz had 'died as he had lived, not believing there exists a Devil or Hell, God or Angel'.⁶

Most of the remaining mutineers were more subdued, some confessing, others not bothering. But the crazed cabin boy Jan Pelgrom began weeping hysterically and begging to be spared as avidly as he had once begged to murder. He screamed to be left on an island so he might 'live a little longer'. For some reason, Pelsaert heard his plea and agreed on account of his youthful eighteen years. The other mutineers went to their deaths as decreed by Pelsaert and the council. In those days, hanging was not an efficient method of execution, death occurring by strangulation rather than snapping of the neck. The mutineers dangled a long time before they stopped breathing.

Between the interrogations of the mutineers and preparations for the dispatch of some, the rescuers and those survivors who had remained loyal to the VOC began to salvage the *Batavia*'s rich treasures. They also scoured the reefs and islands for anything else that might be valuable, useful or of interest to their masters awaiting the *Sardam*'s return in Batavia Castle. It was a massive task. The *Batavia* herself 'was lying in many pieces', Pelsaert wrote, and most of the structure above the waterline had been washed away and lay strewn in broken sections around the site. 'There did not look to be much hope of salvaging much of the money or the goods.'

Foul weather prevented the divers from reaching the chests of treasure remaining in the *Batavia*'s shattered hold. While they waited for the weather to improve, Pelsaert had all able-bodied hands out searching the reef and islands for any scrap of useful material. During this extensive beachcombing exercise, another five men were lost in a boating accident as they searched for salvage on the outer islands in mid-October. Bad weather forced their small craft out to sea and they were never seen again. There was a hasty search for them. Smoke was later seen rising from the mainland but no other traces were found. Although the smoke was probably from Aboriginal fires, perhaps one or more of them made it to the mainland, unknown to Pelsaert and the survivors.

But, delayed by the bad weather, Pelsaert had no time to waste. He was worried about the potential for a renewed mutiny among the ragged band at his command. A further five mutineers were tried and sentenced to keel-hauling, being dropped from the mast, a flogging or a loss of wages. Sometimes they suffered a combination of all four punishments. By the time the divers had recovered ten of the twelve VOC treasure chests from the sea floor and the islands had been picked bare of useful items, it was mid-November. Pelsaert set sail for Java.

Begged from death

On 15 November the *Sardam* carried away the remaining seventy-seven survivors of the wreck, the majority of them, including the promoted Wiebbe Hayes, loyal to the VOC. As they sailed north they spotted smoke on the mainland. Hoping it might be the missing five men, the *Sardam* managed to moor in an inlet. They soon saw that the place was inhabited but found no trace of their shipmates and saw no indigenous people. There was fresh water, though, and Pelsaert decided this would be a good place to carry out the sentences of Jan Pelgrom and another mutineer, Wouter Loos, condemned to marooning for taking over as leader of the mutiny after the capture of Cornelisz by the defenders.

Why Pelsaert decided to spare, if only for an unknown time, the lives of these murderers and rapists, we will never know. Perhaps he hoped to reinforce his shaky position with the council in Batavia by telling them he had left a couple of men on the Southland to pursue the company's interests. But as the first-known European settlers on the continent, they were chillingly uninspiring. What little we know of them comes from Pelsaert's journal:

> Jan Pelgrom de Bije of Bemmel, aged about 18 years, late cabin servant on the ship Batavia, who according to his own freewill confession has behaved in a godless manner in words and deeds, more fitting to a beast than a man, has also murdered on Seals Island a boy and Janneken Gist, wife of Jan Hendricxz from the Hague, gunner, and has also helped Andries Jonas to kill. And on 16 August required very urgently that he should be allowed to behead Cornelis Aldersz of Ylpendam, hooploper [young sailor], but this was allowed to Mattijs Beijr, about which he wept. He also has had carnal knowledge of Zussien and Trijntgien Fredricxsz, both sisters, and Anneken Bosschieters, all married women.

Loos was around twenty-four years of age, a soldier from the German city of Maastricht. It was said at his trial that he had 'let himself be drawn aside from the way of humanity and of reasonable creatures, and through his innate corruptness has let himself be used by the Godless, Epicurean villain Jeronimus Cornelisz'. Among his many crimes of murder and rape was that testified by Judick, surviving daughter of the minister, who had witnessed Loos use an adze to batter in the head of her brother. The council's verdict was that:

> We have preferred grace in place of rigour of the Justice to foresaid Wouter Loos, and have sentenced him as we sentence hereby, that he shall be put here on the same Southland as a death-deserving delinquent, together with Jan Pelgrom de Bije van Bemmel, who was sentenced on 28 September, to the gallows on account of his misdeeds, but has been begged from death, in order to make himself familiar with the inhabitants of this land and to search out what is happening here, and to be rescued some time by ships that may happen to fall hereabout, and to be of some service to the Company.

And, of course, all Loos' wages and belongings were forfeit to the company.

The two men were landed at what is now Wittecarra Gully, south of the Murchison River. They were given a small boat, or *schuijdt,* so they would be able 'to put ashore there or here, to make themselves known to the folk of this land by tokens of friendship'. These tokens, supplied to them by Pelsaert, included some cheap wooden toys and novelties known as 'Nurembergen', as well as knives, beads, bells and small mirrors, 'of which shall give to the blacks only a few until they have grown familiar with them'. It was instructed that once they had made friends with the natives, and if invited 'into their villages to their chief men', the castaways should 'have courage to go with them willingly'. Pelsaert confidently pronounced that 'Man's luck is found in strange places' and 'if God guards you will not suffer any damage from them, but on the contrary, because they have never seen any white men, they will offer all friendship'.

Most importantly, while Pelgrom and Loos were making their way in an unknown world, they were enjoined to:

Observe with all diligence what material, be it gold, or silver, happens there to be found, and what they esteem as valuable. So that, having come to perfect friendship with them, you may be able to ask, by signs and by learning their language, that a look out should be kept for ships, or for people coming from the side of the sea, in order to obtain from them more of such goods as iron, copper, or Nurembergen, of which you have with you several samples which without doubt will please them greatly.

Pelsaert reminded them that most VOC ships passed that part of the coast between April and July and that they 'must look out keenly at that time, and seeing any, give suchlike signs as shall appear to be done with purpose, be it with smoke or otherwise'. Finally, he advised, 'Above all, keep God in mind, never forget him, and without doubt he will keep you close in his shadow and will yet vouchsafe, at the last a good outcome.'

What 'good outcome' the merchant could have had in mind is difficult to imagine. Reading his journal, it is possible he had a hazy notion of establishing a VOC trading post, perhaps to curry some much-needed favour with his company masters. Whatever Pelsaert's motivations, Pelgrom and Loos were never seen again by any European, though the import of their existence on the Southland—however brief it might have been—continues to the present.

After a rapid three-week voyage back to Batavia Castle, the survivors found the siege lifted and Governor-General Coen dead, replaced by Jacques Specx. Pelsaert's judgements on the fourteen mutineers remaining alive were ignored and the men were re-sentenced. Five were hanged. The rest were variously flogged, branded, exiled or otherwise punished. One man, a stonecutter named Pietersz, had taken a prominent role in the mutiny and some of the murders. He was sentenced to be broken on the wheel, an especially slow and agonising way to die.

A handful of those who had played some part in the mutiny and the murders managed to escape VOC retribution and faded into history. So did most of the survivors. The minister Bastiaensz wrote an account of his ordeal for the VOC but received no sympathy for his losses. Instead, he was persecuted for signing one of the oaths of allegiance to Cornelisz, an action thought unworthy of a man of God. He remained under a cloud with the Council of the Indies but was eventually allowed to preach again. He remarried two years after his Southland ordeal but in 1633 died of dysentery, a common end in the Indies. His surviving daughter, Judick, was subsequently married and widowed several times. She eventually received a handsome compensation payment from the VOC and became a woman of substance in Dordrecht, though her ultimate fate is unknown.[7]

The woman at the centre of the lusts and greed of the mutineers, Creesje Jans, finally arrived at her destination. But the husband she had left Holland to rejoin was dead. She later married again and returned to Holland where she lived on until at least the early 1640s.

Fortunately for Pelsaert, he had been successful in recovering the bulk of the company's money. He was sent off to fight the Portuguese and eventually died in September 1630, probably of the same mysterious but persistent disease he had suffered at least since the *Batavia* set sail from Texel.

The mutinous skipper, Ariaen Jacobsz, had been imprisoned since the longboat arrived in Batavia in July 1629. He was interrogated and tortured but refused to confess. He was still in the dungeon in June 1631 but after that there is no further record of his fate. It was probably unpleasant.

For the company itself, the *Batavia* incident became the textbook example of what not to do in case of shipwreck. All VOC merchants and skippers were from then on forbidden to leave survivors without authoritative command. Over the next fifteen years, a few VOC ships were told to look out for Pelgrom and Loos as they coasted the

Southland's shore. None ever saw them. Yet, sixty-eight years after the marooning, Willem de Vlamingh searched for water where the men were left. He recorded that he came across a hut constructed in the European style with a sloping roof, very unlike the dwellings erected by the local Aboriginal people.

Once the story of the wrecking and its horrors became public knowledge, it stimulated a publishing industry in its own right. There were no newspapers as we know them at this time. Instead, individuals wishing to air their opinions or ideas published pamphlets. Some of these were eyewitness accounts by survivors and circulated widely through Dutch society, as did a few street ballads lamenting the sensational events at the other end of the known world. Later, larger pamphlets, or proto books, appeared which contained bits and pieces of Pelsaert's journals, what purported to be the accounts of survivors, as well as letters by various hands, including that of the minister, Gijsbert Bastiaensz.

But over time, the *Batavia*'s story faded and outside a small circle of maritime historians, was little known in the English-speaking world, despite the occasional surfacing of a translated journal or other document. It was not until Henrietta Drake-Brockman's *Voyage to Disaster* provided the first full English translation of Pelsaert's journal in the early 1960s that a serious interest was taken in relocating and investigating the wreck. Since then, a number of writers have tackled the theme in various ways, bringing the dreadful events of the *Batavia* wreck to a wider audience.[8]

Rediscovering the graveyard

As far as we know, it was not until 1840 that another ship visited Batavia's Graveyard. Commanding the famous *Beagle* that once carried Darwin around the world, Lieutenant Lort Stokes surveyed the still isolated and forbidding Houtman Abrolhos. He found wreckage he believed to be that of the *Batavia*, or possibly the

Zeewijk, and believed he had established the location of the various islands on and around which the survivors had played out their bloody drama.

An expedition led by newspaperman Malcolm Uren in 1938 presented a conclusion that did not fit well with the few known facts and suggested that the wreckage sighted by the later *Zeewijk* survivors had not been the *Batavia* at all but one of the other missing VOC ships of the period. It would not be until the 1950s that historian and author Henrietta Drake-Brockman began to deploy her local Abrolhos contacts and archival sleuthing abilities to argue that the real location of the *Batavia* was more than 100 kilometres further north than the position suggested by Lort Stokes.

A number of local discoveries of skeletons and artefacts were made in the early 1960s. One of these items was a trumpet mouth, or bell, bearing the date of manufacture. It was a definitive 1628. The remains of the instrument were found where few had suspected to be the site of the wreck, a windswept cay by then known as Beacon Island.

Then, in June 1963, a party of divers located the *Batavia* at the south-eastern tip of Morning Reef, very close to the area suggested by Drake-Brockman.[9] Hugh Edwards, who would later write a book on the *Batavia*, led the next expedition, which was supported by the Royal Australian Navy and the Western Australian Maritime Museum.

Over the following decades, archaeologists scoured the area, much as the survivors had under Pelsaert's salvage instructions more than three centuries before them. Eventually they found the stone structure on Wiebbe Hayes' island known as the 'fort'. Whether or not the crude building is where the defenders mounted their resistance to the blood-crazed mutineers, it is generally said to be Australia's earliest European structure. The broken and coral-encrusted remains gave up cannon, anchors, arms, money and a great variety of objects from the everyday life of the early seventeenth century.

Eventually the ship that once carried these objects gave up her bones. A large section of *Batavia*'s hull has been resurrected and reassembled in the Shipwreck Gallery of the Western Australian Maritime Museum in Fremantle. Along with a replica stone portico[10] that the ship was carrying as cargo is a stone sarcophagus containing the hacked skeleton of a murdered castaway. The information provided for the visitor is a chilling précis of the *Batavia* story and the vicious way in which the person in the coffin met his end. Professional research on the site has continued on and off since then and the wreck is now part of an official 'trail' of wrecks for recreational divers.[11] A full-sized replica of *Batavia* was built in the Netherlands and visited Australia in 2000.

Batavia's grim story was only the first of a number of shipwreck sagas, lost treasures and survivor mysteries along the western shores of the unknown Southland. But in the years immediately following the deathly reign and ignominious end of Jeronimus Cornelisz, the VOC would send out one notably unsuccessful expedition and another that would change the maps and charts forever.

5

Paper voyages

Even by the bloody standards of the time, the *Batavia* mutiny was a shocking event. More worryingly for the company, it was an expensive exercise. As well as losing a valuable ship and a sizeable portion of its rich cargo, further resources had to be diverted to the rescue and return of the survivors. The VOC issued new standing orders forbidding the skipper and upper-merchant to leave stranded crew and passengers in any future wrecks. There was also now a vital need to obtain accurate charts of the Southland and its surrounding reefs and islands—if, in fact, that was what they were. No one knew. Someone had to be sent to find out.

An ill-fated expedition
In April 1636, Gerritt Thomas Pool was given command of *Cleen* (or *Klein*), *Amsterdam* and *Wesel* (variously described as *jagts* and *shallops*), which were destined for the discovery of the lands situated east of Banda, and furthermore, of the Southland. Pool was to visit the places discovered by the *Pera* and *Aernem* thirteen years earlier—as the VOC decreed, 'You will endeavour to ascertain

what may be obtained from there, whether these lands are peopled, and what the natives subsist on.'

Pool was also charged to seek a passage through to the South Seas. Failing that, he was to sail west, then down the western coast of Southland, looking out for the rocks on which the *Tryall* had foundered and also the 'two Dutch delinquents', Jan Pelgrom and Wouter Loos, marooned by Francisco Pelsaert after the *Batavia* disaster. 'You will grant passage to the said persons, if they should be alive to show themselves, and should request you to be brought hither,' the VOC instructed. He was also to look for 'refreshments and fresh water' to provision VOC ships on the long haul from the Cape of Good Hope to the Indies and take careful note and record of everything seen.

There were extensive instructions on dealing with the natives. As well as trading, where possible:

> In landing with small craft you will use great circumspection, and your treatment of the natives that should allow you to come to parley, must and ought to be marked by great kindness, wary caution, and skillful judgment; slight misdemeanours on the part of such natives, such as petty thefts and the like, which they should commit against you, you will suffer to pass unnoticed, that by so doing you may draw them unto you, and not inspire them with aversion to our nation.

Sage advice was offered on the character traits required when questing for new lands: 'Whoever endeavours to discover unknown lands and tribes, had need to be patient and long-suffering, noways quick to fly out, but always bent on ingratiating himself.' But the orders soon came back to the main item of business:

> We have put on board your ships various kinds of merchandise and minerals, which you will show to the people whom you should

come to parley with, partly that by so doing you may come to know whether any of these goods are produced by their country, partly in order to see what desire and inclination they evince to our mercantile commodities, and what goods they might be ready to offer in exchange for the same.

While juggling these injunctions, Pool and his men were to pay close attention 'to the disposition of the people, their character, condition and humours; to the religion they profess and to their manner of government; their wars, their arms and weapons; the food they eat and the clothes they wear, and what they mainly subsist on'. In contrast to other voyages, Pool was cautioned: 'You will not carry off with you any natives against their will.' But if any were willing to sail with him, the company allowed him to grant them free passage.

The VOC's instructions demonstrate a very different approach to the natives and indicate some rethinking by the company. The detailed commands and considerable resources made available for this expedition marked a serious attempt by the company to sort out the Southland question, including whether or not it was connected to New Guinea. They were 'convinced' that it was but were willing to explore further.

However, their high expectations for the expedition were dashed when Pool was killed early in the voyage in a skirmish with 'wild Southlanders'. He went ashore with some of his crew and almost immediately encountered a group of indigenous inhabitants. At first they were friendly 'but acted afterwards in a hostile manner'. The commander and his steward were surrounded by their assailants who 'cut these two men to pieces, and carried them into the wood; but it never could be discovered what they did with them'. Two other crewmen suffered a similar end.

Although the Dutch believed their attackers to be Southlanders, they were not. Pool's flotilla was, in fact, still in New Guinea.

The super-cargo Pieter Pietersen became captain and attempted to carry out the instructions Pool had been given. But, as the company report put it: 'On the 9th of June, being duly revictualled, he had set sail again from the said native village of Taranga, shaping his course to southward in order to endeavour to get to eastward by some means or other, so as to accomplish his ordained voyage.' He seems to have made contact with the Southland, but briefly:

> When he had got to southward as far as the 11th degree of latitude, he had not only found and met with the east- and south-east winds blowing constantly with great vehemence and hollow seas, but had also come upon a new land; in such fashion that, seeing no chance of getting to eastward for the accomplishment of his voyage, since such voyage will have to take place in the beginning of the western monsoon, he resolved with his council to give up further investigations to eastward, to explore and survey the situation of the newly discovered Van Diemensland[1], also called Arnhems or Speultsland, and, having gathered the required information, to run northward again for the purpose of obtaining perfect knowledge of the islands of Timor and Tenember; and all this having been duly effected, to return to Banda.

Pietersen reported an experience much like that of many other VOC sailors. He surveyed east and west for 20 miles: 'He has seen many fires and frequent clouds of smoke, but no natives, houses, prows [boats] or fruit trees, although he has paddled close along the shore with an orangbay [ship's boat], and gone ashore in sundry places, finding the land wild and barren; wherefore, not having been able to come to parley with any of the inhabitants.'[2] These events took place around the region of what is now Melville Island.

Whether the expedition was being careful to avoid contact with the native inhabitants after their commander had been killed, we cannot know; though it seems remarkable that no Aboriginal or Torres Strait people were encountered at all during these months of voyaging. Pietersen's sorry flotilla slid back into Batavia on 6 October 1636 with nothing further to report.

The grand gentlemen of the VOC were still no wiser about the Southland and considerably poorer for their efforts to find out. But they had not given up. Six years later they would again equip an ambitious expedition to discover more about the stubbornly enigmatic land. In the meantime, the company continued to develop its extensive trading interests and the creaking management structure that held it all—more or less—together. The whole enterprise depended on ships and those who sailed them, the organisation of the company and the maritime information jealously guarded from its many competitors.

The business of the VOC

Many sailors on both naval and merchant ships of this period were not necessarily seamen, but cheap labour, possibly press-ganged or 'crimped', perhaps convicts, criminals or heretics on the run. They were—and are—mostly anonymous. Even quite senior officers were unnamed in merchant ships. Discipline was harsh, severe or even on occasion sadistic. The captain was, literally, 'the master'.

Ships were cold and damp in winter, poorly ventilated and stifling in summer conditions. Crews were often poorly fed, with scurvy and other ill-effects of malnourishment contributing to the sometimes astonishingly high death rates.[3] Especially in tropical regions, they also commonly suffered from dysentery, malaria, yellow fever, typhus, possibly smallpox and frequently venereal diseases. Other vitamin-deficiency problems included beriberi, pellagra and possibly night blindness. They slept and ate in cramped quarters among decomposing refuse, urine, vomit and the stink of always-damp ballast. Ships were infested with vermin, as were those who sailed them. Once fresh supplies ran out, the rest of the lengthy voyage from Europe to the South Seas was supplied only with dried foods and salted meat. Often this was ruined in the damp storage conditions, producing maggots, weevils and what would elsewhere have been inedible food. But the sailors had no choice, other than to leave it to the rats that lived aboard all ships.

Although 'Jan Company', as its employees called the VOC, was a Dutch enterprise, those who sailed its ships or sailed in them, or who provided the armies of administrators needed to run the empire, came from many parts of Europe. The Seventeen Gentlemen—pinnacle of the hierarchy—ordered a count of the VOC's employees in the Indies (Asia) in 1688. The tally is incomplete, but it tells us that there were around 11,500 employees on land, 7800 being military. More than half of these soldiers came from outside the Dutch provinces: from Germany, Poland, Switzerland, England, Scandinavia, what is now Belgium, as well as from the Baltic region. At sea were approximately 4000 sailors[4] and while the survey does not seem to have included their countries of origin, we know from many other sources that the crews of VOC ships were usually a very mixed bunch.

These sketchy figures are only for the Indies locations of the VOC's mercantile empire. The scale of their activities also included a massive managerial, administrative and commercial intelligence structure in Amsterdam and elsewhere. It is often suggested that a primary, though not the only, reason for the company's eventual bankruptcy was its massive human scale. It was simply too big to run and, in any case, its management structure was unable to do the job.

The VOC had been formed through what we would today call a corporate merger. Companies with an interest in the Indies trade were already operating in various Dutch seaport cities. Six of these cities formed the chambers of the organisation. The largest chamber was Amsterdam, controlling eight seats on the board of the Seventeen Gentlemen. The other five cities of Enkhuizen, Rotterdam, Hoorn, Middleburg and Delft made up the remaining chambers—with nine gentlemen representatives among them. These chambers continued to operate their own business, though now everything had to first be approved by the board. Once approved, the chambers would carry out the board's decisions.

In the Indies, the VOC established a council to operate as a kind of sub-board and, under supervision of the Seventeen Gentlemen, to conduct company business in that lucrative part of the world. The 'Council of the Indies' was a very powerful group, headed by a 'governor-general' who controlled the business, military and political activities of the company throughout the region. Each of the company's trading bases had its own governor and so there was another vast bureaucracy supporting this large-scale and complex activity—though one thing always remained paramount, the maintenance and furtherance of trade.[5]

While the VOC had a well-defined and all-powerful board, the problems of distance, communication and regulation meant that the vast bulk of the human iceberg beneath their well-heeled shoes effectively operated as they saw fit. While there were very clear rules and regulations promulgated throughout the company, the realities of seventeenth- and eighteenth-century life meant that those who wished to, or needed to, could flout the rules without worrying much. As the company became increasingly bloated, so these inbuilt tendencies within its structure became more pronounced. Personal trading, always allowed, became greater and greater, as did the corrupt practices that often accompanied it.

To better pursue their trading ambitions, the VOC developed what was essentially a think-tank, or commercial intelligence unit. Headquartered in Amsterdam was the company training college. All charts and associated information from the VOC's far-flung operations were transported back to Amsterdam. Here, they were copied and filed to form the basis of the next generation of charts, maps and atlases. As new information arrived, it was meticulously reviewed and, if found useful and accurate, turned quickly by scribes into the latest must-have for *stuurleiden,* or steersmen, the main navigators aboard VOC craft.

So great was the demand for such charts, not only by the VOC but also the many private traders, that a vigorous network of independent mapmakers and suppliers thrived in the harbour towns of the Dutch Republic. In 1617 the great mapmaker Hessel Gerritz became the VOC's exclusive supplier, and from then all mapping and navigation matters became in-house operations, even though those who made them worked from their own premises rather than company headquarters. Not surprisingly, the contracting mapmakers were required to keep the valuable information at their fingertips a closely guarded secret. Later in the seventeenth century, some mapmakers began producing their own charts and collections, or mapbooks, independently of the VOC and making use of the developing technology of print and bookmaking.

The mapmakers also assumed greater responsibility for training navigators as time went on. VOC captains and steersmen were obliged to use only company charts on their voyages and were supplied with the latest relevant editions as well as the necessary navigational instruments.

Although the dominant Amsterdam chamber held the lion's share of intellectual property, the smaller chambers managed to retain some control over their mapmaking needs. And, far away in Batavia, the governor-general and council also maintained a substantial local map- and chart-making operation responsive to regional needs, maintained military forces and generally kept control of whatever needed to be controlled in the interests of furthering company business.[6] Looming ever-larger in this business was the whereabouts and character of the unmapped Southland.

In 1642 after considerable discussion, Governor-General Anthony van Diemen received from Master Pilot Franz Visscher[7] a 'memorandum concerning the discovery of the Southland'.

Visscher was a skilled navigator and amateur geographer with an extensive knowledge of VOC activities in the Indies. In his opinion, the Southland would be found by travelling east from Mauritius to New Guinea. Van Diemen valued Visscher's knowledge and appointed him to the role of chief navigator on a new attempt to be mounted under the command of Abel Tasman.

Tasman's island

Borne on a north-east wind and with good weather, Abel Jansz Tasman and his ships *Heemskerk* (175 tons) and *Zeehan* (50 tons) left Batavia behind on 14 August 1642 'for the discovery of the unknown Southland'. The VOC had decided to make what we might today call a targeted investment in discovering the great south continent. They were also anxious for Tasman to confirm the stories of fabulous golden riches in the land of 'Beach', as they called it at the time. Tasman, a tough 40-year-old Calvinist, was selected to captain this momentous undertaking based on his long experience. As a result of this and a later voyage, he is generally considered among the great navigators of sail, although many of his discoveries were known only to a few until well into the eighteenth century.[8]

Tasman's voyage did not begin well. On the evening of the first day, the *Zeehan* ran aground on a local island. She was soon refloated during the night, but it was not a good start to what was to be a very rough voyage to Mauritius. Six weeks sailing from Mauritius brought him to the island now known as Tasmania, though he gave it another name: 'This land being the first land we have met with in the South Sea and not known to any European nation we have conferred on it the name of "Anthony Van Diemenslandt" in honour of the Honourable Governor-General, our illustrious master, who sent us to make this discovery.'

Tasman sailed around his discovery, though a storm blew him far back out to sea on 29 November. But three days later Tasman's ships were able to anchor in what they named Frederick Henry's Bay (now Blackman Bay), after the leader of the Dutch Republic.

Early the following morning, Pilot-Major François Jacobsz took a party of men armed with muskets, side arms and pikes ashore. They came back in the afternoon carrying 'various samples of vegetables which they had seen growing there in great abundance'. The Dutch had heard 'certain human sounds and also sounds nearly resembling the music of a trump or a small gong', which they determined was not far from them, though they saw no one.

On 3 December, Tasman and his men made several further foraging expeditions around the bay in which they had anchored, concluding that the still unseen natives must be 'of very tall stature, as the steps cut into trees to allow access to bird's eggs were fully five feet apart'. Tasman's journal describes how he and his men went to the south-east of the bay during the afternoon: 'We carried with us a pole with the Company's mark carved into it, and a Prince-flag to be set up there, that those who shall come after us may become aware that we have been here, and have taken possession of the said land as our lawful property.'

About halfway across, the wind blew so severely that the smaller cock-boat of the *Zeehan* was forced to turn back, though Tasman continued on in the larger pinnace:

> When we had come close inshore in a small inlet which bore west-south-west of the ships the surf ran so high that we could not get near the shore without running the risk of having our pinnace dashed to pieces. We then ordered the carpenter aforesaid to swim to the shore alone with the pole and the flag, and kept by the wind with our pinnace; we made him plant the said pole with the flag at top into the earth, about the centre of the bay near four tall trees easily recognisable and standing in the form of a crescent, exactly before the one standing lowest.

The Dutch then returned to their ships, 'leaving the above-mentioned as a memorial for those who shall come after us, and for the natives of this country, who did not show themselves, though we suspect some of them were at no great distance and closely watching our proceedings'.

What the natives made of these activities of possession can only be surmised.

When the storm died down, Tasman made a dash for a better harbour, an anchor broken. They saw columns of smoke billowing from the shore again but not those who made the fires. By 5 December, Tasman was at sea again, away from the land that would now begin to be known as 'New Holland'[9].

Heading east, Tasman reached New Zealand, falling into conflict with the Maori which resulted in fatalities on both sides. He then continued on to discover and chart the Pacific islands of Tonga and Fiji, among others, before returning to Batavia in June 1643.

Tasman's second voyage

Despite his discoveries, Tasman did not return to his masters in triumph. Instead, his voyage was deemed, at best, a moderate success as he had found nothing the company could exploit, certainly no lands of golden riches. In January 1644 he was dispatched again, this time with three ships—*Zeemeuw*, *Limmen* and *Bracqu*—to extend knowledge of New Guinea and attempt to sail down the east coast of Southland. The Dutch already suspected that Southland was 'the largest island in the globe' and wanted Tasman to prove it. Only the sailing orders and a chart from this voyage have survived. But these are far more than a bare list of instructions. They contain the entire VOC knowledge of the Southland up to that date. The details of discovery and disaster are rehearsed, and it is clear that the company's view of the place was largely negative:

The several successive administrations of India, in order to enlarge and extend the trade of the Dutch East India company, have zealously endeavored to make an early discovery of the great land of New Guinea and other unknown east and southerly countries, as you know by several discourses, and maps, journals, and papers communicated to you. But hitherto with little success, although several voyages have been undertaken.

Observations on previous sightings, encounters and disasters such as the *Batavia* story were given: 'In this discovery were found everywhere shallow water and barren coast; islands altogether thinly peopled by divers, cruel, poor, and brutal nations, and of very little use to the Company.'

The orders then came to Tasman's previous voyage. They were, for the VOC, highly congratulatory:

After the little success in these voyages nothing further was attempted on discovery to the eastward, but last year (under your direction) the discovery of the remaining unknown south lands was assiduously reattempted; and in that remarkable voyage was that great unknown Staten and Van Diemen's Land discovered from 35 to 43 degrees south latitude, and at the same time the (so long wished for) passage to the South Sea.

Tasman was being rewarded for his modest previous success with another big task. The company wanted to find out 'whether New Guinea is one continent with that great south land, or separated by channels and islands lying between them'. They also wanted to know if Van Diemen's Land was attached to the larger landmass and what islands might be found between New Guinea and 'the unknown south land'. The VOC masters were confident that Tasman 'will with courage, vigilance, prudence, good order, and the requisite perseverance, skillfully direct this important voyage in such a manner as to be capable to give an account on your return fully to our contentment'.

With these precise commands, together with several more pages of the VOC wish list, Commander Tasman, as he was now styled, departed in January 1644. But, like everyone else except Luis Vaez de Torres, he missed the straits that would have taken him to the east coast. Instead, as his orders allowed in case he could not find a way through, he sailed westward in the wake of many who had gone before, charting the coasts from the Gulf of Carpentaria across to the west coast where he was to conduct a VOC treasure hunt: 'You shall steer along the Land of Eendragt to Houtmans Abrolhos; and when you have found a proper place thereabouts for anchoring, you are to endeavour to find a chest containing 8,000 rix dollars, that was lost in the wreck of the ship *Batavia* in the year 1629.'

Not only was Tasman instructed to look for the missing portion of the *Batavia* treasure, he was told to search for the 'two Netherlanders [Jan Pelgrom and Wouter Loos], who, having forfeited their lives, were put on shore by their Commander Francisco Polsert [Pelsaert]'. Furthermore, the company instructed, if the men were found alive, 'you can enquire of them concerning the country; and, if they entreat you to that purpose, give them a passage hither'.[10]

But the castaway mutineers of the *Batavia* were not found. Tasman returned to a mostly successful further career with the VOC, voyaging, trading and fighting the Spanish. In 1649 he was removed from office after a drunken fit in which he hanged one of his sailors. The incident took place while Tasman was in Manila attacking Spanish treasure ships. Normally this would not have been much of an issue in the VOC, but Tasman's inebriation caused him to execute without the nicety of a trial. He paid compensation to the dead sailor's family and was reinstated by January 1651 but retired shortly after. He is thought to have died wealthy in Batavia, probably in 1659.

The Bonaparte map

Recognition of Tasman's significant discoveries was a long time coming. This was due mainly to the VOC's concern to keep its commercial information in deep confidence. A map known both as 'the Tasman map' and as 'the Bonaparte map' shows the navigator's discoveries during his two famous voyages, combined with those of other Dutch explorers. It is famous for the very early and accurate representation of the whole of Southland, a fact that suggests it was made later than the mid-1640s. While it was once thought that Tasman supervised the drawing of this map on fine Japanese paper, it is now believed that the work is from the mid-1690s and so reflects later knowledge of the continent.

The history of this map is mysterious. It is assumed that, like everything else of potential informational value, its contents would have been used to prepare updated charts for VOC sailors. What happened to it up to 1860 is unknown, but it probably remained in the hands of the Van Keulen business of VOC cartographers. In that year, the cartographers published a lithograph of the original as a supplement to an edition of Tasman's journal.

By 1891 the map had come into the hands of the bookseller Frederick Muller. It then gained its second name of the 'Bonaparte map' when it was purchased by Prince Roland Bonaparte. It seems that the New South Wales government were also interested in purchasing the map, but probably could not better the prince's deeper pockets. Bonaparte was closely interested in the history of Australia and is said to have wished the map to be donated to the Australian people at his death.

Nothing happened until 1926 when the always-intriguing Daisy Bates entered the story. She wrote to the head of the Public Library of New South Wales, as it was then known, drawing attention to the prince's wish and suggesting that the Trustees of the Mitchell Library should follow it up. They did so, discovering that the map was held by the nobleman's heir, the Princess George of Greece. In 1933, the princess donated the map to the Mitchell Library, where it remains today. In 1943 a marble mosaic of the map was revealed in the foyer of what was then the new library building.[11]

However, as with most historic maps, things are not straightforward. There is, in the collection of the National Library of Australia, a previously unrecorded map of Tasman's two voyages. Thought to have been published in 1648, the very fine work by Amsterdam mapmaker Cornelis Danckert (the elder) shows a reasonably accurate version of the western side of the continent and of Tasmania.[12] If the dating of this map and of the Tasman/Bonaparte map are correct, then Danckert's is the oldest known representation of Australia including Tasmania.

Sailing instructions, charts, logs, journals, business letters and records were as much part of the revelation of Australia as epic journeys of discovery and enigmatic first encounters. These practical documents were complemented by more thrilling accounts of danger and discovery penned by those who had been there, as well as many who had not. The demand for factual or fabricated adventures about the end of the earth was so high that they were a staple of book publishing and street literature for centuries.

But little more than a decade after Tasman's additions to the European knowledge of the Southland, another of the VOC's mighty ships would splinter on the cruel corals of the western coast. The story of her survivors and the subsequent search for them, preserved only in a few sheets of paper, is one of the most intriguing mysteries in the history of shipwrecks, treasure hunting and marine archaeology.

6

Death of the dragon

The *Golden Dragon*, as her English name suggests, was a fine vessel of which the VOC could be rightly proud. Officially called *Vergulde Draeck*—which is sometimes translated as *Gilt Dragon*, she was built at Amsterdam in 1653 and was a 260-ton yacht[1], almost 42 metres long and 10 metres wide. Sadly, though, her time in service with the VOC was short and she would famously founder on the distant shores of the Southland. The fate of her survivors, her lost treasure and her legends continue to puzzle and dismay us to the present day.

The dragon's end

It was to be the *Vergulde Draeck*'s second foray to the East Indies, and she left Texel in the Netherlands on 4 October 1655, the holds filled with eight crates of coin and trade goods worth a total of around 185,000 guilders. The voyage was without significant incident apart from the loss of two men overboard on the passage to the Cape of Good Hope. Here, Captain Pieter Albertsz resupplied and on 13 March 1656 set a course for Batavia with 193 men aboard. He followed the route pioneered by Hendrik Brouwer, catching the trade winds across the vast Indian Ocean, then north to the Spice Islands.

After six weeks of voyaging along this course, the first day-watch was just beginning on 28 April when, without warning, the ship ground into a reef on the west coast of the Southland, about 5 kilometres off the coast, a little north of present-day Moore River. The strong, near-new vessel immediately disintegrated on the cruel corals. Passengers and crew had no chance to salvage anything except themselves. Albertsz and his under-steersman struggled ashore with seventy-three others. The rest of the ship's company was stranded aboard the wreck, being rapidly pounded to smaller pieces by relentless waves. A few items and some provisions were washed up on the shore but otherwise the survivors had only what was on their bodies.[2]

Fortunately, one of the ship's boats—a small sailing craft known as a *schuyt*—had survived the ordeal and it was decided to send it to Batavia, more than 2500 kilometres away, with a small crew of survivors. The under-steersman and six others set out on their near-hopeless voyage aboard the tiny boat a few days later.

Those who remained scavenged whatever was washed ashore from the wreck and either resolved to stay and wait for possible help to arrive from Batavia, tried to repair the other ship's boat which was half-buried in the sand, or went inland in search of food and water. Quite possibly they did all these things, perhaps splitting into three, or even more, parties to maximise their chances of survival. Whatever did happen to the sixty-eight men on the beach after the *schuyt* left to seek rescue, nobody has yet discovered.

But, incredibly, after a harrowing four-week ordeal, the battered *schuyt* and her crew made it back to Batavia on 7 June. News of the wreck, a presumed large loss of lives and, not least, the rich cargo, galvanised the VOC. The company immediately dispatched the *Witte Valk* and what turned out to be the ironically named

Goede Hope to rescue the survivors and, with the provision of Macassan 'black divers' among the crews, perhaps the money.

Victualled for a five-month voyage, the *Witte Valk* sailed from Batavia the day after the *schuyt* brought the bad news, rendezvousing with the *Goede Hope* in the Sunda Strait. Even within such a short time, the VOC scribes were able to produce the usual detailed sailing orders. The ships were to 'steer for the coast of the Southland and having arrived, with God's help, at the people of the *Draeck*, they will distribute them over the two ships which must do their utmost to stay constantly together'. After that, the rescue ships would 'try to recover in the most careful way, whether diving or otherwise, if it is possible, firstly the cash and then as much as is practicable and possible of the cargo, the guns and what else is particularly valuable'.

Searching for survivors

The two ships sailed straight into violent storms and were, as the VOC had feared, quickly separated. The seas were so bad along the coast that the smaller *Witte Valk* dared not even try a landing and battled her way back to Batavia, arriving on 14 September with nothing to report. But the *Goede Hope* managed to get to the location given for the wreck. They put a boat and crew ashore and investigated, they claimed, several miles inland. Not only was there no sign of a wreck or survivors, but three men became lost in the 'wood' beyond the beach. A party of eight went to find them, but they also disappeared without trace. The *Goede Hope* had added another eleven to the *Draeck*'s casualty list and, possibly, deposited another group of early settlers on the uncharted coast.

The boat in which the landing crew had come ashore was found broken beyond use on the beach. The weather was so bad that the master feared losing his ship as well as the remainder of his men. He sailed back to Batavia, arriving exactly a month after the *Witte Valk* and with an even grimmer tale to tell. In fact, due to the inaccuracy of seventeenth-century navigation, the *Goede Hope* had landed her rescue boat at least 50 kilometres away from the wreck.

A second attempt to rescue the survivors of the *Vergulde Draeck* got underway early the next year, but this was also plagued with problems. Believing that any survivors might still be alive, it was decided to try sending smaller ships from the Cape of Good Hope to look for them. One of these was the fluyt *Vincq*, which sailed from the cape on 27 April 1657. In the pitch darkness of the night of 8 June, she anchored at 25 fathoms, (around 45 metres) well off the coast. When the sun came up the skipper found he was anchored to a long reef with large breakers all around. He immediately sailed north into violent storms, arriving in Batavia with no news. Even if he had been able to land and conduct a shore search, the luckless captain would have found nothing as he was a good 150 kilometres north of even the inaccurately recorded position of the *Draeck* and her survivors if, by then, there were any.

In December 1657, the governor-general convinced the Council of the Indies in Batavia that yet another attempt should be made to rescue any survivors, perhaps salvage the cargo and also chart the treacherous reefs along that coastline. The fluyt *Waeckende Boey* and the smaller galiot *Emeloordt* were selected for this expedition. Their respective captains, Samuel Volkerson and Aucke Pieters Jonck, received the usual detailed instructions from their VOC masters. Their orders rehearsed the sad tale of the *Draeck* and the abortive rescues. They expressed 'very little hope that these people will still be found alive, but we have great fear that they have perished through hunger and misery or have been beaten to death by savage inhabitants and murdered'.

Jonck and Volkerson were to proceed to the believed site of the wreck, light large fires on the beach and fire the occasional cannon to attract the attention of any who might still be alive. As the time of year was summer, it was expected that the two ships would enjoy better weather than the previous winter expeditions. As always, they were to chart anything and everything they came across. The experience with the earlier rescue attempts, particularly that of the *Goede Hope,* had left their mark on the VOC hierarchy and there were detailed directions to the captains about how they should handle any landings.

They were to always be fully armed, keep together and must leave either the master or mate aboard the ships, along with sufficient men to crew them home if disaster struck the shore party. If they came across any inhabitants, they were warned not to trust any friendly advances 'as there can be no doubt that if any inhabitants appear they will be a savage and barbarous people which cannot be trusted'. However, in case the inhabitants were interested in trade, the captains were provided with trade goods and cloth 'to see what they may be able and willing to exchange for these which could yield a profit for the Company'.

While the orders expressed little hope that the *Draeck*'s cash could be retrieved, the captains should see if there was an opportunity to do so. And there was an incentive: 'For this purpose, in order to make the crew more zealous, we have approved that out of what shall be acquired and salvaged by them a proper share be apportioned to be distributed among them individually.' The VOC was very keen to have its treasure back, even at a cost.

The captains were strictly enjoined to keep their ships together and, indeed, were told that 'we have decided to employ two ships for this exploration for which otherwise one would have been sufficient'. The two ships, although relatively recently built, turned out to be sadly mismatched in terms of their sea-going qualities. Jonck's *Emeloordt* was in structural trouble early in the long voyage, worsened by regular atrocious weather. He had to stop frequently to effect repairs and rest his exhausted crew. Volkerson's *Waeckende Boey* suffered relatively little difficulty and continually outpaced Jonck, a source of growing frustration to Volkerson who seems to have been very much a man on a mission. Jonck was a

more laid-back character and these differences in the men's personalities played into the tensions between them and their vessels.

As well as having the better ship, Volkerson was also lucky
to have an outstanding first mate or upper-steersman. He was a
man named Abraham Leeman,[3] whose little-known story would
become one of the greatest epics of seafaring.

It began after the *Emeloordt* and *Waeckende Boey* had sailed from
Batavia to round the southernmost tip of the Southland, probably
near what is now called Canal Rocks in Western Australia, mostly
at a distance of 1600 kilometres or more out in the empty ocean.
Turning north-west after seeing the massive seas pounding this
part of the coast, Jonck began one of his assigned tasks, mapping
the western shores of the Southland. The morning of 27 February
found him and his men sailing north towards a rendezvous
previously agreed with Volkerson at the site of the *Vergulde Draeck*
disaster. On the way he named 'Draeck's Reef'. As it turned out, this
was in fact where the ship had died, though the Dutch believed the
spot was actually about 50 kilometres north at a location that Jonck
named on his chart 'The Draeck Headland'.

The following afternoon, the two ships rejoined as agreed, after
having lost sight of each other for more than two weeks. They
were now close to where they thought the bones of the *Draeck* and
probably her people were to be found. They saw no signs of life
along the dunes that fringed the shore. After sailing together for a
little while, the ships were again separated by foul weather.

On 8 March, the *Emeloordt* was about 50 kilometres off the
coast when smoke was sighted. Jonck believed these to be signals.
He wrote in his journal, 'We replied with three guns and showed a
big flag from the main topmast.' But there was no response. They
remained in the area that night and observed a fire lit ashore,
bearing east-north-east. Fires were again lit ashore the next
morning. Jonck then fired three cannon shots and was rewarded
with the sight of more fires on the land. A boat was prepared with a

crew of ten and a load of provisions, arms, tools and other items for the survivors. But as soon as the boat touched the shore, the flames were extinguished.

It was now late in the day, and the boat returned to the ship. 'I suspect that this fire is no honest work,' wrote Jonck. They discharged more cannon and flew the large flag again, but received no response. Next day, the small boat and its provisions were launched once more. It was a repeat performance of the previous day, with fires being lit ashore at the same spot, cannons fired on the hour and the flag flown. The small boat crew spent the night ashore. The *Emeloordt* continued burning lights and firing cannon, hearing sounds of musketry from the beach camp around 9 p.m.

Nothing else occurred that night and the boat returned again to the *Emeloordt* at sunrise. The men, however, had an unsettling encounter to relate. In their journey into the interior they had come across 'five persons of distinction and of very tall build'. These people were near what the men described as three 'houses' and beckoned to the Dutchmen as they 'sympathetically put their hands under their heads as a signal of sleep'. The Dutch, 'not being simple enough to put ourselves in the hands of such savage people', went back to their boat. The natives followed them to the beach but would come no closer, despite being given encouragement, and left at dusk. The shore crew claimed to have foraged inland for 3 *miljen*, or about 15 kilometres, finding 'seeding land which they burn off in some places', some fragrant herbs but no water or trees, mainly sand dunes. At night they saw 'many fires being lit'.

Jonck—oddly perhaps—concluded that there was little else to be learned from this area and sailed south, looking for signs of the *Draeck*. But there was nothing. After fifteen days of this, the *Emeloordt* headed north on 11 March, charting as they went. The men were now showing extreme signs of exhaustion with sore eyes and sickness. The weather worsened and *Emeloordt* took on a lot of water from heavy rain. Jonck set sail for Java. All he had to show for the efforts of himself and his crew were his charts of the southern coast and a description of the inhabitants: 'The men are of robust build, naked except for their genitals which are a little covered, with a crown on their heads; very black.'

While the *Emeloordt* was undertaking these tasks, a few hundred kilometres south, the *Waeckende Boey* was battling heavy weather around what is now Rottnest Island, just off the coast near Perth. On 24 February she was about 12 kilometres offshore, around modern-day Two Rocks. As Jonck and his men had witnessed further north, fires were lit ashore. One of the ship's two boats landed under the command of upper steersman Abraham Leeman. He and his men, well armed, made a thorough investigation of the beach and some distance inland. When daylight faded, they lit a fire and camped. Volkerson placed a signal light at the stern of the *Waeckende Boey*.

Next day the weather worsened and the men on the ship began to worry about the safety of their comrades. They saw smoke rising from fires but by evening there was still no sign of the shore crew. That night the ship dragged her anchor and they sent the second boat ashore next morning. Halfway there, they met Leeman's boat and crew returning with exciting news. They had found the remains of the *Vergulde Draeck*.

The wreckage on the beach included beams, oak planking, a keg, buckets, chests and other wooden items. And although Leeman and his men 'had gone far and wide, both inland and along the beach', they had found 'no footprints nor any place where people had lived'. There was one curious find that seems to have puzzled Volkerson and his men, and has been the subject of ongoing controversy to the present day. Leeman told Volkerson that 'a number of pieces of planking had been put up in a circle with their ends upwards'.

Waiting no longer to reflect on the finds, Volkerson 'resolved to weigh anchor and to sail north along the coast'. But as the cable was hauled up, it snapped and the anchor was lost, followed quickly by the loss of Leeman's small boat. Now the *Waeckende Boey* had only a single lifeboat. Nothing could be done about the situation, so they sailed north against the southerly current that had deposited the wreckage of the *Draeck* where Leeman found it. A few kilometres north of present-day Moore River, the remaining boat was sent ashore with Leeman in command. Again, nothing was found.

Volkerson then proceeded directly to the reported site of the wreck, passing the actual site on his way. About 40 kilometres north of that sad spot, he anchored and again sent the Leeman's party ashore. As the small craft neared the land, the men aboard saw fires being lit. But, with considerable difficulty in the heavy swell, the boat returned in the afternoon with no further news. They managed to get their precious remaining boat safely aboard just as the *Emeloordt* hove in from the south. But the weather was so bad that the ships were soon separated again and, despite Volkerson's best efforts, they did not reconnect.

Volkerson sailed south again in foul weather. Bolstered by a ration of the south-east Asian liquor known as 'arrack', he and his exhausted crew reached Rottnest Island on 18 March. The next day the weather improved and Volkerson decided to have the ship careened while Leeman again took the boat to investigate the island. He returned with little to report and two days later the *Waeckende Boey* turned north once more.

The searchers now adopted a method of sailing their ship along the coast while the boat, with Leeman and a crew of around thirteen men, went ashore and searched for wreckage and signs of survivors. On some occasions, the upper-steersman and his men spent the night on the beach. In this way, they came across several more items of wreckage from the *Vergulde Draeck*, including pulley blocks and sections of the ship's shattered structure. On 22 March they were carrying out this procedure again when Leeman noticed the weather changing for the worse. Mindful of their recent storm experiences that had damaged the boat, he called his men together and made for the *Waeckende Boey*, anchored to their south.

Leeman's small boat quickly got into trouble as the men tried to row against strong winds and high seas. In fear of imminent swamping, they desperately signalled the ship with musket fire, expecting Volkerson to raise his anchor and come to their aid. But their captain did nothing. The *Waeckende Boey* remained tethered to the sea floor seemingly not caring that some of its crew, including the first mate and the only remaining lifeboat, were all about to disappear beneath the crashing breakers. Almost at the last possible moment, the strong winds broke the anchor cable, blowing the ship towards them so that the men in the stricken boat were able to catch a rope and get aboard.

Instead of welcoming them safely back, Volkerson told the bedraggled boat's crew they were lucky the cable had parted because he would not have helped them otherwise. According to the astonished Leeman, 'He repeated this diver [many] times to the crew, which made my heart to ache and I was very sad.'

Then, unbelievably, the captain ordered Leeman and his men back ashore. The wind was already howling through the rigging and the breakers were high enough to block out the view of the land.

Leeman protested: 'If, when I go ashore, I get this bad weather, where shall I go, because there is no bay or island for shelter? And if I am washed against the shore, we will die; I cannot beat out to sea—it is foul and full of rocks. Also, if I have to go now with the evening coming, there will not be enough visibility.'

But Volkerson's only reply was, 'It's beautiful weather.'

It clearly was not, and Leeman continued to object.

Volkerson called him a coward. The captain then consulted the bookkeeper, who was one of the merchant's staff and no sailor. Despite all evidence to the contrary, he cravenly agreed with Volkerson.

Leeman and his thirteen companions now had no choice. They had been given a direct, if inexplicable, order by their captain and must obey.

The tribulations of Abraham Leeman

While it was unusual for a VOC boat to have a senior officer who was not of Dutch birth, it was not unknown. Then, as now, merchant seafaring was an international occupation and men with the necessary skills and experience were in demand to sail the company's many craft around the known world. How Abraham Leeman came to be on the shores of the Southland was a result of the Protestant reformation that began officially with Martin Luther's defiance of papal authority in 1517. Religious dissension caused massive disruption in European politics and in daily life. Those areas now known as the Netherlands and Belgium were largely under the control of the Catholic Spanish at this time and Protestants were persecuted and ejected from many communities.

In 1560, Elizabeth I of England allowed around twenty-five Flemish families to settle in Sandwich, an ancient medieval seaport at the mouth of the River Stour. It is likely that the town already had links with the various protestant groups and sects in Europe and that some had already settled there, though perhaps not in such numbers. The newcomers were known as 'Strangers' to the locals, but brought spinning and weaving expertise, together with market gardening skills, into the seaport town. A flourishing wool trade through the port provided them with steady employment and the Strangers seem to have been accepted readily by the townspeople.

A few years later, in 1564, plague broke out in the town. In an attempt to stop the spread of infection, the church of St Peters was given to the Strangers for their exclusive use; it remained their church from then on and they became an accepted part of the local community. A man named John Leeman, said to have been one of a number of 'aliens borne', is recorded as living in Sandwich in

1622.[4] He may have been the father of Abraham, though we will probably never know.

The Strangers belonged to a branch of Protestantism usually known as 'Anabaptists'. Within this group were many factions, including Mennonites, Hutterites and the Amish, among others. Most of them held the belief that it was only possible to be truly entered into the Christian religion through adult, as opposed to infant, baptism. This act was necessary in order to exercise the free will of a mature human being, something a child could not do. Links between these groups, who were widely persecuted by other Protestants as well as Catholics, were clandestine yet strong, often involving family connections and extending across European countries and across the channel to similar communities in England. It was not unusual for members of such families and groups to move between countries in search of work, safety from persecution, or both. Anabaptists, of various kinds, were commonly employed by the VOC as shipbuilders and seamen, their often-austere work and life ethic making them excellent employees. Unfortunately, as Jeronimus Cornelisz and the bloody sequel to the wreck of the *Batavia* revealed, some members of these sects harboured sociopathic tendencies. While we cannot know for sure, Abraham Leeman was quite possibly an Anabaptist, but in his case the religious, moral and physical qualities engendered by that affiliation made him the Southland's first European hero rather than its first madman.

Obeying Volkerson's orders, Leeman and his thirteen companions clambered back into the ship's remaining boat and headed towards the breaking surf. They cleared the reef but then heard the massive breakers before them. They were nearly 5 kilometres from the beach, in darkness and without means of escape to the open sea where, in any case, their captain would not wish to receive them. Leeman tried to anchor the boat but the wind was so strong that they could only tack north before it. They managed to stay afloat, anchored once more then waited until dawn. The wind and sea continued to batter them, though at least they had light. They hauled up their anchor and set off again through the stinging spray. Then the rudder broke. Oars were put out but the wind was increasing. Without a rudder, they had no chance.

They cried out in fear, looking to their leader for salvation. Leeman's faith came to the fore. He got unsteadily to his feet and stood in the pitching stern of the small boat, yelling through the wind and spray: 'We all have to die some time, men. Come, let us trust God and turn towards Him.' They prayed and this, together with whatever comforting words Leeman could muster, seemed to help.

Leeman's little crew continued at the mercy of the weather and the sea until around mid-afternoon when they spotted what looked like a small cove where they might be able to land. The cove lay between two rocks around which the waves burst and sucked. The only chance was to put on sail and go through the gap between the rocks as quickly as possible. Under sail, the boat sped towards the rocks, almost capsized and was thrown by the surf onto a rocky ledge beyond, the wooden keel grinding across it. Some of the crew were washed out of the boat and onto the shore, while Leeman and the others managed to cling to the boat and float it onto a small beach. 'We live again,' Leeman wrote. The men rejoiced that they had been mercifully deposited on the island without being wrecked and drowned.

But that was most of the good news. As they took stock of the situation, they found that all they had was a few pounds of soggy bread, four slabs of bacon and a cask of water, and were stranded somewhere on edge of the dangerous Southland with a broken boat. Although the island was home to many seals and birds and the crew ate well that night, Leeman began rationing the water, already fearing they had lost their ship.

In the morning, the situation seemed a little brighter. The winds were slackening and damage to the boat's rudder and mast was less than imagined. Leeman went up onto the rocks and saw nothing but more rocks and sea. Having 'called on God from my heart for help and succour', he went back down to the beach and 'had the crew make prayers'. They began repairing the boat and assessing their situation. The water cask was already half empty, leaving about 30 litres. They found brackish but drinkable water in the rock hollows. Later, the leader of the bedraggled sailors repeated his climb up the rocky hill to pray for help. When he returned to the camp, he had his men pray together again and 'I admonished them to keep God in mind and to beware of temptation for we were in great peril and God was the right steersman who could lead us back.' Some of the men wept.

The crew spent another night beneath the rock on the mainland side of their island and the next day continued to forage for food and work out a plan. There was no way to sail back through the rocks they had already barely survived. But by carrying their battered boat across to the mainland side of their location, they could sail between the beach and the reefs. They readied the vessel, gathered their meagre supplies and slept another night on the island that was now the closest thing they had to home. Early the next morning, Leeman visited his hilltop to seek divine guidance and then imparted his belief in this to the crew as they again prayed together.

The plan was to sail south in search of the *Waeckende Boey*. It was a difficult passage, with reefs and breakers to be negotiated. They managed to land on what was probably Lancelin Island. After another meal of local seal meat, Leeman left his men for one more solitary survey of the scene and a prayer. He saw nothing but sea, sky and shore and once again 'called upon God with all my heart for help and succour in this time of great need'.

The next day they continued south, past the spot where the *Draeck* lay, seeing yet more of her bleaching remains. The winds turned their boat north again and a grim despair took hold of the lost mariners. Leeman wrote in his journal that he felt the entire burden of their survival lay on his shoulders—'The worries were all mine. I prayed to God in my heart for guidance.' They also began to feel the effects of thirst, eking out their fast-disappearing water with seawater mixed with urine.

Eventually they found an island, probably part of what are now known as Green Islets, which was well populated with seals and they also dug successfully for fresh water. They ate again and their leader posted a watch in the faint hope that their ship would still be looking for them. Towards evening, a miracle. The lookout cried, 'A sail, a sail!'

They could just make out a small patch of white against the darkening skyline about 16 kilometres away. It was the *Waeckende Boey*. 'We live again,' the crew cried in gratitude. Leeman had a fire set on the beach, then a second one in case the ship mistook their signal for the deceitful flames they had experienced before. The ship was now only 10 kilometres away and a cannon shot roared out across the waves. They lit the second fire as the men danced around in joy, wanting to launch their boat for passage back to the *Waeckende Boey*. But Leeman pointed out that it was too dark and dangerous for such an attempt. So they kept watching.

They watched all through the night for a sign that their ship would rescue them. But when the sun came up, there was nothing but empty sea before them. They launched their boat and went north in search of the ship. But she was nowhere to be seen. Despair turned to anger and the upper-steersman decided to return to the island. Here, he again sought solace from his God up in the rocks. This time he returned to his men with an odd instruction. He asked them to dry the skins of the seals they had killed and eaten.

By now, the water quality of the small wells they dug was decreasing and the men were becoming ill. Like the survivors of the *Tryall*, the *Batavia* and the *Vergulde Draeck*, they were now cast away on an unknown continent, thousands of miles from their version of civilisation, with little food or water and probably surrounded by large numbers of natives they had been told to think of as savage, deceitful and unmerciful. On 1 April, four days after their last sighting of the *Waeckende Boey* and during his regular conversations with God, Leeman finally abandoned any hope of rescue. He gave the men orders to cut 'stanchions' to heighten the sides of their boat for the dangerous trip back to Batavia.

The men ignored him. Leeman told them that he would leave behind any man who did not help. Then he took an axe and went to work himself, piling nine staves of wood on the beach. At this, the crew took him seriously and joined in. Leeman detailed their labours:

> I had the carpenter prepare the stanchions, and hammered them into the openings for the rowlocks. I took the rope guards from the boat and made rope-yarn of [them]. We still had four pikes, and I instructed the crew how I wanted them tiled along the stanchions to give stiffness. I had some rope-yarn plaited to make sheets and braces of the rope guards. I took the seal skins and cut them into pieces as long and wide as they would go.

Although they had little equipment, they did at least have a large nail: 'We made holes in the skins at both ends, and we sewed them together with rope yarn, then tied these onto the stanchions that had been knocked into the boat. I had the rowlocks knocked off and took the nails to nail down the skins around the boat, together with a rope plait.'

They spent the next few days adapting their craft for what Leeman knew was an impossible voyage. The conditions in which the crew existed gave them severe diarrhoea and made them weak and unmotivated. According to Leeman's account, his men looked to him as their only saviour. He prayed on his hill more and more. Even though they were sick and desiccated, the men clawed their way up the hill to bring him meals of seal and seabird. Without the upper-steersman and his knowledge of navigation and seamanship, they knew they had no hope at all.

As the water quality decreased, along with the seal and bird population, Leeman decided it was time to launch their makeshift vessel. They dried seal meat, found some drinkable water for their cask and improvised a storm sail. Leeman carved a crude map of their position and destination in the boat's stern and made two sets of wooden dividers for basic navigation. On the morning of 8 April, he prayed on his hill for the last time and asked God to help them reach Batavia. All fourteen men climbed into their leaky craft then 'set sail in the name of the Lord'.

With Leeman strictly rationing the precious water and ensuring the crew kept watch as they would aboard ship, the frail container with its hopeless human cargo sailed north for the Java coast, 2000 kilometres away. Even if they made that landfall, Batavia was more than 300 kilometres further. They found only one island where it was safe for them to land and replenish their water. Otherwise, the reefs and the awesome breakers of what is now the Zuytdorp Cliffs kept them well out to sea.

Again they began to suffer from thirst, drinking seawater and their urine, sometimes fighting over whose it was after it had cooled in the communal shell they used for a latrine as well as a bailer. They stopped eating their dried seal meat and even the parsley-like herb harvested on their only island respite. They became weak and reluctant to bale the leaking boat. Leeman punished those who did not work by reducing their already pitiable water ration.

The first man died on 19 April. It was the day that the *Emeloordt* and the *Waeckende Boey* returned to Batavia. Unaware of this tragic irony, Leeman and his remaining companions struggled to raise and lower their sail. Their compass was broken in an accident and the leader had to do his best to set their course by starlight. All the time the men groaned and wailed in the extremity of their misery. They could barely make their way from stem to stern in the relentless heat.

The second and third men died on 26 April. Two days later the water cask was almost empty. Leeman feared that this was the end. He lied to the men that he expected to be in sight of land very soon and ordered them to keep a sharp lookout. The one who first saw it would have an extra drink of water. Incredibly, a man in the stern at last called out 'land'. By then, the survivors would have dismissed the sighting as an hallucination. But the next wave lifted them high enough to see Java. 'There was such great joy as if we had become new men.'

They sailed west all that night. Leeman wrote that, 'By then we had been drinking our water and seawater for 15 to 16 days. My mouth and tongue were so raw that I could hardly speak because of the burning feeling caused by my own water.'

Next morning the men were desperate to land. Leeman was worried about the natives of the jungle and the hazards of the coast, but by 9 a.m. had found somewhere to moor. He told the carpenter to take his axe and four men ashore to look for coconuts and water. The men swam to land, cut down a coconut tree and began eating and drinking. Leeman and the men remaining in the boat called out for them to pull the water cask ashore so they could drink as well. But the five men ashore simply ignored them.

Leeman then sent the youngest member of the crew ashore to get the carpenter and his companions to fill the cask so they could drag it back to the boat and slake their own thirst. But the boy promptly joined those ashore, drinking and eating and likewise ignoring the five remaining men in the boat. Later, Leeman sent another man ashore with the same orders, and he performed exactly the same act of inexplicable betrayal.

Too weak to swim ashore himself, Leeman was left with only three men who could not swim. Then their mooring line parted and Leeman had to make a fateful decision. He signalled to the men ashore that he was sailing. They simply motioned him to bring the boat to shore. Fearing the boat would be lost in the rising sea, Leeman sailed off to a safer mooring.

Next morning they found somewhere to land and two of the four remaining crew went to locate the treacherous seven ashore, now fed and watered. But the jungle was too thick for them to proceed. Fortunately, they found a nearby stream to slake their painful thirst. They used a cutlass to fell a coconut tree and resupplied the boat.

Sailing back to—generously, in the circumstances—pick up the seven ashore, the boat was swamped in the surf. Weak and short-handed, they could not save their craft as a monsoonal squall roared in to smash the vessel and wash the exhausted men ashore. '[We] looked sadly at each other, not knowing what to do. We ate some palm shoots and suddenly it began to blow and rain so hard that we could not keep our eyes open. We crept into the sand together and remained lying like this until the next day.'

In the morning they saw the wreckage of their boat. Asking what they had done to displease God, Leeman wept. His three companions were alarmed but their leader soon recovered his composure and prayed again for deliverance. They all agreed there was no way now for them to contact the others and their only option was to trek along the coast. They had three cutlasses and a gun between them. Using the cutlasses, they eventually managed to fell three coconut trees. They ate the flesh and drank the milk of the welcome fruits and then moved unsteadily westward.

Unknown to the four men, they were very far from where they had hoped to land—more than 600 kilometres further east than their intended destination. To reach Batavia along the coast, they would need to walk more than 1100 impossible kilometres, traversing jungle, mountains and rivers, avoiding wild animals and the indigenous inhabitants who they assumed were unfriendly. Living on shellfish, coconut and anything else they could forage, the four survivors struggled over mountains, along precipitous cliffs and dripping rainforest. Leeman feared for his sanity and clung even more tightly to his faith in God.

After five weeks or so of this dreadful struggle, the men again became weak and depressed. Water was getting scarce. Their cutlasses had broken and they could only obtain coconuts by climbing the trees. Leeman was unable to do this and so the men considered splitting into two groups to better their chances of survival. Another range of mountains compelled them to stick together, though, and after scaling these heights they found a small bay where four Javanese houses stood. The place was deserted but there was food. They had a narrow escape from a tiger, then moved on to find yet another inhabited bay, complete with two *praus*, or Javanese fishing boats. Their attempt to launch one of these boats was dashed by violent surf. They abandoned this but soon saw another *prau* sailing towards them.

The two Javanese aboard landed on the beach, where the survivors were in full view. Leeman quickly buried his gun in case of misunderstandings and went to meet the two men, addressing them in Malay. They did not know this language but fortunately were friendly, feeding and accommodating the four sailors. After two months of hopeless trekking, and more than three months of desperate sailing, Leeman and what was left of his crew at last had some good luck.

Their Javanese friends took them to another group of indigenous people. One of the Dutchmen had hurt his leg and he was given assistance to make the journey. But when they arrived, it soon became clear that they were to be hostages rather than guests.

After three weeks or so as captives, they were taken to Mataram, a Javanese stronghold, with their injured companion mounted on horseback. In Mataram they were interrogated by members of Prince Tommagon Mati's court and eventually managed to convince their captors that their tale of terrible struggle and survival was true.

Sometime later a Dutch man named Michiel Zeeburgh arrived and assisted Abraham Leeman to write to the VOC representative at the port of Japara, some 400 kilometres from Batavia. Zeeburgh took the message to Japara and rapidly returned with clothes and money. Even better, negotiations for their release were underway. These went for some time until Leeman and his three companions were freed. 'Our joy was so great, as if we were going to Heaven,' wrote Leeman.

On 23 September they finally reached Japara and 'came again to our people, for which the Almighty God must be thanked and praised everlastingly, amen'.

However, like unwelcome ghosts, Abraham Leeman and three of his men had inconveniently returned from the dead. Marooned, battered, betrayed and abducted, they had more than earned survival through their ordeal. Leeman's journal of the momentous voyage of survival undertaken by the passionate leader and his sailors was transcribed in the neatly detached hand of the VOC clerk and handed to the council.

Retribution was now about to fall on the treacherous master of the *Waeckende Boey.* The tone and content of the official VOC documents tell the tale. These briefly recount the details of the *Draeck's* sinking, the rescue attempts and Leeman's extraordinary escape from the Southland. Of the seven men who had deserted Leeman's boat at landfall in Java to save their own lives, 'nothing more was heard'. The report then turned to the actions of Volkerson, noting: 'Thus of this expedition again the only result was that the crew of the *Waeckende Boey* abandoned a boat with fourteen of their comrades, including the upper steersman, and that in a manner but too reckless as it afterwards proved.'

Volkerson's self-serving account of the abandonment of his men was shown to be largely false. What his fate might have been when the remaining survivors of the marooning turned up in Batavia, we can only speculate. Volkerson was killed in an accident of some kind just a few weeks before the hostages were released.

A few more VOC ships were asked to keep an eye out for survivors of the *Vergulde Draeck* as they passed along the Southland's western coast. But nothing was found. The Seventeen Gentlemen in Amsterdam wrote to the governor-general and Council of the Indies in Batavia on 21 August 1660: 'Now that all missions have been fruitless, we will have to give up, to our distress, the people of the *Vergulde Draeck*, who have found refuge on the Southland.'

Meanwhile, the extraordinary seafarer and survivor Abraham Leeman disappears from history, his even more extraordinary story preserved only in the official VOC copy of his journal.

Quest for the dragon

After Leeman and his men retrieved the broken pieces of the *Vergulde Draeck*, the wreck was left to become one with the sea, sand and rock in which she lay. But odd bits and pieces began appearing quite soon after Western Australia was settled.

In 1846, a group of Juat people turned up at the frontier missionary town of New Norcia carrying an urn discovered at a water source around 20 kilometres south of the wreck site. Sections of a mast and some domestic implements turned up in 1890. Several kilometres north, a skeleton was uncovered at Eagle's Nest in 1932, though there appears to be no record of the eventual fate of this possible relic of the wreck. The year before, a cache of forty silver coins had been found in sandhills north of Cape Leschenault, about 30 kilometres south of the wreck site. Then, in 1957, skin-divers reported that they had found the *Draeck* about 5 kilometres off Ledge Point. But the 'cannon' that the divers claimed to have discovered turned out to be natural features of the waters in the area.

No one knew what these sporadic finds meant, though there were some clues in translations of the original VOC documents relating to the wreck. These appeared in 1859 and subsequently in 1899. To anyone interested enough to inquire, the records made it clear that the *Vergulde Draeck*'s last resting place was very probably hiding a fortune.

The gold seekers were not deterred by the inaccessibility of the wreck and the dangerous location in which she was gradually returning to the sea. At uncertain times in the twentieth century, unknown persons did locate the wreck and attempt—possibly successfully—to salvage her rich cargo. But it was not until 1963 that a youthful Graeme Henderson, spearfishing in the area with family and friends, again located the *Vergulde Draeck*. There was soon at least one attempt by treasure hunters to blast the wreck. Legislation protecting VOC wrecks was rushed through the Western Australian parliament the following year, so vulnerable to looting and destruction were the *Draeck* and other early wrecks along the coast.[5]

Once the news was out, more treasure hunters were not too far behind. The year following the finding of the wreck, a father and son team, Frank and Kevin Moore, began excavating a sand dune at what became known as Dynamite Bay, around 13 kilometres south of the fishing settlement of Leeman. They graduated to explosives and then to a mechanical excavator, creating an enormous hole that would bottom out at around 18 metres. Despite attracting investors and conducting further test-drilling of the beach after their initial hole turned out to be devoid of treasure, nothing was found and the Moores and their backers gave up.

This escapade had been sparked when, according to a newspaper interview with Frank Moore, he was given 'an old piece of parchment' by a friend of Dutch extraction. This turned out to be a map of the whereabouts of the *Draeck*'s treasure. The friend, known only as 'Harry', claimed to be 'a direct descendant of one of the men who had sailed in the Gilt Dragon'. The map had been handed down through his family for generations. When Harry and Frank Moore visited Dynamite Bay, he confirmed that this was the correct location of the treasure and then, according to Moore, 'In front of my eyes he burnt the map, saying: "No one else has seen this, and no one will." Later he died.'

When the Western Australian Maritime Museum was finally able to make a professional archaeological survey in 1972, it revealed that the wreck site is about 50 by 40 metres, with a honeycomb reef running along one side. The reef depth varies from 1 metre at low tide to 8 metres at high tide. The archaeologists found that most of the wreck is covered in weed, with the cannon and anchors concreted together. There were a number of small yellow bricks all around the site, presumably part of the cargo. Excavations of the site, official and unofficial, have revealed African elephant tusks, tobacco pipes, ceramics, bottles, beardman or Bellarmine jugs, brass and bronze utensils, tools and armaments. There is little mention of the guilders, at least in official documents.[6]

As well as the enduring lure of sunken treasure, there is the more important mystery of the fate of those who survived the tragedy. While it is known that a large group of men made it to the beach, it is not impossible that one, even a few, of those left aboard the wreck may have survived, perhaps blown south on a spar by the strong current. The discovery of old Dutch coins, almost certainly from the *Vergulde Draeck,* at a significant distance south of the wreck, together with the mysterious skeleton, gives some support to this possibility. On the other hand, a group of the beach survivors may have made their way south in search of help. Speculations like these, together with expeditions and the assiduous work of a small group of researchers, have generated an intriguing mix of history, artefacts and folklore. A central element of this is known as 'the ring of stones'.

An admiralty surveyor named Alfred Burt was part of a coastal survey in 1875. He and another member of the party, Harry Ogbourne, were struggling through thick wattle scrub around 250 kilometres north of Perth. They unexpectedly came into a small clearing in which was a ring of small stones or boulders, a little more than a metre in diameter. Burt thought that this was unusual but apparently said no more about it until 1930 when a journalist interviewed him about another presumed VOC disaster known as 'the Deadwater Wreck'. During the interview, the journalist mentioned the *Vergulde Draeck* treasure story and so reminded Burt of his youthful discovery fifty-five years before. Burt, and the journalist, made a connection between the stones and the *Draeck*, generating a belief that the ring of stones somehow marked the location of the ship's treasure. Burt wrote to the commissioner of police about it, enclosing a crude map locating the ring.

Every good lost treasure legend needs a map. This one has two. Together with Burt's recollections, the map was convincing enough to inspire serious interest. In May 1931 an official search was initiated, involving the police, Burt and local people. The country is rough and the scrub frequently impassable. Nothing was found and a second attempt was made in February 1932. Burt was not involved in this, but the police enlisted local farmers and also members of the Juat people to burn out sections of the scrub. Again, this proved unsuccessful.

The next year, a farmer from Three Springs, Mr King, reported finding a mile-long line of stones running east and west, apparently connecting a prominent sand hill and Woodada Well to the east. There was some occasional police activity on the story, but it was not until 1937 that another treasure hunter, J.E. Hammond, a friend of Burt's, spent a couple of weeks searching for the ring, and possibly the even more enigmatic line of stones also reportedly found in the area. In March 1938 school children discovered more Dutch coins and in December that year, a ring of stones was discovered by Jack Hayes and Gabriel Penney. They described three groups of stones in a clearing, a circle in the middle, with a rectangle on each side, one with a base line around 20 metres in length. Believing that this structure was a pointer to the treasure, they dug beneath it but found nothing.

It seems that whatever Hayes and Penney found was not what Burt claimed to have seen in 1875. Even though the location of both finds seems to be more or less the same, the Hayes and Penney structure is clearly larger than that described by Burt. Neither of these structures is the same as that described by King. It seems that there are three distinct stone structures in this area, all subject to intense speculation as to their origins and meaning. Were any of them made by the survivors of the *Vergulde Draeck*? If so, for what purposes? Are they some sort of Aboriginal ceremonial structure? Or perhaps they were constructed for completely different reasons? It is difficult to imagine why anyone would take so much trouble to build such structures in such inaccessible locations unless they had a very important purpose.

The key researcher in this field, the late Rupert Gerritsen, who himself searched the scrub for these artefacts, did not believe they were Aboriginal structures, or associated with stock routes.[7] Gerritsen and colleagues tried to locate the sites a number of times. They tried again in 2008, and this time they were assisted by the discovery of the documents Burt had provided to the police in the 1930s, including his map. This radically altered understandings of where Burt's original find was located. Gerritsen revisited the area in the light of this new knowledge. He did not find the ring of stones but instead stumbled upon yet another rock structure. It appeared to be a grave.[8]

Now there were at least four unidentified stone structures in the area. The possible grave, of course, also in a clearing, had to be investigated by the police. They found that it was a pile of rocks with a limestone slab beneath. As of 2009, that was where the matter lay. Gerritsen then felt that none of these enigmatic assemblages was the original one found by Burt in 1875. If that can be relocated, it may well hold a clue to the fate of the *Vergulde Draeck* survivors.[9] The search continues.

7

Cliffs of fire

It is likely that Western Australians would now speak French if a proposal to the government of France around 1700 had been approved. In 1687 Captain Abraham Duquesne-Guitton sailed along the western coast of the Southland, and thought one particular area attractive and suitable for settlement. Twelve years later his brother-in-law, Gédéon Nicolas de Voutron, submitted a proposal to the French government for a colony on the river that the British would later call the Swan. His submission was rejected.

While these ideas and proposals about the southern continent developed in France, the English were still interested in knowing more about it. Commissioned by the admiralty, William Dampier made landfall at what is now Shark Bay with his Royal Navy ship *Roebuck* in 1699. But this official visit was not his first voyage to these regions. Under very different circumstances he had been here before.

Dampier the pirate
William Dampier was a man of 'firsts'. He was the first Englishman to land on the mainland of *Terra Australis*, the first European to

collect and preserve the flora and fauna of the southern continent, and the first navigator to circle the globe three times. He is also usually considered to be one of the finest navigators of sail, among some very elevated company that includes Walter Raleigh and James Cook. Dampier was also a best-selling author and successful early show business entrepreneur. And he was quite often a pirate. Between and during these and other activities, Dampier was probably the first British person to land on the Southland on two occasions, separated by twelve years.

Dampier's first visit came towards the end of an epic stint of eight years 'privateering'—a form of licensed plundering of enemy ships. He sailed from North America, down the east coast of South America, through the Pacific, to China, the East Indies and, in January 1688, to the western shores of the Southland. After various disagreements and partings among the numerous 'captains' he encountered, Dampier ended up aboard the *Cygnet* under the command of Captain Read. On 5 January 1688, *Cygnet* anchored 3 kilometres from the shore and 53 metres over 'good hard sand and clean ground'. The crew relaxed and careened the ship while Dampier added extensive details about the local ecology and people to the journal of his travels.

These later appeared in his classic, *A New Voyage Around the World*, published in 1697.[1] He wrote, 'New Holland is a very large tract of land. It is not yet determined whether it is an island or a main continent; but I am certain that it joins neither to Asia, Africa, nor America. This part of it that we saw is all low even land, with sandy banks against the sea, only the points are rocky, and so are some of the islands in this bay.'

Dampier went on to further precise observations:

The land is of a dry sandy soil, destitute of water except you make wells; yet producing divers sorts of trees; but the woods are not thick, nor the trees very big. Most of the trees that we saw are dragon-trees as we supposed; and these too are the largest trees of any there. They are about the bigness of our large apple-trees, and about the same height; and the rind is blackish and somewhat rough. The leaves are of a dark colour; the gum distils out of the knots or cracks that are in the bodies of the trees. We compared it with some gum-dragon or dragon's blood that was aboard, and it was of the same colour and taste. The other sort of trees were not known by any of us. There was pretty long grass growing under the trees; but it was very thin. We saw no trees that bore fruit or berries.

Always comparing against the known, as all the newcomers inevitably would, Dampier provided details of the country, its wildlife and its people. They saw 'the tread of a beast as big as a great mastiff-dog' but no other traces of wildlife other than 'a few small land-birds but none bigger than a blackbird; and but few sea-fowls'. Dampier added that, 'Neither is the sea very plentifully stored with fish unless you reckon the manatee and turtle as such. Of these creatures there is plenty but they are extraordinary shy; though the inhabitants cannot trouble them much having neither boats nor iron.'

And then he penned his frequently quoted depiction of the Aborigines:

The inhabitants of this country are the miserablest people in the world. The Hodmadods of Monomatapa[2], though a nasty people, yet for wealth are gentlemen to these; who have no houses, and skin garments, sheep, poultry, and fruits of the earth, ostrich eggs, etc., as the Hodmadods have: and, setting aside their human shape, they differ but little from brutes. They are tall, straight-bodied, and thin, with small long limbs. They have great heads, round foreheads, and great brows. Their eyelids are always half closed to keep the flies out of their eyes; they being so troublesome here that no fanning will keep them from coming to one's face;

and without the assistance of both hands to keep them off they will creep into one's nostrils and mouth too if the lips are not shut very close; so that, from their infancy being thus annoyed with these insects, they do never open their eyes as other people: and therefore they cannot see far, unless they hold up their heads as if they were looking at somewhat over them.

Dampier pandered to his already-prejudiced readers with even more physiological details, again in an unflattering way. According to Dampier the inhabitants were 'coal-black' and had 'great bottle-noses, pretty full lips, and wide mouths'. Men, women and children were all missing their upper two front teeth, though he did not know how or why. They had long faces, short, black curly hair 'like that of the Negroes'. He thought they were 'of a very unpleasing aspect, having not one graceful feature in their faces'.

This negative description of Aboriginal physiognomy was followed by an account of their bodily adornment and dwellings: 'They have no sort of clothes but a piece of the rind of a tree, tied like a girdle about their waists, and a handful of long grass, or three or four small green boughs full of leaves thrust under their girdle to cover their nakedness.' He observed that they had no houses, 'but lie in the open air without any covering; the earth being their bed, and the heaven their canopy. Whether they cohabit one man to one woman or promiscuously I know not; but they do live in companies, twenty or thirty men, women, and children together.'

The Aboriginal people he encountered subsisted mainly on fish: 'which they get by making weirs of stone across little coves or branches of the sea; every tide bringing in the small fish and there leaving them for a prey to these people who constantly attend there to search for them at low water'. He added that these small fish seemed to be all they could catch, as 'they have no instruments to catch great fish should they come; and such seldom stay to be left behind at low water.'

The English fared little better, Dampier admitted, even with their supposedly superior angling technology: 'nor could we catch any fish with our hooks and lines all the while we lay there.'

Dampier also observed that, 'In other places at low-water they seek for cockles, mussels, and periwinkles: of these shellfish there are fewer still; so that their chiefest dependence is upon what the sea leaves in their weirs; which, be it much or little, they gather up, and march to the places of their abode.'

This description of fishing runs into an account of its role in the social life of Aboriginal people, which was almost certainly superior to that of European society in terms of aged care:

> There the old people that are not able to stir abroad by reason of their age and the tender infants wait their return; and what providence has bestowed on them they presently broil on the coals and eat it in common. Sometimes they get as many fish as makes them a plentiful banquet; and at other times they scarce get everyone a taste: but be it little or much that they get, everyone has his part, as well the young and tender, the old and feeble, who are not able to go abroad, as the strong and lusty.

The Aborigines did everything as a group. Dampier said that after they had eaten together, they all lay down to sleep and 'then all that are able march out, be it night or day, rain or shine, it is all one; they must attend the weirs or else they must fast: for the earth affords them no food at all.' He claimed that he saw 'neither herb, root, pulse, nor any sort of grain for them to eat ... nor any sort of bird or beast that they can catch, having no instruments wherewithal to do so'.

Dampier clearly felt more pity than disgust for the people he encountered, though his observations were based on very superficial contact, as shown by his lack of knowledge, or perhaps simply his lack of understanding, of Aboriginal spiritual life—'I did not perceive that they did worship anything.'

Nor did he find their weapons very impressive:

These poor creatures have a sort of weapon to defend their weir or fight with their enemies if they have any that will interfere with their poor fishery. They did at first endeavour with their weapons to frighten us, who lying ashore deterred them from one of their fishing-places. Some of them had wooden swords, others had a sort of lances. The sword is a piece of wood shaped somewhat like a cutlass. The lance is a long straight pole sharp at one end, and hardened afterwards by heat. I saw no iron nor any other sort of metal; therefore it is probable they use stone-hatchets, as some Indians in America do.

At first, Dampier and those with him made little contact with the indigenous people who preferred to keep well away from the strange visitors. The Englishmen searched for native dwellings but found only 'many places where they had made fires'. They left 'a great many toys ashore in such places where we thought that they would come', but had no success with these gifts or with finding water. It was not until they visited the islands in the bay that they came face to face with 'a great many of the natives'. They were hostile, according to Dampier:

At our first coming ashore [they] threatened us with their lances and swords; but they were frightened by firing one gun which we fired purposely to scare them. The island was so small that they could not hide themselves: but they were much disordered at our landing, especially the women and children: for we went directly to their camp. The lustiest of the women, snatching up their infants, ran away howling, and the little children ran after squeaking and bawling; but the men stood still. Some of the women and such people as could not go from us lay still by a fire, making a doleful noise as if we had been coming to devour them: but when they saw we did not intend to harm them they were pretty quiet, and the rest that fled from us at our first coming returned again. This their place of dwelling was only a fire with a few boughs before it, set up on that side the winds was of.

The English stayed for some time, during which the Aboriginal men 'began to be familiar'. The English thought to make them gifts of clothing in return for the labour involved in carrying casks of water to the ship. They put their old clothes upon the Aborigines 'thinking that this finery would have brought them to work heartily for us'. They then took them to the well and laid six-gallon barrels of water on their shoulders. But to the apparent surprise of the English, the local men were not interested in labouring for the newcomers and in his disappointment Dampier lapses into the ancient European slur:

> But all the signs we could make were to no purpose for they stood like statues without motion but grinned like so many monkeys staring one upon another: for these poor creatures seem not accustomed to carry burdens; and I believe that one of our ship-boys of ten years old would carry as much as one of them. So we were forced to carry our water ourselves, and they very fairly put the clothes off again and laid them down, as if clothes were only to work in. I did not perceive that they had any great liking to them at first, neither did they seem to admire anything that we had.

The Aborigines did not make use of canoes, but swam from island to island as necessary. The sailors plucked four of them from the water one day and fed them 'boiled rice and with it turtle and manatee boiled'. According to Dampier, the Aborigines 'did greedily devour what we gave them but took no notice of the ship, or anything in it, and when they were set on land again they ran away as fast as they could'. At one point the pirates repelled an imminent attack when the captain had the ship's drum purposely and vigorously beaten 'to scare the poor creatures'. He reported that, 'They hearing the noise ran away as fast as they could drive;

and when they ran away in haste they would cry "Gurry, gurry," speaking deep in the throat.' Dampier noted the poor eyesight of the Aborigines, which made it easy for the pirates to capture them, though 'we did always give them victuals and let them go again'.

During these encounters, Dampier almost got himself marooned for trying to persuade his companions to sail from here back to England, a suggestion that did not fit in with the captain's plans. 'This made me desist and patiently wait for some more convenient place and opportunity to leave them than here: which I did hope I should accomplish in a short time.'

After repairs, *Cygnet* sailed for the Cocos Islands on 12 March. Dampier would have many more adventures before returning to England in 1691. These are described in his book, which is still an excellent read today, regardless of its level of inaccuracy. Dampier was keen to present his buccaneering activities as the result of coercion by Captain Read and other desperadoes: 'Being sufficiently weary of this mad crew, we were willing to give them the slip at any place from whence we might hope to get a passage to an English factory.' There is an account of him and two others being set ashore in the Nicobar Islands, a kind of agreed marooning, in order to be free of Read and his crew. They subsequently escaped in a modified native canoe, pursued by hostile 'Indians'.

When Dampier does eventually get back home, he is penniless, except for two slaves he purchased on his travels: the heavily tattooed Prince Jeoly and his mother. He makes a living by exhibiting them in sideshows and private exhibitions in the period while he is writing and publishing his book. Eleven years later, he would be back in New Holland as it was then widely known. In the years between, others followed in his wake.

'A pewter plate hammered flat'
Willem de Vlamingh sailed from Holland aboard the frigate *De Geelvinck* in May 1696 as commodore of a small fleet. He was

accompanied by his son Captain Cornelis de Vlamingh aboard the galiot *Weseltje,* and Captain Gerrit Collaert on the hooker *De Nijptang.* They had orders to search for the missing *Ridderschap van Holland*, lost two years earlier.

Ridderschap van Holland, or 'The Nobility of Holland', was a veteran VOC ship of more than 500 tons, built in Amsterdam in 1682. She left the Netherlands in mid-1693 and spent a month in Cape Town to resupply and recuperate from the voyage to that point, as was usual VOC practice. On 5 February 1694 she set a course for Batavia carrying around 300 passengers and crew—and has not been heard of since.

At one point, it was thought that the ship had fallen victim to pirates, but it has also been claimed that she was wrecked at Manantena, near Fort Dauphin, Madagascar, in July 1699.[3] What the ship was doing in this part of the world is a puzzle—and seems to have puzzled the VOC as well. There was a suggestion that her mainmast had failed during the passage round the Cape of Good Hope and she may have lost the ability to steer. No one knew then, just as no one knows now.

De Vlamingh was ordered to look for her first in these waters and then, if unsuccessful, to try the west coast of Southland. Finding no sign of *Ridderschap van Holland* elsewhere, de Vlamingh came in sight of the Southland on 29 December. Next day they took their guns in a small boat to an island now known as Rottnest. Returning to the island the following day, they found evidence of a wreck, 'a piece of wood from our own country, in which the nails still remained' and 'three or four leagues from us some smoke was seen to rise at different points of the main land'.[4]

Over the next few days, the Dutchmen noted large numbers of fires and rising smoke ashore. With eighty-six armed men, de Vlamingh landed on the mainland and marched an hour eastward on 5 January and found a hut 'of a worse description than those of the Hottentots'. The Dutch saw human footprints but saw no men, women or children.

They found more signs of habitation the next day, then made themselves ill by eating bush nuts before returning to the ships with two young black swans. Over the next few days, they conducted several more expeditions ashore and along the river, always seeing fires, smoke, huts and other human signs. De Vlamingh had it in mind to abduct someone from the Swan River, but was never given the opportunity by the people now called Nyungar, who watched him and his men carefully without ever revealing themselves.

De Vlamingh sailed north after ten days, landing at numerous points but finding no humans. Ashore again on 28 January, the chief pilot observed 'three or four men, and several more on the little downs beyond, all quite naked, black, and of our own height'. But he had 'not been able to get near them on account of the current'. They continued north, always viewing enticing signs of human activity but seeing nothing beyond footprints, a hut and a few wild animals.

At the beginning of February the Dutchmen were anchored near Dirk Hartog Island. Intending to erect a commemorative tablet of his visit[5], de Vlamingh sent two boats ashore. Two days later the upper-steersman of the *Geelvinck* returned from the island carrying 'a tin plate, which in the lapse of time had fallen from a post to which it had been attached', and on which was cut the name of the captain, Dirk Hartog, as well as the names of the first and second merchants and the chief pilot of the vessel *De Eendragt*.

De Vlamingh then had his own 'pewter plate hammered flat', inscribed and erected on a wooden pole. The wording (here with modern punctuation) incorporated that of Hartog's earlier message and documented the presence of de Vlamingh and his men:

> *1616 the 25 October is here arrived the ship*
> *Eendracht of Amsterdam, the uppermerchant*
> *Gillis Miebais of Liege, skipper Dirck Hatichs of*
> *Amsterdam. The 27 ditto* [the same ship] *set sail for*
> *Bantum, the undermerchant Jan Stins, the first mate*
> *Pieter Dookes van Bil. Anno 1616.*

1697 the 4 February is here arrived the ship Geelvinck
of Amsterdam, the commander and skipper Willem
de Vlamingh of Vlieland, assistant Joannes Bremer
of Copenhagen, first mate Michil Bloem of Bishopric
Bremen. The hooker Nyptangh, skipper Gerrit
Colaart of Amsterdam, assistant Theodoris Heirmans
of ditto [the same place], first mate Gerrit Geritsen
of Bremen. The galiot Het Weseltje, master Cornelis
de Vlamingh of Vlieland, mate Coert Gerritsen of
Bremen and from here sailed with our fleet to further
explore the Southland and destined for Batavia—#12
[on the 12th] *VOC.*

Continuing north in poor weather, still no contact was made with the natives. They lost at least three crewmen through mishap and possibly illness. The fleet sailed on without further incident and on 21 February, aboard the commodore's ship *Geelvinck*, 'five cannon shot were fired and three from our vessel, as a signal of farewell to the miserable South Land'.[6]

The three ships returned to Java. De Vlamingh had Hartog's original plate with him and, like most things not pilfered by their servants, it went back to VOC headquarters in Amsterdam to be carefully squirrelled away with all the other records of the company's business.

Return of the pirate

It was in the morning of 6 August 1699 that William Dampier returned to the Southland. No longer a pirate but a naval officer, he anchored the leaky HMS *Roebuck* 3 kilometres from shore in 15 metres, over clean sand. He sent a boat party forward into the mouth of a sound he called Shark's Bay. The boat crew searched for water ashore but found none. Neither did Dampier when he landed the next day, contenting himself with cutting a supply of wood.

In *A Voyage to New Holland*, Dampier describes the gently sloping land around the bay, though there was 'a steep shore against the open sea'. As before, he took careful note of the local plants: 'The grass grows in great tufts as big as a bushel, here and there a tuft: being intermixed with much heath, much of the kind we have growing on our commons in England.' His observations are still prized for their detailed depictions of native plants and wildlife, describing the size, shape, colour and other characteristics, and his ability to make comparisons with those he had seen elsewhere during his extensive travels:

> Most of the trees and shrubs had at this time either blossoms or berries on them. The blossoms of the different sort of trees were of several colours, as red, white, yellow, etc., but mostly blue: and these generally smelt very sweet and fragrant, as did some also of the rest. There were also beside some plants, herbs, and tall flowers, some very small flowers, growing on the ground, that were sweet and beautiful, and for the most part unlike any I had seen elsewhere.

The birdlife was not especially abundant, but Dampier noted and drew a number of species he had not previously seen on his many travels. He described 'iguanas' (presumably goannas), sharks, rays, skates and turtle on which they dined happily. According to Dampier, they also caught and ate a great many sharks, and inside one 11-foot long beast they found 'the head and bones of a hippopotamus; the hairy lips of which were still sound and not putrefied, and the jaw was also firm, out of which we plucked a great many teeth, two of them 8 inches long and as big as a man's thumb ... The maw was full of jelly which stank extremely.' There was a great diversity of shellfish, including mussels and periwinkles, for Dampier to collect, but unfortunately he would lose most of his best specimens in the disaster of his return journey.

The *Roebuck* stayed until midday on 11 August then sailed further into the bay, but found little of interest and left three days later. They coasted north-east until they 'might commodiously put in at some other part of New Holland'. Dampier's observations of fauna continued unabated: 'In passing out we saw three water-serpents swimming about in the sea, of a yellow colour, spotted with dark brown spots. They were each about 4 foot long, and about the bigness of a man's wrist, and were the first I saw on this coast, which abounds with several sorts of them.' They also came across more sea snakes, dolphins and herds of whales.

On 22 August they anchored at 'the easternmost end of an island', about 25 kilometres in length and 5 kilometres wide. There was nothing to detain them here and the need for water was becoming urgent so they continued north, finding another island. The sounding boat again went out but returned to say the land was bare and dry. Dampier decided to bring his ship into the islands and shoals of the area in the hope that he might find fresh water, or perhaps ambergris, the valuable whale vomit used for perfume or 'some rich mineral'. He went ashore with men and shovels, finding flowers, birds, shellfish, turtle, sharks and water snakes, but no drinkable water. They saw evidence of burning and some smoke from an island about 20 kilometres away but, after consulting his officers, Dampier decided to keep sailing north as their anchorage was a poor one.

With fine weather and abundance of fish, whales and sea birds, the *Roebuck* continued until 30 August, when 'we made the land again, and saw many great smokes near the shore'. There was an eclipse of the moon that night and next morning Dampier went ashore with a group of men in search of water and 'armed with muskets and cutlasses for our defence, expecting to see people there; and carried also shovels and pickaxes to dig wells'. When they came near the shore, they saw 'three tall black naked men on the sandy bay ahead of us: but as we rowed in they went away'.

Dampier sent the boat offshore in case the natives tried to seize it while the remainder of the armed sailors went after what was now a group of about a dozen 'black men' who ran off. They came to the top of a hill and saw 'several things like haycocks standing in the savannah; which at a distance we thought were houses, looking just like the Hottentots' houses at the Cape of Good Hope: but we found them to be so many rocks'. Again they searched fruitlessly for water 'but could find none, nor any houses, nor people, for they were all gone'.

Dampier and his men went back to his landing place and began to dig. As they worked a group of about ten Aborigines assembled on a small hill nearby:

> [They] stood there menacing and threatening of us, and making a great noise. At last one of them came towards us, and the rest followed at a distance. I went out to meet him, and came within 50 yards of him, making to him all the signs of peace and friendship I could; but then he ran away, neither would they any of them stay for us to come nigh them; for we tried two or three times.

Taking two of his men with him along the beach, Dampier tried to capture an Aboriginal to find out where they obtained their fresh water:

> There were 10 or 12 natives a little way off, who seeing us three going away from the rest of our men, followed us at a distance. I thought they would follow us: but there being for a while a sandbank between us and them, that they could not then see us, we made a halt, and hid ourselves in a bending of the sandbank. They knew we must be thereabouts, and being 3 or 4 times our number, thought to seize us. So they dispersed themselves, some going to the seashore and others beating about the sandhills.

Knowing that his crewmen could outrun the Aborigines, Dampier sent 'a nimble young man' to chase them. The crewman soon overtook them and they turned to fight. The sailor had a cutlass, while the Aborigines had wooden lances, 'with which, being many of them, they were too hard for him'. Dampier was himself chasing two other Aborigines along the beach but returned to help his outnumbered crewman.

> I discharged my gun to scare them but avoided shooting any of them; till finding the young man in great danger from them, and myself in some; and that though the gun had a little frighted them at first, yet they had soon learnt to despise it, tossing up their hands, and crying pooh, pooh, pooh; and coming on afresh with a great noise, I thought it high time to charge again, and shoot one of them, which I did.

But still the Aborigines did not take fright and instead renewed battle. Dampier and his crewman, together with another man who had not taken part in the fray because he had come ashore unarmed, managed to escape. 'I returned back with my men, designing to attempt the natives no farther, being very sorry for what had happened already.'

Even while fighting, Dampier managed to observe one who he thought was the leader of the Aborigines:

> He was a young brisk man, not very tall, nor so personable as some of the rest, though more active and courageous: he was painted (which none of the rest were at all) with a circle of white paste or pigment (a sort of lime, as we thought) about his eyes, and a white streak down his nose from his forehead to the tip of it. And his breast and some part of his arms were also made white with the same paint; not for beauty or ornament, one would think, but as some wild Indian warriors are said to do.

Then Dampier returned to the stereotypes of his day, feeding his audience with comparisons that such an intelligent man must have known to be absurd:

All of them have the most unpleasant looks and the worst features of any people that ever I saw, though I have seen great variety of savages. These New Hollanders were probably the same sort of people as those I met with on this coast in my Voyage round the World; for the place I then touched at was not above 40 or 50 leagues to the north-east of this: and these were much the same blinking creatures (here being also abundance of the same kind of flesh-flies teasing them) and with the same black skins, and hair frizzled, tall and thin, etc., as those were: but we had not the opportunity to see whether these, as the former, wanted two of their foreteeth.

He found ample evidence of the Aboriginal use of fire and saw 'a great many places where they had made fires; and where there were commonly 3 or 4 boughs stuck up to windward of them; for the wind (which is the sea breeze) in the daytime blows always one way with them; and the land breeze is but small'.

The Aborigines lived mainly on shellfish gathered from the rocks at low water. The English saw no evidence of seafaring as 'they have neither boats, canoes or bark logs'. Instead, they seemed to swim from island to island, often in groups. They were thought to be fully nomadic as Dampier found no houses, 'and I believe they have none, since the former people on the island had none, though they had all their families with them'.

After making these observations, Dampier returned to the main party of his sailors to the news that they had not found fresh water. They tried again the next morning, but the men came back with only a small supply of brackish water that was not fit to drink, though it was good enough to be boiled up with oatmeal to make 'burgoo' for their breakfast. As they worked in the hot sun through the rest of the day, Dampier complained that they were 'sadly pestered with the flies, which were more troublesome to us than the sun'. They did not encounter any more of the natives, but saw the smoke of their fires about 3 kilometres away.

Despite finding an abundance of flowers, trees, shrubs and wildlife, including lizards, a small snake and what were described as 'raccoons', there was no water. His men saw 'two or three beasts like hungry wolves, lean and like so many skeletons, being nothing but skin and bones'. Dampier described crows, hawks and seabirds of many kinds. In the sea were 'the largest whales that I ever saw; but not to compare with the vast ones of the northern seas'. There were more turtles, sharks and shellfish, and Dampier gathered the last shells he would collect in the Southland. However, having still not found fresh water or anywhere to careen his ship, he had decided it was time to move on: 'And it being moreover the height of the dry season, and my men growing scorbutic for want of refreshments, so that I had little encouragement to search further, I resolved to leave this coast and accordingly in the beginning of September set sail towards Timor.'

Dampier then proceeded around New Guinea and the surrounding islands but was unable to carry out the planned survey of the east coast. Despite her size and fine design, *Roebuck* was sinking. She had to be run ashore at Ascension Island in February 1701. The crew waited five weeks ashore before being rescued by a passing East Indiaman, finally returning in August that year.

Dampier was then court-martialled on several charges, mainly relating to the earlier part of *Roebuck*'s voyage. He had ordered an officer to be jailed in Brazil, an act that was considered to be 'hard and cruel usage'. He was found guilty of that charge and discharged from the navy.

But in 1703 the apparently unstoppable Dampier was appointed to go privateering again. Commanding the *St George*, Dampier's attacks on Spanish shipping and the Panamanian town of Santa Maria ended in fiasco and the abandonment of his ruined ship. After being captured by the Spanish and then imprisoned by the Dutch, he limped back to England late in 1707. The next year he went as sailing master aboard the privateer *Duke* under the command of Woodes Rogers. On this voyage he took part in the rescue of Alexander Selkirk, the model for Daniel Defoe's Robinson Crusoe and the world's best known castaway.

The real Robinson Crusoe

William Dampier's privateering voyage of 1703 and 1704 consisted of two craft: his own, the *Duke*, and the *Cinque Ports*. The *Cinque Ports* was commanded by Thomas Stradling and the sailing master was an argumentative Scotsman named Alexander Selkirk. The two ships separated in May 1704 and by September the *Cinque Ports* lay off an uninhabited island in the Juan Fernandez archipelago looking for food and water.

By now, the ship had become unseaworthy and Selkirk wanted Stradling to repair it. The captain was of a different opinion and when Selkirk rashly declared he would rather be left behind than sail in a leaky boat, Stradling obliged him. The complaining Scotsman was put ashore with his belongings, arms and supplies. Stradling sailed away and, true to Selkirk's fears, the *Cinque Ports* sank near present-day Colombia. The Spanish captured Stradling and other survivors and harshly imprisoned them.

Meanwhile, the castaway Selkirk had to learn to live off the land, build dwellings, make his own clothes and contend with the isolation and loneliness of his situation. Spanish ships visited the island on two occasions but, in a difficult dilemma, Selkirk decided to hide, avoiding capture but condemning himself to continue a miserable existence.

After almost five years of privation, Selkirk was overjoyed when the *Duke*, commanded by Woodes Rogers and piloted by William Dampier, anchored off his island. When the news reached England of his rescue, Selkirk's story became widely known. He featured in Woodes Rogers' book A *Cruising Voyage Around the World* and became a minor celebrity. He seems to have been a sailor for the rest of his roistering life. Ironically, he died as member of the Royal Navy while chasing pirates in 1721.

Selkirk is usually said to have been the inspiration for Daniel Defoe's even more famous book *The Life and Surprising Adventures of Robinson Crusoe,* published two years after Selkirk's death. Defoe would certainly have known Selkirk's tale, but research has shown that there were many inspirations behind the now-classic castaway yarn, including other chronicles and narratives published in the seventeenth century.[7] In any case, Selkirk, Robinson Crusoe and the desert island castaway became firmly fixed in popular culture from this time, assisted by the real-life events of castaways on the mysterious Southland.

Dampier's legacy

William Dampier is thought to have died in London in 1715, though the circumstances of his death are unknown. He seems never to have received his share of the booty from the *Duke* voyage, which was outrageously successful, taking more than 17,000 pounds worth of Spanish treasure, which would be valued at many millions today. One of Dampier's many contributions was to establish the popularity of travel narratives about the Southland. While the mercantile voyages of discovery and trade continued to produce, in some cases, tangible results in the form of goods, profits and maps, the southern landmass continued to attract fantastication.

In 1693 a book was published in France under the title *A New Discovery of Terra Incognita Australis, or the Southern World.* The book was 'authored' by James Sadeur (though in another edition, the author's name is printed as Nicolas Sadeur), who claimed that he had been cast away on the Southland as a young man and survived there for not less than thirty-five years. Sadeur said that he had adopted the manners and customs of the indigenous peoples and described the plants and animals of the place.

According to the 'back story', these memoirs were deemed to be so unusual and sensitive that a minister of state had to keep them under lock and key until Sadeur's death. Like many such works, including those of William Dampier, they were very popular with European readers. This fantasy went into several editions, including an English translation. The difference with Dampier's book was that he had actually visited the Southland, though he was not above enhancing his original journal entries for the titillation of the reading public and in accordance with the stereotypes and prejudices already established in the European psyche.

These fictions and travel narratives were often only slightly more sensational and puzzling than the reality. Other than a lot of charting and the occasional ocean-edge encounter with Aborigines, almost nothing was known of the continent, or even if it was one at all. The few accounts of indigenous people were often contradictory and bewildering to Europeans in almost every way. None more so, perhaps, than in what was probably the first European contact with the Tiwi people.

Meeting the Tiwi

In January 1705, a VOC fleet of three—*Vossenbosch*, a fluyt, *Nova Hollandia*, a 'patsjallang' [small war ship] and the sloop *Wajer*—cleared Batavia under the overall command of Maarten van Delft. His task was to explore the northern coast of the Southland and to locate a possible gulf that was thought to penetrate deep into the interior of the mysterious continent.

It was the second day in April, a month's sailing from Timor, when they saw smoke on the shore of a large island. The crew later landed between what are now Cook's Reef and Karslake Island, and here there was a volatile encounter. In a report to the VOC, it was described: 'Between these two islands or headlands some natives were met by our men on April 23rd, who did not indeed retire, but nevertheless ran together toward an eminence, and with all sorts of movements and gestures attempted to drive our men from the land.'

In the fight, a Tiwi leader was wounded by musket fire. However, van Delft went on to state, rather matter-of-factly, that the two groups then made peace and the wounded man was treated and gifts were exchanged.

Friendly relations persisted, with the Tiwi coming aboard the Dutch ships, bringing fish, and the Dutch giving presents of clothing, knives and beads. It was observed that the Tiwi men went naked and were often decorated with ceremonial scars, while the women covered 'their privy parts with leaves or the like'. The Tiwi ate 'sparingly and moderately' and appeared to live exclusively on fish, roots and vegetables rather than birds or other animals. 'They have neither iron nor anything like minerals or metal; for a stone which has been grounded serves as their hatchet; have neither houses nor huts, and occupy themselves with fishing by means of harpoons of wood, and also of little nets, and putting out to sea in little vessels made of the bark of trees, which are so fragile they have to be shored up with cross-beams.'

The Dutch also witnessed a large night-time gathering of perhaps five hundred Tiwi 'round several fires among the bushes'. But they lost interest in the gathering when they observed that 'nothing however was seen in their possession of any value'. This was around mid-June and was by far the largest group of Aborigines to have been reported, suggesting that the gathering (presumably a corroboree) was of great ceremonial significance.

It seems that van Delft was under instructions only to bring home any natives who wished to accompany him: 'Our men might also easily have taken and brought over to Batavia with them, two or three of the natives who daily came on board, but the skipper of the *Vossenbosch*, following out his instructions to the letter, would not allow them to be taken without their full consent, either by falsehood or fraud.' Whether this was an act of Christian decency or of simple practicality, it is difficult to tell, but according to the surviving account, 'as no one understood their language, nothing was to be done in the matter, consequently they remained in their own country'.

The three Dutch ships then sailed east around the island. They met with another Tiwi group and established the same friendly relations as previously. But, at the last moment when the Dutch were on the point of departing, two sailors were attacked and wounded by eight natives. It was believed that the natives had attacked 'with the hope of taking possession of their cloth, and that after having conversed with these people for weeks, eaten and drunk, been aboard, examining all things in admiration, having received presents, and on their part had regaled our men with fish and crabs'. The Dutch were perplexed and dismayed by this apparent breach of trust, though from the Tiwi point of view their visitors may have been seen to be departing without exchanging the appropriate amount of goods in return for the hospitality they had received.

Continuing to follow instructions, the Dutch left for the Cobourg Peninsula, looking for a passage into the interior. At one location 'a tiger was met with' and while anchored near Maria's Island, the inhabitants attempted to tow the *patsjallang*. They met with no success and so tried to bring up the anchor. But it was too heavy and they returned to the shore. It is not clear whether the Aborigines wished to tow the ship to their shore or to tow it away.

Van Delft also landed on Greenhill Island for water before his little fleet returned home in August with crews much depleted from 'severe sickness, principally fever, acute pains in the head and eyes, and above all, dropsy' (fluid accumulation in body tissue). Van Delft was dead, as were his two steersmen.[8] The voyage had not been what the VOC would class as a success, with the loss of sailors, many of the logbooks and charts, and no new potential for trade with those the Dutch now considered of 'rude and barbarous character' and with a 'malicious disposition'. Nor was there a conveniently quick passage into the centre of the continent.

The Tiwi of Melville Island confirmed their reputation as fierce warriors long after these events took place. In May 1818 the colonial-born navigator Phillip Parker King, destined to circumnavigate Australia three times, attempted to land on the island. He and his men were driven off by the Tiwi. Between 1824 and 1829, a British fort was established there. Fort Dundas was the first British settlement in the north of Australia. It was under what was effectively continual siege by the Tiwi until it was abandoned.

Maarten van Delft's report of his experiences with the Tiwi provides a first-person account of what happened when a group of Europeans met a group of Aborigines for the first time. Just seven years later on another shore of the Southland, an event took place that left no such documentary testimony, only a still unsolved mystery.

8

The ship of doom

There are many ghosts haunting the castaway coasts of the Southland. The fate of perhaps 250 people thrown onto the desolate shore
in the winter of 1712 is still unknown. In the empty space between
certainty and a few tentative facts, there has always been speculation about the wreck of the *Zuytdorp*.

Built in six months over 1700–1701, the ship was named after
the southern Zeeland settlement of 'South Village' or Zuiddorpe.
A very fine vessel of the VOC's largest class, more than 45 metres
long and nearing 12 metres wide, the *Zuytdorp* could carry cargo
of more than 1100 tons. Like most merchant ships of the time,
she was well armed with forty cannon and strongly built for the
rigours of voyaging to and from the East Indies. The *Zuytdorp*
suffered storm damage on her maiden voyage in early 1702 but
spent a successful few years trading in Asia and playing a significant role in the blockade of Surat. She returned to the Netherlands
in 1710, departing once again the following year. But almost from
the moment it began, this voyage was doomed.

A deadly voyage

The *Zuytdorp* left the Netherlands for Batavia via the Cape of Good Hope in the summer of 1711. Commanded by Marinus Wysvliet, she sailed in company with the smaller *Belvliet* commanded by the more experienced Dirck Blauuw. Wysvliet had not voyaged to the East Indies, while Blauuw had two previous Asian voyages to his name and had occupied senior ranks. Blauuw was in overall command of the two ships, but among the many mysteries of the *Zuytdorp* is why the fledgling Wysvliet was skippering one of the VOC's largest and newest vessels to the far end of the globe.

This fine ship was carrying an estimated treasure of almost 250,000 silver guilders. The rest of the cargo was the usual assembly of food, implements and arms necessary to keep the ship and her 286[1] sailors, soldiers, officers and passengers alive for the many months of the journey to the cape.

The ships made reasonable progress until they entered the region of infrequent winds known as 'the doldrums' at the end of September. By early November they had hardly moved any distance and many aboard were ill through malnutrition and the appalling lack of hygiene that was usual on sailing ships. *Zuytdorp* had forty-eight down with scurvy and not expected to live unless fresh food and water could be obtained. Against orders, they sailed for the island of São Tomé in the Gulf of Guinea. Fresh supplies were obtained but as the two ships loitered in these tropical climes men began to desert rather than face the rest of the deadly voyage.[2] They were wise. After the ships left the island, those aboard began to die even more quickly.

At that time, it was the custom for the goods of those who died during a voyage to be auctioned off to the survivors, the proceeds being returned to their widows and grieving families back home. The journal of the *Belvliet* notes many of these often-pathetic dispersals of the sometimes-negligible goods of sailors. One man had only a little tobacco and a couple of pipes to his name. Others seem to have been better off, depending on their rank. The highest paid man, of course, was the master.

Blauuw also fell ill and instructed his first mate to ensure that his goods were not auctioned aboard the ship but retained until they could be sold in Batavia, presumably because they would fetch a better price there. Blauuw died on 22 February. He was given a 'seaman's burial', with twenty-two guns fired over him and his body carried all round his ship three times before being committed to the deep.

By this time, wind and currents had separated the two ships for almost a month. They would not be reunited for another two months when both sailed into Table Bay within four days of each other. The *Belvliet* had continued to suffer a high mortality rate, but the *Zuytdorp*'s toll was even greater, with 112 dead, with another twenty-two ill. The death rate was near 40 per cent, almost ten times higher than the average four-month voyage from the Netherlands to the Cape of Good Hope.

The eight-month ordeal had encouraged scurvy, and probably malaria and other tropical diseases contracted in the notorious São Tomé, to ravage both ships. The cramped and unhygienic living conditions of the crew and soldiers also contributed to the carnage. No matter how often the decks were scrubbed with vinegar and the surgeon administered strange-sounding potions, the scourge of disease stalked all. Even the surgeon and his two assistants became ill, and then threw themselves raving into the ocean rather than face the dreadful end they knew to be inevitable aboard the death ship *Zuytdorp*.

After a month at the cape, the *Zuytdorp* was resupplied with food and people, two hundred of them. There would later be some suggestions that Wysvliet, who survived the voyage, had been hoarding food in order to sell the surplus in Batavia on his own behalf, a not uncommon practice. But that insinuation would mostly come later after his ship inexplicably failed to arrive at her destination. She left the cape in company with the *Kockenge* on 22 April. The faster *Zuytdorp* soon left the smaller vessel in her wake, and then vanished for more than two centuries.

The sinking

In Batavia, the VOC governor-general and council began to worry about the *Zuytdorp* after a few months. In November 1712 they wrote back to Amsterdam, stating 'to our regret the fine ship Zuytdorp has not arrived so far'. They wrote again in January 1713—still no news.

Oddly, the loss of such a new and expensive ship, together with a substantial amount of silver, does not seem to have aroused much concern. No search was ever made for her, even though she could conceivably have lain wrecked along the western coast of the Southland. It seems that the VOC simply assumed that the *Zuytdorp* had sunk at sea with all hands, as probably had the *Ridderschap van Holland* fifteen years before. Willem de Vlamingh had been sent in search of that ship, but found no trace, and the VOC seemed content to leave it at that, as with the *Zuytdorp*.

If only a survey ship had been sent down the west coast, it might have rescued many castaway souls.

Probably in a winter storm during the first week of June, the *Zuytdorp* had ground into jagged reefs and smashing breakers beneath the towering cliffs of the Southland's western shore. Perhaps only thirty, perhaps many more,[3] managed to get themselves ashore onto a rock platform at the base of the cliffs. Here they huddled together in cold, shock and injury great or small as waves broke over them. Clutching broken pieces of wreckage, a few personal items and perhaps some supplies, they scrambled up the rock scree to the top of the cliffs. They built a large fire, for warmth and as a beacon to any would-be rescuers.

A number of VOC craft are known to have passed this way in the weeks immediately after the wrecking. It is difficult to believe that the large signal fire on the stark cliffs was not seen. If it was, the flames and smoke may have simply been mistaken for just another of the many fires lit by Aborigines, and therefore tragically ignored.

When the *Zuytdorp* grounded, she hit the reef head on. The waves then forced her sideways with stern and middle sections close to the rocky shore. Masts and rigging crashed down; though this allowed any survivors not crushed beneath or already drowned to claw their way ashore across the heaving mass of canvas and broken spars. At some point, possibly quite soon after her grounding, the heavy seas split the *Zuytdorp* into three and sank her. Her hold spilled its cargo into the waters at the edge of the rock platform. The chests of silver carried in the stern of the ship went straight to the bottom, but many items washed onto the shore were fairly easily retrievable.

The survivors were able to salvage barrels, clay tobacco-smoking pipes, navigational instruments and even bottles of gin. They made their first temporary camp near the cliff edge and close to their signal fire. Broken gin bottles found near this site suggest they kept themselves warm with the contents. It seems that they were able, for some time at least, to reach the wreck and obtain supplies and other necessities. But then what?

Fate of the survivors

Research into the behaviour of shipwreck survivors suggest that they fairly quickly adapt the structures and attributes of their wrecked ship, which itself is a microcosm of the society that built it. Chains of command from shipboard life are usually rapidly reasserted among survivors, especially if the master is among them. Otherwise, if officers have survived, the tendency is for these individuals to assume command and for those who were their inferiors—sailors, soldiers not of officer rank, and any passengers—to acknowledge and accept that leadership.[4] If these authority structures were preserved among the *Zuytdorp* survivors, they would have fairly quickly been organised to retrieve whatever was available from the wreck, as indeed the *Zuytdorp* people appear to have done. They were also able to bring the metal breech blocks ashore from the wreck. These were needed to fire cannon and it seems that the survivors planned to bring one of the smaller swivel guns ashore for signalling. There is no evidence that they succeeded in salvaging any cannon. Only the breech blocks found in modern times remain to allow this conjecture.

From whatever bits and pieces were available, and using the many and diverse skills practised by those aboard a sailing ship, they would have tried to re-create a material culture necessary for survival. Shelter would be the first need, probably provided by sails fixed to spars to form tents or a basic hut. They had the means of making fire, probably from flints, so warmth and cooking were possible—as long as there was anything to cook. Bacon was a staple aboard VOC ships and at least some of this might have been plucked from the boiling seas, or even hurled ashore by the surf. Implements for cutting and for protection might have been available in the same way, including knives, pikes and perhaps muskets, though the powder would need to be dry before these were usable. Clothing was initially what they stood up in, perhaps later complemented with sodden garments dragged from the sea.

The major problem was drinking water. The *Zuytdorp* had cast its occupants onto one of the driest places on the coast of one of the continent's most arid regions. Without a reliable source of drinkable water, all would perish very quickly. Unbeknown to the survivors, the nearest permanent source was around 13 kilometres away at Billiecutherra soak, though there were seasonal sinkholes in rocks used by Aborigines around the immediate area. These sources of water may have been later shown to the survivors by the Malgana or possibly Nunda people, between whose traditional lands they had been stranded. Other than obtaining water, there was little chance for the survivors to live off the scrubby land in which they found themselves, unless they had been able to save muskets, powder and ball from the wreck. Shellfish and fish were available, as long as they had the strength and some basic implements to obtain them.

But we know they managed to live for at least a little while. There is evidence of a second and possibly a third site where the survivors camped. Artefacts have been found here, including dividers used for navigation. As well as those items at the wreck site, coins and other artefacts almost certainly from the wreck have turned up. An Aboriginal man found a coin around 40 kilometres north of the wreck in 1869. A Dutch tobacco tin lid made of brass turned up in 1990, recovered more than 50 kilometres north of the site.

Were these items rescued and transported by Aboriginal people, or by survivors? We cannot tell. But other potential evidence for the *Zuytdorp* survivors moving beyond their initial campsites has been put forward from time to time. A human bone was discovered near one of the campsites. A curious rock painting of what appears to be a two-masted sailing ship has been seen at Walga Rock since at least the late nineteenth century. The painting and the pseudo-writing beneath it have been examined but the results are inconclusive. It is likely that the painting is a nineteenth-century hoax.

Did one of the stricken ship's boats survive the wrecking? Experts think it unlikely. Another possibility might have been to build a seaworthy craft from the remaining timbers of the ship. This would have required skills and equipment, though is not an impossibility as the *Zeewijk* survivors demonstrated in 1728. But there is no evidence of construction at the site and the savage nature of the coast would make it very difficult to launch any such craft.

Despite these rational analyses and theories, haunting facts hover around the *Zuytdorp* story. Why are there no skeletal remains? None have been found in or near the remains of the ship. None have been found on the rocks or on the cliff top. Apart from the one bone found at the possible third campsite, there seems to be no evidence of burial, incineration, even decomposition. As none of their own people knew where they were, the lost voyagers of the *Zuytdorp* had no other chance of survival than the assistance of the local Aborigines. Did they receive it? We do not know for sure, but there is a good deal of circumstantial evidence that at least some of them did.

As early as the 1840s, settlers in the region reported seeing fair-skinned, light-haired Aboriginal people with European features. Similar reports appear in the 1860s, one in the form of a legend. In this story, two tribes live along opposite banks of the same river. One is black, the other white. Although originally on friendly terms, the white tribe suddenly cuts communication with the black. Then one day it begins to rain for so long that a great flood arises. When the rain stops, there is no trace of the river, only a wide sea beneath which the white tribe has disappeared.[5]

Further mythological, linguistic, botanical and other evidence can be mustered to support the theory that the *Zuytdorp* survivors did interact significantly with Aboriginal groups.[6] There may also be some genetic indications that this took place. But before such modern methods of investigation could be deployed on the *Zuytdorp* puzzles, the treasure hunters arrived.

Treasure hunters

One April day in 1927, a man is out trapping dingoes along the desolate cliffs north of Geraldton. The country is so thickly wooded that he literally has to cut his way through it to reach the coast. When he does, he decides to take a break from his work to go fishing. As he scrambles down the cliff scree towards the rock platform below, he sees broken bottles and pieces of wooden debris, not especially remarkable along this wild coast. He throws his line into the sea, hooking a couple of fish for dinner. On the way back he notices some green cylinders, which he picks up and scrapes with his knife. They are metal. So are the eight-or-so small discs he scoops up next. His mind now turning back to the task he has been contracted to carry out for a local farmer, he slips the discs into his pocket and gets back to his traps.

From this point on, almost everything about Tom Pepper's discovery of the *Zuytdorp* is disputed by one or more interests. Some even deny that he was the first to find what was left of the stricken ship and her treasure.[7] Whatever the truth of the claims and counter-claims, at least part of a 200-year-old mystery was solved. Marine archaeologists would later confirm the last resting place of the *Zuytdorp* beneath the cliffs that now bear her name. But the fate of the 200 to 250 people aboard has been debated ever since.

The story of the *Zuytdorp*'s rediscovery is one of treasure seekers, artefact hunters and newspapers looking for a sensational story. Perth's *Sunday Times* newspaper funded the first attempt in 1941. At this time, the wrecked ship had not been identified. Despite finding a few more coins and metal objects, the expedition made no major discoveries, other than to speculate that the wreck might be the *Zuytdorp* rather than the *Vergulde Draeck*. The items that were discovered were taken back to Perth but, like many artefacts reclaimed from historic wrecks, subsequently vanished and have not been seen since.

The next organised expedition to the site was in 1954. It was financed by another local newspaper, the *Daily News*, and included Phillip Playford. Fascinated with artefacts, museums and wrecks since childhood, Playford consulted extensively with Tom Pepper about his earlier finds and became a self-taught authority on the subject of VOC wrecks. He would later write a book about the events and his intimate experience with the *Zuytdorp*'s story over many years. The plan was to dive on the wreck. Although conditions prevented that, the group was able to locate the wreck, scrape up more coins—some with the help of explosives—barrel hoops, breech blocks and many wooden fragments, including a large section of a yardarm. They also found evidence of the survivors' fires and campsites.

Four years later, Playford was back at the site, again supported by the *Daily News*. Once more, the immense waves pounding the cliffs prevented diving. Fragments of clay pipe were found, together with two keys and a variety of other items all confirming occupation of the area by the survivors for some time. More blasting revealed no artefacts but caused some environmental damage that was not rectified for many years. Against Playford's wishes, the wooden items were taken back to Perth where they were supposed to be housed in a public museum in the headquarters of the newspaper company that had funded the expeditions. These objects have since disappeared.

Despite these expeditions and finds, no one had yet dived on the wreck itself until 1964 when a successful dive was made, discovering cannon, anchors and lead ingots. Further dives were achieved in 1967 and 1968, during which the famous 'carpet of silver' was found. This consisted of a mass of coins cemented together on the sea floor by centuries of tide and waves. Dives were made by personnel from the Western Australian Museum in 1971 and again in 1977. Over this period there were also dives by persons unknown.

In the late 1970s a new identity entered the story. The eighth nizam of Hyderabad, Prince Mukurram Jah, owned Murchison House station, not far from the *Zuytdorp* wreck site. He used the property as his holiday home and for indulging his interest in earth-moving and other heavy equipment. When the prince learned of the wreck and its history, there were immediate resonances with his own family history and the political history of Southern India and its attempts to resist colonisation. He became an enthusiastic and generous supporter of the project, grading roads and an airstrip and installing equipment at his own expense.

Air access allowed museum staff to make another dive in 1978, which confirmed the wreck had been recently looted. Fearing further plundering and damage, a caravan and permanent watch-keeper were placed at the site in June that year. In October 1980, while the watch-keeper was away, an arsonist poured petrol through the caravan windows and burned it to the ground, together with other nearby equipment. The police investigated, but no one was ever apprehended for what was a well-planned and efficiently executed crime.

A local abalone diver was then employed on a part-time warden basis, a position he held, firstly on a paid basis and then in an honorary capacity, until 1994. At that point, the Commonwealth government issued an amnesty for anyone who admitted unlawfully taking items from historic shipwrecks. The warden confessed that he had been taking items from the *Zuytdorp* for twenty years. He had amassed an impressive and valuable collection of coins and other items, described by Phillip Playford as 'the largest and most valuable collection known to have been taken from the *Zuytdorp*'.[8]

However, the warden was not the only treasure hunter.

In 1981 a group of divers claimed to have discovered a trove of silver worth millions. Claims for ownership of the wreck and its treasure began to be made. In the absence of effective legislation protecting historic wrecks from predatory behaviour, a serious conflict arose between private interests and the Western Australian Maritime Museum, eventually involving the Commonwealth government and the government of the Netherlands. There were more unauthorised and illegal dives made on the wreck site, physical violence, threats, more dynamiting and various legal actions. Out of it all came workable legislation for the protection of Dutch shipwrecks and their contents and surrounding sites, together with the authority for qualified marine archaeologists to control access and investigation.[9]

Official museum work on the wreck site began again in 1986. Between 1978 and 1986, possibly 90 per cent of the *Zuytdorp*'s treasure disappeared. By April 1996 the Museum of Western Australia expedition found that the 'carpet of silver' no longer existed. Along with the silver went many historically—and commercially—valuable relics. None of this haul is known to have reappeared, leading to speculations that it might be secreted along the forbidding immensity of the Zuytdorp Cliffs. Numerous dives were subsequently made throughout the 1990s and many more coins, cannon, anchors and even domestic items recovered for the museum.

The 300th anniversary of the *Zuytdorp*'s death was commemorated in June 2012. A stainless-steel plaque can now be seen on a hill overlooking Chinaman's Beach. It was commissioned by the Shire of Northampton and the Embassy of the Kingdom of the Netherlands, and includes information about the ship, the discovery of the site in 1927, and the continuing mystery of the survivors and their fate.

The El Dorado factor

The conspiracies and controversies surrounding the treasures and artefacts of VOC wrecks such as the *Zuytdorp* are modern continuations of some very old themes. The fascination for fabled treasures in far-off lands was a major motivation in the expansion of mercantile empires in the seventeenth and eighteenth centuries. The classic formulation of the myth is the 'El Dorado' tale of a lost city of fabulous wealth, around which the Spanish focused much of their conquest of South America. But these beliefs were not restricted to national or ethnic boundaries. From around 1717 a Swiss employee of the VOC named Jean Pierre Purry proposed that the company should colonise the south-western parts of the

Southland. He called the country 'The Land of Nights' and spiced up his plans with claims that these areas were rich with untold wealth. This suggestion was taken up by others, including the English mapmaker Emmanuel Bowen who published a work on the subject in 1747.

While such myths have usually turned out to be illusory, there is a sense in which they have come true. The wrecks of sailing ships laden heavy with gold, silver and now-rare artefacts are magnets for modern-day treasure hunters. There is a thriving illegal industry within Indonesia and elsewhere in the world which involves the looting of sunken vessels.[10] Precious metals may be melted down for sale, while artefacts may be sold to private collectors and even to museums and galleries that do not inquire too closely into the provenance of their purchases. Certainly the Southland wrecks have been mostly looted, despoiled or otherwise interfered with, and there is much that has gone missing.

Just a few years after the disappearance of the *Zuytdorp*, two other VOC ships went missing. Bound for Batavia out of Cape Town on her maiden voyage, the 800-ton *Fortuyn* failed to reach her destination in early 1724. Only two years old, she was described as a frigate, about 45 metres long, with a complement of 225. Her fate remains unknown, though it is possible that she was wrecked on the Southland. The survivors of the *Zeewijk* wrecked in 1727 reported the remains of a wooden ship that might have been the *Fortuyn*, though there is some evidence that she might have gone down near Christmas Island.[11]

The wreckage sighted by the *Zeewijk* men might also have been that of *Aagtekerke*, which was lost between Cape Town and Batavia in 1726 with no known survivors. At 280 tons, *Aagtekerke* was a sister ship to the *Zeewijk* but unlike her was carrying a cargo of elephant tusks. Elephant tusks have been found at Half-Moon Reef, leaving investigators to conclude that both ships were wrecked at the same location. The chances are great against two sister ships foundering at the same Southland graveyard within two years of each other. But the number of cannon and anchors at the *Zeewijk* site could exceed the usual complement for one ship.[12] *Aagtekerke* was carrying 3 tons of silver coins. If coins are found, it will be proof of the theory as all the *Zeewijk*'s money chests were accounted for and returned to the VOC in Batavia. While agreeing that there was a wreck prior to that of *Zeewijk* on the Half-Moon Reef, not all experts accept the theory that it was *Aagtekerke*, claiming that it might have been a wreck elsewhere in the Houtman Abrolhos. Nevertheless, investigators are now taking this unlikely possibility seriously.[13]

Yet another intriguing possibility concerns the 'Deadwater Wreck'. In 1846 the surveyor and explorer Frank Gregory reported the 'remains of a vessel of considerable tonnage ... in a shallow estuary near the Vasse Inlet ... which, from its appearance I should judged [sic] to have been wrecked two hundred years ago'.[14] The next recorded sighting of the wreck in the section of the Wonnerup Inlet known as 'the Deadwater' was in 1856, though the account stated that it had been visible 'for years past'. It seems there is a credible line of documentation back to the earliest years of European occupation in this area during the 1840s. There is also the usual folklore surrounding this mystery. Unverified local tradition claims that Aboriginal people were massacred by early settlers to obtain gold ornaments they possessed from some unknown source.[15]

The decomposing ship was plundered in the 1860s, though almost certainly not by Aborigines, but there have been no credible sightings of it since. That has not quashed speculation and investigation about the ship's identity. Serious research and fieldwork into the wreck was carried out by one of the leading authorities of this area, Rupert Gerritsen, and a group of like-minded inquirers. Based on estimates of the length of the Deadwater Wreck, Gerritsen's group suggested that the ship is a VOC *hoeker* named the

Zeelt.[16] This class of ship was around 30 metres in length and built in the high-stern style of many early VOC craft, according to some descriptions of the wreck before its disappearance beneath the sand and mud. The small 90-ton *Zeelt* went missing as early as 1672 on only her second voyage. The careful work carried out by Gerritsen and his group may have revealed the identity of the Deadwater Wreck, but there is also research suggesting *Zeelt* actually went down in southern Madagascar.[17]

Modern wreck hunters persist in their quest for many reasons. For some, it is simply the possibility of great wealth, or adventure; for others it is the discovery of historical truth and the preservation of maritime heritage. The more complicated possibility is that the enthusiasm is fuelled by a combination of all these elements. Just as modern-day seekers may be motivated by a number of sometimes conflicting passions, so the people who found themselves cast away on the great Southland in the seventeenth and eighteenth centuries—or possibly before—were energised by a mixture of motives. The lure of strange new lands and experiences beyond the known world certainly inspired many adventurers. The 'El Dorado' factor was another powerful dimension, either in the form of gold and silver or the more prosaic but sometimes even more valuable spices, herbs and other exotic products. These could be had for next to nothing and sold for eye-watering sums in the markets of Europe.

Few had any interest in human contact and interchange. We might find this callous and narrow. But we are looking at the past from the vantage of what we like to think is a more enlightened present. The era in which the uncharted Southland was gradually revealed was, by our standards, extremely tough, as were the people of the period. Despite pious words in official documents and sermons, human life was cheap and had very little meaning. The lives of indigenous peoples even less. Even men of the Enlightenment, such as James Cook and Joseph Banks, would slip easily into stereotype and prejudice when describing their first and subsequent contacts with people who had inhabited the land for tens of thousands of years but the like of which the Europeans had never encountered. The legacy of those intrinsic values and attitudes ensured the disintegration of traditional societies. We still live with the consequences, and even the skin and bones.

9

Skeleton coasts

On Monday 26 April 1728 the Council of the Netherlands Indies in Batavia received a desperate letter:

> My High Excellency, together with the Council of the Nether-landish India, I pray of you most urgently to send me help and assistance against these robbers of the money and the goods of the wreck Zeewyk, who have divided the money and goods among themselves. I am stark naked; they have taken everything from me. 0, my God! They have behaved like wild beasts to me, and everyone is master. Worse than beasts do they live; it is impossible that on board a pirate ship things can be worse than here, because everyone thinks that he is rich, from the highest to the lowest of my subordinates. They say among themselves, 'Let us drink a glass to your health, ye old ducats!' I am ill and prostrate from scurvy.

Jan Steyns, the skipper, and Jan Nebbens (sometimes Nobbens or Nibbens), the under-merchant, had been wrecked with their crew when the near-280 ton *Zeewijk* went aground on the treacherous reefs now known as the Houtman Abrolhos. On her maiden voyage from Flushing in Zeeland, *Zeewijk*'s passage to Cape Town was marked by sickness, twenty-six deaths and a close shave with pirates. Reprovisioned and with her crew strengthened to more than two hundred, she left Cape Town for Batavia on 21 April. Another eleven men died on this leg of the voyage. In defiance of his VOC orders and over the protest of his steersman, Steyns set a course straight towards the western coast of the Southland, or the Land of Eendracht as the Dutch were generally calling it at this time. The ship's master also entered a false note in the ship's log to the effect that the decision of the ship's council to sail east-north-east was 'decided unanimously'. It was not, and this act would eventually ruin Steyns.

Half-Moon Reef

It was during the first watch of the evening of 9 June. The lookout on the ship's foreyard noticed white flecks on the sea before the ship. He watched them for half an hour or so and decided that they were reflections of the moon. But around 7.30 p.m. the *Zeewijk* struck and foundered in heavy surf around a reef shaped like a half-moon. The under-steersman, Adriaen van der Graeff, described the disaster:

> At dusk, therefore, we were running under small sail, i.e. foresail and both topsails double-reefed, but at about 7.30 in the evening Jan Steyns, the master, together with the under-merchant Jan Nebbens came up on to the quarterdeck from the master's cabin and asked the third mate Joris Forkson who had the watch at the time 'What was that which could be seen ahead?' answering himself at the same time 'My God, it is surf, lay your helm to starboard!' and called the first and second mates who were in the former's cabin setting out the course on the charts. The under-merchant came to warn us, coming to meet us from the awning. We had heard the shout in the cabin and jumped into the waist to the sheets and braces, but before the foresails had been braced to the wind, the ship crashed with a great shock into the cliff on

her starboard side and turning her head in the wind round the SW knocked her rudder out of the helm port.

Hearing and heeding the master's orders:

I, Adriaen v.d. Graeff, second mate, made my way to the steerage and found there to be 8 feet of water in the ship, whereupon our main mast fell overboard. We then decided to cut away our fore and mizzenmasts and found our ship to be lying in 10 to 11 feet of water, so that we prayed the Almighty for a propitious outcome. While terrible waves washed over us constantly we attempted to cut away the top hamper. A seaman named Yuriaen Roelofsen was washed overboard together with the fore mast and bowsprit, so that we looked at one another sorrowfully and prayed for surcease from the terrible punishment which the Almighty was sending us. We asked the lookout who had been sitting on the foreyard whose name was Pieter de Klerck van Apel, whether he had not seen the surf; he confessed at once that he had seen it for at least half an hour, but had imagined that it was caused by the sky or the moon.

The men of the *Zeewijk* were trapped aboard. 'We could see nothing but surf, which washed over the ship in an awful way,' recollected van der Graeff. Attempts to get off were dashed by the sea and they soon found their craft was beginning to come apart. They began making life rafts and, on the Black Friday of June 13, only just saved the life of a crewman who volunteered to swim ashore with a rope. Next day some of the men began breaking into the stores and rampaging drunkenly through the wreck. The officers, soldiers and many of the crew swore an 'oath to God to be loyal to one another and to be faithful to the authorities and to punish together, be it even with death, all evildoers and malignant'.

They managed to get a line from the grinding wreck to the reef through the bravery of some of the crew who at first swam through the deadly surf and then managed to get ashore on a small catamaran they had roped together. There were now four men on the reef with the rest still stranded on the shifting wreck, unable to help them further. One seaman died aboard the wreck in the afternoon and at sunset they managed to drift some supplies to those on the reef. But that night the seas rose again and shifted the rapidly disintegrating ship from one side to the other, 'so that now the surf assaulted the larboard side so much more that we thought we would be overturned with each sea'. More praying ensued: 'We therefore fell at the feet of the Almighty and prayed together for His help and succor.'

Amazingly, the Dutchmen's prayers were answered and the wind dropped. Next day various attempts were made to launch small boats with men and supplies. Eight men drowned and they lost more supplies, but they managed to establish twenty-two survivors on the reef. Ominously, during these tragic events, those on the reef 'found a filled hand-grenade, also old rope and ship's skin, these belonging to a ship or ships which the same fate had struck here'.

The following day, the weather improved. Fresh water was found on an island near the reef and more men and provisions ferried over. By Wednesday, only three officers and sixty-nine crew remained on the wreck. The senior officer was the under-steersman van der Graeff. As he sat in the master's ruined cabin that night, dutifully writing up the ship's journal, a crew member was discovered stealing knives and sharpening them for unknown purposes. The man, presumably addled from shock, was put in irons. But it was another gloomy hint of what was to come.

On Thursday, van der Graeff planned to float the remaining survivors off the *Zeewijk* onto the reef. But many of the crew mutinied, refusing to leave the wreck:

We could not move the hardened hearts of many of the crew, since about half of those malignants would not help us, saying that they wanted to remain on the wreck, so that we found ourselves compelled to help one another of those who had decided to leave the wreck. Therefore we threw overboard the victuals which we had barrelled, lowered away our rafts and so floated to the reef at God's mercy, which we reached with the help of God Almighty without any of us being lost.

By Saturday 21 June, ninety-six survivors shivered together on the island, including the master, officers and a good number of petty officers, most of whom were tradesmen with useful skills. They also had meat, bread, butter, wine and brandy. These they began rationing and van der Graeff noted that there were plenty of seals on the island, together with enough scrub to build cooking fires.

On Monday they were able to revisit the reef, secure one of their boats, find some more supplies and pick up a few stragglers. One, a boy, refused to go back to the island in the longboat. On Wednesday, survivors began dying. On Thursday, the carpenter started to improvise a mast for the longboat's voyage to Batavia. 'I am hoping for the rescue of us all,' van der Graeff wrote. On Saturday, a soldier died at dawn, and a seaman died the next morning. The survivors on the island could see two others walking around on the reef but 'we could not help them'.

It was Monday again and another week of misery and death had passed. They took the longboat to the reef 'with great difficulty'. There they found the reluctant boy still alive. The men left aboard the wreck had floated some supplies to him. They waved and signalled to the wreck for more supplies, including sailcloth. Some wine, brandy and butter were delivered, together with a sail they could fit to the newly built mast of the longboat.

Next morning at seven, the tent in which the officers were sheltering on the island was invaded by 'all petty officers and the common hands, most of whom were drunk'. Van der Graeff reported:

The men walked into our tent with a great deal of clamour and confusion of argument and counter-argument, all shouting at the same time, telling the master that they wanted the long boat to sail to Batavia and that they wish to appoint as her chief the 1st officer Pieter Langeweg and no one else, and 10 of the best seamen with him whom we are to select. They would hear of no further counsel, saying that they will carry on their affairs and that they have collected some good seamen whom they deem to be capable of handling a long boat and have made them draw lots and have appointed 10 of them according to the lots drawn to sail in the boat.

No more is heard about this incident and its aftermath but van der Graeff's journal goes on to describe negotiations with those still on the wreck. They now wanted to be taken off with the longboat, though the weather conditions were so bad that this was impossible. Also, those on the wreck had lost most of the remaining supplies needed by those on the island. However, a deal was done and some more alcohol, butter and kegs of salted fish were floated across from the wreck on Thursday 3 July. That day, the sail-maker also began to improvise the sails for the longboat.

The seal population was now disappearing and by Monday 7 July, the survivors were down to a pitifully small list of victuals: '8 barrels of bread, 4 aums of wine, 3½ aums of brandy, 4 aums of sweet oil, 1 aum of wine, 7 kegs of butter, 6 kegs of anchovy, 9 cheeses, 4 sides of bacon, 3 hams.'

That day another man died on the island. By Wednesday they were stocking the longboat for its arduous trip and at sunset the next day, it set sail with '12 souls in all'. Pieter Langeweg was in command, as the men had demanded earlier. There was probably unofficial distribution of wine and the survivors' remaining boat, the skow, came back from a hunting trip to the other islands around the reef with twenty-four seals 'at which we rejoiced greatly'.

There were now around eighty men on the island and an unknown but probably significant number still on the wreck or otherwise unaccounted for. They were within sight of the mainland, though had no desire or need to attempt to reach it. Instead, the survivors began fighting among themselves. Under the stress of the situation, excess alcohol and fear, men began to draw knives against each other and some began to act irrationally, throwing scarce victuals into fires and threatening their fellows. The council had four manacled and marooned on another island, 'as we fear that, staying here, they will persist in their recalcitrant behaviour, which they had affirmed incessantly to me and to several other people during the past night while they were in irons'.

On Sunday 13 July the skow went to the reef and came back with another frightened boy and a small amount of ham and wet bread. Over the following days, the wine ration was finished, but edible vegetation began to sprout on the island, making a welcome addition to the sparse diet. The survivors established a routine of taking the skow to the reef to bargain for supplies with those still in the wreck. They also used the little boat for seal hunting and transport between the islands. On Wednesday 23rd, the four men marooned on one of these were flogged and 'at the intercession and request of the common hands they were permitted to remain here in the island, upon their promise to lead henceforth a Christian life'.

The following day saw the second mate and eight men float off the wreck on a small skow they had fashioned. It was August and becoming colder. On Monday 4th they discovered that their freshwater supply had dried up. They prayed for rain, cleaning out the small wellspring to find seven live crabs in it, a certain sign that any water that might bubble from it would be undrinkable. Next day five men took one of the skows without permission and rowed to another island about 3 to 4 kilometres away. On the Thursday, while most of the officers were away fishing, the ship's hands and petty officers took away to their own tents the water previously held by the officers on behalf of all. The authority of the officers was now under serious challenge from the crew. From then on, the ship's hands and petty officers doled out the water to the master and other officials rather than the other way around. The men also insisted on maintaining the daily ration of half a loaf of bread a day, rather than accept the master's recommendation that they reduce it to a quarter loaf. Fortunately, it rained the next day and further supplies were obtained from the wreck, together with some seals from the surrounding islands.

The days dragged by with much the same routine, punctuated by occasional acts of disobedience and hoarding of supplies. The occasional additional man also arrived on the island, having forsaken the wreck. On 22 August another man died. According to the second mate's meticulous record, there were now ninety-five on the island.

The situation was severe enough for the survivors to send out an expedition to the mainland in search of possible future supplies. Six men left for the Southland on 24 August, returning at sunrise three days later. What they had taken to be the mainland was in fact an oblong island about 6 kilometres long by 1 kilometre at its widest point. They had found another one of the *Zeewijk*'s boats that had become separated during the grounding. They had also come across 'a piece of a ship or wreck, finding the figurehead lying under a cliff, of which they could discern that it had been the figure of a woman'.

Two more men died on 29 August. There was a dwindling but significant number aboard the wreck controlling the supply of food and drink, other than that available naturally, mainly the declining seals and flocks of dark birds that were described as being the size of a small duck.

There was alarm among the men when the master proposed taking both skows to explore the other nearby islands. He placated them by promising he would return as quickly as possible and bring more seals, and so he and eighteen others were allowed to leave. They returned as promised four days later, together with the gig that had escaped the wreck, a valuable addition to their chances of survival. Steyns, apparently in confidence, also told van der Graeff that they had found another wreck, along with other items washed there from the stricken *Zeewijk*.

On 10 September, Steyns and a small crew of ten managed to get out to the wreck and establish a line to the reef, enabling the transfer of provisions. A week later they were able to bring off the five remaining chests of VOC money, the rest having apparently been salvaged earlier. By 21 September all ten of the money chests were together on the island. But supplies of food and water were again dwindling 'so that we beseech the Almighty for rain from the sky'. Three days later another sailor died.

The next Saturday the regular expedition to the reef for further supplies from the ship resulted only in a letter thrown overboard in a container. It was from Jan Steyns, the master, and stated that there would be no further supplies coming from the ship until someone rowed across and got them and, presumably, Steyns and the other men who had earlier accompanied him to the *Zeewijk*. The letter was taken to the under-merchant Nebbens who had command of the sailors on the island in the absence of the master. He penned a testy reply, co-signed by van der Graeff and more than fifty others:

> I under-merchant Jan Nebbens, after the boatswain and the boat-swain's mate have again returned without victuals, having read the letter brought from you and understanding there from that you wish to have us come aboard in spite of weather and violent surf on the reef, which was impossible as the men tell me, wish that you on board were here on the island to make the easy trip to the wreck, this we, the undersigned, declare together, and master Steyne [sic] and your men ought to know that we officers in the island were requested by the hands to issue the wine and the

brandy as long as there was any left, the reason for which being, as you know, that so far it has not pleased the Good Lord to grant any rain, for it is as dry on the island as it has not been before, for the little water which is left in the well is not potable, it being as salty as seawater, and this is the cause that there is no longer any water in the tents, and we declare together that this is the truth, which we are ready to affirm on oath at all times.

The next day another sailor on the island died. He was probably not much lamented as his death meant there was one less mouth to feed from the dwindling supplies. Van der Graeff went to the reef to ask those on the ship for victuals on Monday 29 September, but was refused. Instead, he was given a signal that Steyns wanted to leave the wreck. Fresh water had now become an urgent issue for the islanders 'for we are at our wits' end with thirst'. Fortunately, drinkable water was found on another island 'so that now, God be thanked, we need not ration one another any longer'. But it was too late for one of the boys and another sailor who died over the following few days. 'We now number eighty-nine,' van der Graeff recorded in his stoically non-committal way.

Even with reduced numbers, supplies were consumed quickly. There was further pressure from the men for larger rations and by 6 October they were down to a little bread, some groats or hulled cereal kernels, oil, butter, cheese and some tobacco. They were subsisting mostly on the small birds. That day the master and men returned from the wreck, having built a skow onboard and floated across. Next day Steyns and van der Graeff took the new skow and gig to the reef. As usual, they hauled the craft over the corals hoping to launch into the sea beyond in order to reach the *Zeewijk*. They were unable to do this but some provisions were thrown into the sea for them by those still onboard.

On Friday 10th, van der Graeff and the third mate managed to get across to the broken ship in the gig and to organise some substantial supplies of food, tools and sailcloth. The good weather went on for days, during which a great deal of provisions were either rowed or floated to the reef. A few of those who had never left the *Zeewijk* were also brought ashore. One of the soldiers aboard the wreck died on 21 October, and another less than a week later, but the work continued unabated. Still the weather held. They now began to cannibalise the ship itself for all usable materials, even including the ship's bell. Van der Graeff was relieved of his trans-shipment duties on 29 October and proudly recounted how much he had been able to send ashore. He also apologised for the alleged loss overboard of that part of his journal relating to his weeks back aboard the *Zeewijk*.

The survivors were now in the best situation since the wrecking. They had sufficient food, a supply of fresh water, and enough timber and materials to build a new boat, a large skow. By 30 October, now accepting that the longboat that had left months earlier had not reached Batavia, they resolved to build a new one and to rescue themselves. They laid the keel on 7 November and the stem the following day. In their journal, Steyns and Nebbens noted: 'We called it the Sloepie, that is, the little sloop, made up from the wreck of the Zeewyck.'

Troubled waters

On Thursday 14 November, van der Graeff was again rostered to return to provisions duty at the wreck despite his erysipelas[1] and a wounded leg. The surgeon ordered him to rest and another took his place, returning with more food and shipbuilding materials. The next day van der Graeff reported that there were ninety-five on the island, and that they erected their craft's sternpost. The almost daily expeditions to the wreck now returned with large amounts of timber, nails and other necessities for building a seagoing craft, together with loads of firewood. Progress was good.

But on 30 November the master was informed that two boys, Adriaen Spoor van Sint Maertensdyck and Pieter Engelse van Gent, were found 'committing together the abominable sins of Sodom and Gomorra which fact cries to Heaven and greatly distresses the master and the other members of the ship's council'. Three sailors swore to witnessing the act but the boys refused to confess, despite burning fuses being placed between their fingers. The council, 'with the consent of the commone hands', then determined to 'place these men apart in one of the northernmost islands at the first opportunity which God will grant' and the boys were thus condemned to death 'for the prevention of further evil'.

On 2 December, van der Graeff, under-merchant Jan Nebbens, boatswain Christiaen Radis, quartermaster Jan d'Waeter and six hands 'set out in the gig to take the two persons mentioned to the islands mentioned' and landed about four o'clock in the afternoon on separate islands about 10 kilometres north-east of the wreck site. The boys were left on the islands and never seen again.

By Sunday 7 December, all men had been removed from the wreck and there were now ninety-three survivors on the island. They had taken virtually all they needed from the stricken *Zeewijk*. Van der Graeff refers to the rock on which they struggle to survive as 'our' island.

Escaping the Southland

The routine became one of shipbuilding and searching nearby islands for food and water, of which the latter was eventually found in abundance. But inevitably, supplies were used up again and there were squabbles over the rations and a guard had to be mounted. On 19 December another sailor died. Christmas 1727 then passed without comment in the journal, though the men were issued with a generous 5 aums[2] of wine between them.

At various points the *Zeewijk* was reoccupied. Rations for ten mouths were taken to her on 7 January. The carpenters needed yet more wood and nails for the lifeboat. After some mishaps, these were obtained and the wreck cleared on 10 January, though it was periodically reboarded as further equipment and materials were required ashore.

On 28 January, a party landing on the oblong island to replenish the water supplies found a pair of sailcloth scissors 'which, in our opinion must have been exposed too long for them to be from our ship'. Van der Graeff's entry for Saturday 31 January read: 'During this week we made the main mast out of the foresail yard of our late ship. In the afternoon, evening and early night, the wind SSW, topsail breeze, clear sky, good weather.' His view was that it would not be long before they could escape their castaway island and the horrors of the half-moon reef. The last of the brandy was issued the next day and on Monday 2 February, the sail-maker began to craft the sails.

The under-merchant and some hands were again on the wreck at this time. The weather was too bad to take them off and they were stranded for days until 10 February when they were rescued, though three men and a boy remained aboard, too frightened to trust the breakers. They came off a few days later.

On 16 February, an unnamed survivor died then, a few days later, just as the carpenter was beginning to caulk the new vessel, the carpenter's mate died. That day two sailors were stranded again on the *Zeewijk* as their skow was swamped while they searched for required chandlery items. Work continued, though, and over the next week the hopeful men on the island took turns to revisit the wreck for equipment and search the other islands for fresh water.

Remarkably, by the end of the month, the makeshift craft was ready. She was 20 metres long by 6 metres wide, just big enough to carry about ninety men with enough food, water and equipment to take them to safety. On 28 February, van der Graeff wrote: 'At sunrise we commence the launching of our vessel, which at noon we have waterborne through God's gracious aid and help, so that this evening 3 aums of wine were consumed in the ship yard.'

However, bad weather prevented further progress on the launching and during the storm two men were caught stealing wine and cheese from the communal victuals store tent; they were lucky to escape with a flogging.

Throughout March, preparations for sailing proceeded. By mid month, the company's money chests were placed aboard the new craft, now floating in 6 feet of water. They still had to fit the rudder, stow their supplies aboard and finish a thousand small but essential tasks necessary before they could attempt to sail to Batavia. Meanwhile, three men died during the month. Van der Graeff reported on Wednesday 24 March, 'At 3 o'clock in the afternoon, we read the roll to see if we are complete and find no one absent, being now aboard with 88 souls.'

The first sailing craft known to be built in the Southland weighed anchor at 7 a.m. Friday 26 March. They passed the bones of their ruined ship and set a course due west. Their tiller broke at midnight but was quickly repaired. From then they made good distances without incident, until April 6 when another man died. On April 13, they saw bamboo floating in the sea and pigeons flying in the sky—welcome signs that they were close to land—but two more men died the following day.

Then, on 15 April, in his understated manner, van der Graeff writes: 'Today we make the land of Java N by W of us.' Next day, though, another man died.

The *Sloepie* encountered a VOC ship in the Sunda Straits on 23 April and her crew reported their survival to the master. They came into the vicinity of Batavia on 27 April and the next day transferred the VOC money chest to another company vessel and 'finally arrived on the 30th at the road of Batavia with a land, and a sea breeze, at 5 o'clock in the evening'.

Adriaen van der Graeff and eighty-one others had survived the wrecking of the *Zeewijk* on Half-Moon Reef. They left behind the bones of the other 126 men and boys on the Southland.

The aftermath

The dramatic letter that skipper Jan Steyns and under-merchant Jan Nebbens wrote to their VOC masters, and presumably handed to the first company ship they met in the Sunda Strait, is in stark contrast to under-steersman Adriaen van der Graeff's matter-of-fact account. It seems to reflect events on the island rather than on the relatively untroubled voyage of *Sloepie* back to Batavia. Possibly the two senior officers hoped to mitigate the retribution they knew would be visited upon them by the VOC for disobeying orders and losing a brand new ship.

On reading the letter, the council assembled soldiers and ships to intercept *Sloepie*: 'In order that the ready money might be secured without delay, as much of it, that is, as might still be found. Further, a thorough search was to be made after the remainder, both among the crew and in all the corners and nooks of the sloop, which has been put together by them.'

Other vessels were commanded not to approach the battered makeshift craft:

with the sole exception of that on board of which the commissioners are; so that all possibility may be removed from any clandestine transfer of the stolen booty to another crew, and of the noble company's being thus injured by a complot of a gang of expert thieves. The guilty ones shall be seized and subjected to an exemplary punishment, as a warning to all other evil doers in similar lamentable and fatal occurrences.

As always, the company was taking no chances with its money. They were also interested in the older wreck remains found by the *Zeewijk* men. They speculated that these might have belonged to either the *Fortuyn* or the *Aagtekerke*, both unaccounted for since leaving the Cape of Good Hope in 1724 and 1726 respectively.[3] Although the survivors had brought the money back safely, Steyns was prosecuted for his negligence and for trying to hide this by falsifying his journal. According to one account, he was subsequently executed, though this seems to be excessive, even for the VOC.[4]

The skeleton of the *Zeewijk* and the bones of many of her crew lay in secret on Half-Moon Reef and surrounding islands for many years. In November 1830 Lieutenant William Preston was in command of a vessel investigating the coast north of the Swan River colony, established just a year earlier. The *Zeewijk* survivors had erected a signalling post on their island for use if the first boat to attempt the journey to Batavia resulted in a rescue mission. The post was still standing more than a century later, as noted by Preston.[5] A passing British ship, the *Beagle*, discovered a brass swivel cannon on the island in 1840. They also found signs of another wreck, including a VOC coin dated around 1620 and thought to relate to the *Batavia*. More objects from the wreck were unearthed during guano mining in the 1890s. Several further recorded finds were made in the 1950s and the 1960s, when Hugh Edwards, later to write a book about the *Zeewijk*, took a party of staff from the Western Australian Museum to the main section of the wreck site on the ocean side of the reef that had for so long been the main link between the survivors on the *Zeewijk* and those on the island.

The museum mounted another expedition in 1976 to survey the site and to search for the other wreck the survivors had found during their ordeal. They found signs of unofficial treasure hunting and consequent destruction of archaeological evidence. Nevertheless, and despite the foul weather that the men of the *Zeewijk* often experienced, the remains of three possible campsites were identified, together with the location of numerous cannon.[6]

The events at Half-Moon Reef were the last of the great sagas of Southland shipwreck survival. But there would be more than another century of shocks and surprises. Exploration and contacts with the indigenous peoples continued on every coast and in all manner of modes.

10

Empires collide

The land we now call Australia emerged reluctantly from its myths and mysteries. Its existence as more than a fantasy began with the growth and expansion of Europe's mercantile empires. The desire for trade goods was always accompanied by political interests but also with a fascination for human bodies.

Probably the only documented Chinese contact with the unknown Southland took place in 1751. Searching for turtle shell, a Chinese trader sailed from Timor and landed on one of the Tiwi islands. The local people were described as 'of more than ordinary length and stature, very black and the hair woolly'. After two days, the Chinese sailed away and nothing further was heard of them.

But the arrival of another group of potential rivals did alert the VOC. A report on the resources of the northern coasts of the Southland stated that the area 'produces so far as we know nothing but trepang, being dried jelly fish, and wax'. Although the Dutch were not interested in these humble products, they did commission a new voyage of discovery—just in case. One part of their strategy involved close encounters with the original inhabitants.

The skin trade

Tasked with exploring the interior of the Southland and, if possible, bringing back a few natives, the VOC ships *Rijder* and *Buijs* left Batavia together on 8 February 1756. A storm soon separated them as frequently happened to vessels sailing in company. *Rijder* rode it out and *Buijs* headed for the sanctuary of Banda. Their inadvertently lone voyages added two more sad chapters to the revelation of the Southland and of relations between its original inhabitants and the newcomers.[1]

On 1 April 1756, the VOC barquentine *Buijs* left Banda in calmer weather. She was under the command of Lavienne Ludwijk Van Aschens who, despite his magnificent name, was not a noble but a relatively humble first mate. *Buijs* made her way towards the Southland, anchoring at sunset on 23 April in sight of what is now the Gulf of Carpentaria. After sailing around the region for a week, they anchored near the place Jan Carstenz had earlier called Spelt River, now called Inskip Banks. This was a known watering place and eight men were sent ashore for water and firewood. After a while, those left aboard *Buijs* lost sight of the boat. They waited for almost two weeks but it was never seen again.

Not knowing if their comrades were drowned at sea or had made it to land and been the victim of natives, Aschens decided that the best course was to sail for Timor. He seems to have made no effort to determine the fate of the eight unfortunates, reaching safety with what was left of his crew on 20 May. He may have had no choice in this decision, as he desperately needed water and tinder and may not have had enough men to crew the boat if he lost any more ashore. He probably had no other boat to chance it, as the *Buijs* was a very small ship. Whatever the possible excuses, Aschens was roundly chastised by a VOC mapmaker:

His reports or notes are so misleading that it is clear at the first glance that he can never have had any first-hand knowledge or ocular view of the matters referred to by him, seeing that he has hardly ever been nearer to the land than 3 miles off, at which distance, however, he pretends to have seen a river with an island before its mouth, as well as men, huts, etc.: all which seems to the Undersigned impossible on a flat land, such as this is. Nor has he made any landing on the said coast, although, contrary to Your Worships' orders, he had sailed along it from S. to N. for 40 miles before the misfortune of the loss of the boat befell.

Whatever the rights and wrongs of the case, another eight souls had now been lost somewhere along the coasts of the Southland. There is no record of anyone attempting to rescue them, nor do we know their fates.

While *Buijs* was suffering these misadventures, her partner ship the *Rijder* was having a more fruitful but also a more violent voyage. Commanded by Lieutenant Jean Etienne Gonzal, she spent a good deal of time sailing around the islands of the area and narrowly missing the lost passage through to the Pacific Ocean. On 25 May, *Rijder* anchored about 14 kilometres away from Duyfken Point, about 3 kilometres offshore. They were approached by black men paddling native canoes and inviting the Dutch sailors to come to land, which they did at dawn the next day. The first natives they saw were accompanied by two dogs 'not unlike Bengal tigers', wrote Gonzal. They were dingoes, probably the first to be seen by Europeans.[2] The men with the dingoes ran away but later returned with weapons and a number of women. 'The natives then all of them sat down on the beach near our men, who made signs to them that they were seeking fresh water, upon which the natives rose and signified their willingness to point out the places where water was obtainable.'

The sailors were taken along the beach to where the natives lived in 'a beautiful valley with fine trees' in bark shelters and enjoying a plentiful supply of fresh water, apparently delivered 'through artificial openings'. On returning to the beach, nineteen natives came up to them, 'having their bodies all besmeared with red, and held a frolic with a kind of song. Then they were treated to some arrack with sugar, and shortly afterwards they retired satisfied into the wood.'

Despite these friendly gestures and interactions, the Dutch came ashore again the next morning 'to see if they could not capture a man or two'. They were unsuccessful, but tried again the next day. This time, the natives happily joined the sailors, laying down their weapons, dancing, singing and drinking the mixture of arrack and sugar the Dutch enthusiastically provided. And then, while 'under the influence':

> Two of them were seized, whereupon the others jumped up and set upon our people with their assagays, without, however, wounding anyone; but the ship's clerk, who was trying to get hold of one of the savages, was slightly wounded by him in the hand. Then a shot was fired and one of the natives was wounded and the others fled into the bush. Our people then tried to drag to the boat the two men they had got hold of, but while they were being tied up one of them, by superhuman biting and tearing, managed to break loose and took to flight. Immediately thereafter, upwards of 50 natives came up, preparing to throw assegais, but a single volley put them to flight. Then our men took their one captive on board.

Rijder sailed on, sighting native canoes on one occasion and landing for wood and water. No further contact was made with the inhabitants until 15 June when they went ashore after again having been met by inviting canoe paddlers. On shore, the Dutch were confronted by eleven armed men and five women. Oddly, 'The natives tried to take off the hats of the visitors, which the latter resisted whereupon the natives threatened with their spears. A shot was fired and the crowd fled, with the exception of one youth, who was carried on board.'

Satisfied with a haul of two captives, Gonzal made sail westward. They sighted 'Aernem's Land' along the way and then returned home.

These two European encounters with the Southland included important events, all of which seem to have been mostly passed over at the time and since. Usually the VOC made some attempt to locate company castaways. In the case of the eight men from *Buijs,* it seems that no action at all was taken. The reason was probably that the small boat was simply foraging for supplies and carried no valuable cargo. *Rijder,* however, succeeded in carrying out VOC orders and returned to Batavia with two native prisoners. What happened to them, we are not told, though from accounts of other such incidents, these unfortunate men probably pined away and died of despair, disease or both.

The voyages of *Buijs* and *Rijder* were two of the last VOC adventures on the Southland. Already in deep financial trouble and weakened by wars with other European powers, as well as Asian resistance and revolt, the company was on its last legs. As the Dutch withdrew from the Southland, the French and the British took their place. Instead of taking people away, though, these newcomers were generally more interested in taking information and samples of perplexing animals and plants. They were not seeking to trade, but brought a scientific perspective to bear on the indigenous people. The real and imagined resources of the Southland, its possible strategic value and even its settling would become new elements in its persistent El Dorado image.

Captain Cook's concerns

The fabulous history of the VOC came to a gradual end during the eighteenth century. Little by little, corruption, unsustainable business structure and the sheer extent of the behemoth led to a gradual weakening of money and influence. The once mighty 'Jan Company' was humbled in the fourth Anglo-Dutch war of 1780–84 and the company was bankrupted by 1798. Well before then, VOC shipping around the Southland had faded as the British increased their power almost everywhere and especially in the East Indies. The Netherlands itself became a shadow of its former splendour as other powers took their turn on the world's imperial stage. France was also on the rise and competed with Britain for territory and prestige in a new era of heroic navigation centred, ostensibly at least, around scientific experimentation as well as discovery.

In 1766 Captain Samuel Wallis was dispatched in command of the Royal Navy ships *Dolphin* and *Swallow* to explore the Pacific Ocean with a view to locating the southern continent. The closest the expedition got to the fabled Southland was when the ships became separated and *Swallow* discovered Pitcairn Island, later to become famous in the mutiny on the *Bounty* story and its long aftermath. Wallis also charted many other Pacific islands, preparing the way for the man often considered the greatest navigator of all.

Captain James Cook's famous voyage in the bark *Endeavour* combined the scientific, the nautical and the political. Departing Plymouth in August 1768, Cook was to make a record of the transit of the planet Venus and to further chart the coasts and islands of the Pacific, following on from the work of Wallis. Aboard was the wealthy Joseph Banks with his group of six other scientists and two servants. They boasted state-of-the-art equipment for studying natural history which, at that time, included a close interest in human beings. But Cook also had further, secret orders. He was to search for 'a continent or land of great extent'. If he found that place, he was to claim it 'in the name of the King of Great Britain'.

After documenting the transit of Venus in Tahiti, Cook proceeded on the rest of his mission via a series of Pacific islands and then circumnavigating New Zealand, which he claimed for Great Britain. Finally, on 29 April 1770, Cook and his men became the first known Europeans to reach and then land on the eastern coast of the great southern continent at what is now Botany Bay.

When Cook and a party went ashore for the first time, they were resisted by the indigenous Gweagle people until they were dispersed with musket small shot. Cook, Banks and the others then investigated a small cluster of bark huts, frightened children and some canoes. Cook thought it all 'the worst I think I ever saw'. There were some further skirmishes in the following days but Cook's overall impression was that the Gweagle simply wanted the mariners to go away. Even when the English placed trade goods directly into the bark huts, 'they had not so much as touch'd the things we had left'.

The *Endeavour* then sailed north, encountering the Great Barrier Reef and remaining at the mouth of what they named the Endeavour River in northern Queensland from 17 June to 3 August. Here, the longer sojourn of the mariners led to more prolonged contact with the indigenous people known as the Guugu Yimithirr.

All went well except on 19 July when the sailors refused to give the local people a turtle they had caught. There was a mini-riot aboard *Endeavour* in which the Guugu Yimithirr threw items overboard, stamped their feet and shoved Banks around. They paddled back to shore and lit grassfires to further display their displeasure and to destroy the fishing nets and other equipment left on the beach by the crew. Cook ordered a volley of small shot, injuring one man. The Aborigines then apparently became amenable once more, signalling that 'they would not set fire to the grass again'. The English responded by 'distributing musket balls among them and by our signs explaining their effect'.

Although friendly relations were restored, the Guugu Yimithirr never came to the *Endeavour* again. At one point in late July, Banks noted in his journal that the gifts of clothing they had given to the Aborigines were 'left all in a heap together' in the bush, 'as lumber not worth carriage'. Others of the expedition also documented the inhabitants' lack of interest in clothing, finding a shirt that had been given to them 'torn into rags'[3] and discarded.

As the Europeans could not fail to observe, the Aborigines wore no clothing at all. Just as European customs of ownership and gifting were incomprehensible to the Aborigines, so their needs and values were to Cook and his men. Reflecting upon these experiences in their journals, the navigators generally came to a 'noble savage' conclusion about the inhabitants of the Southland. Their lack of need for more than a few basic material possessions, clothing or significant housing, and what appeared to be a totally nomadic lifestyle, led Cook to write that they 'set no Value upon anything we gave them, nor would they ever part with anything of their own for any one article we could offer them' and to declare unequivocally 'in reality they are far happier than we Europeans'.[4]

This stereotype became as damaging for future black and white relations as Dampier's 'miserablest people' description. Both views are those of the colonial, or proto-colonial, eye and take no account of the indigenous realities, simply because Dampier, Cook or any other European could not possibly know what these might have been. Here, in microcosm, is the entire tragedy of colonisation and post-colonialism.

Unlike the mariners of the VOC, Cook's mission did not revolve around the possibilities for trade. It was primarily scientific and imperial. In completing it, he established his name as perhaps the greatest navigator of sail and added what was almost the final significant page to the secret atlas of the Southland. From now on, there would be little value in the Europeans hiding their explorations and findings as there was more to be gained by publicising them as legal claims of possession and as proof of national scientific discovery.

Also—unlike the Dutch—the French and British ships that sailed to the Southland were naval craft. Their chain of command was that of their respective navies, harsh and rigid, though perhaps not as all-powerful as that of the VOC ships. Officers were commissioned, of course, and the petty officers who controlled the crew and ran the ship were well-established positions. Common sailors might be seafarers, though shortages of men willing or able to go to sea at certain periods meant that press-ganging and other forms of coercive abduction could be the only reasons why some of their crews were aboard.

As most of these voyages took place in the later period of discovery, conditions tended to be slightly better aboard naval ships, particularly the food supplied to sailors and, consequently, the state of their health. One element of James Cook's fame is his insistence on fresh fruit, vegetables and other foods that helped prevent scurvy and the numerous other unpleasant diseases to which sailors were vulnerable in the earlier days of sail. Cook did not fully realise the value of such a diet but he established its efficacy.

Return of the French

Only two years after Cook's east coast voyage, the French became seriously interested in the southern seas. In 1772, Louis de Saint Aloüarn in the *Gros Ventre* reached what is now Cape Leeuwin after becoming separated from the *Fortune* under Yves de Kerguelen, discoverer of the islands named after him. Aloüarn then sailed north to Dirk Hartog Island where he landed and claimed possession of what is now Western Australia in the name of France. He marked this claim by leaving at least two sealed bottles containing coins and a document of claim.

A number of expeditions attempted to locate Aloüarn's bottle, one succeeding in 1998. Subsequent searches of the area by Western Australian Museum archaeologists located a bottle with a French *ecu* coin sealed into its cap, but no document. There was only sand inside the bottle. Sand mites able to penetrate the sealed top might have consumed any documents within the bottle; that is a professional speculation. Local lore has it that a stockman found the bottle in the 1950s and removed the document. It was kept in the area for some time but eventually burned in a fire. In either case, there may well be another bottle in the sand awaiting discovery.

On another coast destined to have more than its share of sorrows, Marion du Fresne arrived in March 1772. He had been at sea since he was eleven, voyaging to the southern oceans and back to France before his twelfth birthday in 1736. Remarkable as this seems today, it was not uncommon for boys as young as or younger than ten to be part of a ship's crew and expected to take their share of the work and danger along with everyone else. Du Fresne was charged, in part, with finding the mysterious land where Binot Paulmier de Gonneville of the *Espoir* had allegedly sojourned with the native inhabitants in 1503, more than two centuries earlier.

At what is now the bay named after him in south-east Tasmania—then known as Van Diemen's Land—du Fresne and his men made contact with the indigenous inhabitants. What followed, as recorded by several of the participants, was another sad tale of mutual misunderstanding.

Du Fresne sent some armed men ashore into 'a beautiful sandy cove' to parley with the inhabitants they had sighted the day before. The natives 'showed themselves gracious', building a fire and inviting the strange newcomers to light it. Du Fresne reported: 'We were ignorant of the meaning of this ceremony, and we lit the pile. The savages did not appear at all astonished; they remained around us without making either any friendly or hostile demonstrations.'

Shortly after, du Fresne came ashore in another longboat, encountering around forty naked Aborigines carrying rocks and spears:

M. Marion, seeing that they did not appear very dangerous and very much wanting to commence, made two sailors undress and go ashore, unarmed, carrying with them some small presents such as mirrors, necklaces etc. The Diemanlanders, seeing them approaching thus, put their spears on the ground and with several gestures which marked their joy and contentment, came leaping to meet them, singing and clapping their hands. Our sailors reached the shore; they [the Aborigines] presented them with fire and then, as if to recognise the good welcome, [the sailors] handed out the trinkets they had brought. The thing that impressed them the most was the mirror. They did not cease looking at themselves in it and grabbing it from one another. After these first impulses, they gestured to the boats to go towards the end of the cove and they themselves followed on land. Our sailors made their way with them—they were two big boys, well-built and very white. The Diemanlanders could not leave looking at them and touching them; often they stopped to do this and on each occasion there were new expressions of astonishment and a lot of talk between them.

The French doled out more trinkets, caressed the natives and generally made every effort to befriend them. In contrast to the indigenous people encountered by the Dutch on the mainland, these locals were fascinated by the newcomers' clothing, 'particularly anything brilliant or of a striking colour and if we had let them have their way we would soon have been dressed Diemansland-style, just like them'. They wanted to trade but had nothing except their spears.

The pleasantries came to an end when du Fresne's boat arrived, the additional numbers alarming the Diemanlanders who began to make threatening gestures. The crew of du Fresne's boat then picked up their muskets, escalating the tension. Spears and stones were hurled, slightly wounding du Fresne and another officer. The French fired a warning volley and the Diemenlanders withdrew. But not for long: 'A moment later they reappeared without showing the least fear.'

The French shore party quickly disembarked and rowed further along the cove, followed by an angry crowd throwing spears and rocks. Eventually one of the Frenchmen was speared and they retaliated: 'We discharged a volley which made them utter frightened cries. There were several dead and many wounded. Some wanted to charge us again; we fired upon them again. They soon fled uttering loud cries.'

Now in command, the French spent a couple of days investigating the bay, finding only 'a few miserable inhabitants there, more like animals than men' who ran away from them.

In reflecting on these experiences, one of the Frenchmen wrote perceptively in his journal that he did not think they had 'other ways of fending off the cold than by lighting fires. Thus they appreciate fire very much and when I saw them come to meet our sailors and offer them fire it occurred to me that this element was the one they found most useful; it was a sign of friendship to offer it to us.'

Elsewhere in the Southland and unbeknown to the Europeans, fire and smoke were also important elements of Aboriginal life. As well as the obvious value of fire for warmth, cooking and light, it is certain that many indigenous groups made use of fire in managing and cultivating their land. Historian Bill Gammage has argued that Australia was effectively 'the biggest estate on earth'. Before European settlement, Aboriginal people used fire to maintain animal habitats, ensure the propagation of plants and generally guarantee the regular and predictable availability of natural resources.[5] The symbolic use of fire as a form of welcome and expression of friendship extends logically from such practices. Du Fresne and his men were welcomed with the most precious resource the Diemenlanders possessed. Their inevitable ignorance of the significance of this ceremony led to violence on both sides.

An English interlude

An Englishman bearing a French surname was the next visitor to Van Diemen's Land when, in March 1773, Tobias Furneaux and his men of HMS *Adventure* went ashore. They were the first English visitors and made several landings in search of water and wood on what is now called Bruny Island. Furneaux described it as a 'very pleasant'[6] land with rich soils and plenty of potentially useful timbers.

Like most observers of the Southland, Furneaux reported many large fires and billowing smoke and offered an explanation: 'The trees are mostly burnt or scorched, near the ground, occasioned by the natives setting fire to the under-wood, in the most frequented places; and by these means they have rendered it easy walking.' Later, as they sailed along the coast, he observed that, 'The country here appears to be very thickly inhabited, as there was a continual fire along shore as we sailed.' Furneaux would name one of the inlets where he saw the evidence of this burning the 'Bay of Fires'. He appears to have made no contact with the local inhabitants, but he did note signs of their presence and make an attempt at communication through gifts:

> There were several wigwams or huts, where we found some bags and nets made of grass, in which I imagine they carry their provisions and other necessaries. In one of them there was the stone they strike fire with, and tinder made of bark, but of what tree could not be distinguished. We found in one of their huts, one of their spears, which was made sharp at one end, I suppose, with a shell or stone. Those things we brought away, leaving in the room of them medals, gun-flints, a few nails, and an old empty barrel with the iron hoops on it. They seem to be quite ignorant of every sort of metal.

Furneaux gave a detailed description of the local indigenous shelters: 'The boughs, of which their huts are made, are either broken or split, and tied together with grass in a circular form, the largest end stuck in the ground, and the smaller parts meeting in a point at the top, and covered with fern and bark, so poorly done, that they will hardly keep out a shower of rain.' The huts featured a central fireplace surrounded with 'heaps of mussel, pearl, scallop, and cray-fish shells, which I believe to be their chief food, though we could not find any of them'. He ascertained that the occupants 'lie on the ground, on dried grass, round the fire'.

Coming to the conclusion that the indigenous people were nomadic, Furneaux wrote: 'I believe they have no settled place of habitation (as their houses seemed built only for a few days), but wander about in small parties from place to place in search of food, and are actuated by no other motive. We never found more than three or four huts in a place, capable of containing three or four persons each only.' He also thought it remarkable that 'we never saw the least marks either of canoe or boat, and it is generally thought they have none.'

As was becoming usual for Europeans, he thought that the indigenous inhabitants of Van Diemen's Land were 'from what we could judge, a very ignorant and wretched set of people'. He stayed only for a few days and then set sail for New Zealand.

Furneaux had been voyaging with James Cook's second expedition of 1772–75 and it was only four years later that Cook himself visited Van Diemen's Land in January 1777, while commanding HMS *Resolution*. Ashore with a woodcutting party, Cook was astonished when a group of nine male Tasmanians walked straight out of the bush towards them. They carried no weapons and made no hostile signs. The locals seemed content, according to seaman John Martin who observed, 'They have few, or no wants, and seemed perfectly Happy, if one might judge from their behaviour, for they frequently wou'd burst out, into the most immoderate fits of Laughter and when one Laughed every one followed his example Emediately.'[7]

David Samwell, the first mate to Cook's surgeon, described the indigenous child-carrying technique: 'The Men had not been long with us before they were joined by ten or twelve Women, some of them carrying their Children on their Baks supported by the skin of some wild beast thrown over their Shoulders and tyed before.'[8]

Another man who served with Cook early in his career also voyaged south, leaving England in April 1791, though he later became known for other significant deeds. George Vancouver was not yet in his mid-thirties when he commanded the sloop *Discovery* in company with the *Chatham* on a lengthy voyage that was to include exploring the south-west coast of the mainland to determine whether it was joined to Van Diemen's Land or not.

Vancouver entered a vast harbour in September 1791 that he named 'King George the Third's Sound', claiming it and the surrounding area for Great Britain. These claims were marked with a cairn enclosing a bottle with details of the claim on Point Possession and another on Seal Island. Vancouver met the people of the region and made notes of their customs in the usual manner of the time. He then sailed off to chart that still unknown section of the coast described in his orders as 'a real blot in geography'[9]—the Great Australian Bight. Repulsed by bad weather he turned for Van Diemen's Land where he also encountered indigenous people. Vancouver then mostly sailed out of Australian history to a much greater role in the Pacific and North America.

The next known visit to King George Sound was in 1799 when whalers fished the area. Like many before and after them, they also left their mark in the form of an inscribed metal plate, subsequently recovered by Matthew Flinders the following year. This stretch of coast now became a very busy place, a worrying development for the British.

Looking for La Perouse

In 1792 Antoine d'Entrecasteaux sailed in the *Esperance* to the Southland in search of a lost French expedition. Jean-Francois de Galaup, Comte de la Perouse, had sailed with two ships in August 1785—*La Boussole* and *L'Astrolabe*. His mission was to prove that France was an ocean power to be taken seriously in the

South Seas and was designed to last four years. La Perouse and his team of navigators and scientists sent regular reports home for publication and promotion of French marine mastery. Just four days after the First Fleet made landfall, La Perouse's expedition sailed into Botany Bay to the considerable surprise of the British. The French stayed until March, when they sailed for home. They never returned to France. Both ships sank in the Santa Cruz Islands (now part of the Solomon Islands) and the remains of *L'Astrolabe* were not discovered until 1826.

In his quest to determine the fate of La Perouse's prestigious expedition, d'Entrecasteaux made several landings along the southern coast, including in King George Sound and at what is now Esperance, and completed some important charts. His scientist Jacques Labillardière later published an account of the expedition, including their two stays in Van Diemen's Land, the first for five weeks in 1792 and the second sojourn the following January. Labillardière described the flora and fauna of the eastern side of the island in considerable detail, including the use of fire by the indigenous people.

But the French found it very hard to make contact with the inhabitants, though they did glimpse one fleeing from the sound of a gunshot long enough to see that he was naked. The sailors discovered a burned female body but Labillardière refuted the suggestion of cannibalism, preferring the explanation that the natives burned their dead. During the lengthy period spent in the area, the French only saw the natives at a distance, and according to Labillardière, 'those who observed us having always fled with great precipitation'. They never found any weapons of defence, there did not seem to be many local inhabitants and they seemed to live mainly on shellfish. Labillardière speculated that the reluctance of the natives to have anything to do with the French was a result of their experience of firearms during du Fresne's visit.

The *Esperance* made another landfall elsewhere on the island and did encounter some local people cooking shellfish near their huts. The French observed that the natives produced fire by striking two flint rocks together, a practice apparently unique to Van Diemen's Land. Goods and food were left for the people, some of which they took. On a couple of occasions, the French came across other groups of inhabitants but these folk were reluctant to have much to do with them, despite accepting some gifts. An elderly woman, attempting to escape from the French, was run down by the sailors. They presented her with a handkerchief, which she appeared happy to accept but then became afraid and leapt down a 40-foot or more precipice, possibly in fear of the sailors' intentions, Labillardière speculated.

During the second visit of d'Entrecasteaux in 1793, the French first stayed in the 'haven' of Recherche Bay, as they named it, after one of their ships. This time they enjoyed extensive contact with the local people, a group of ten men, fourteen women and twenty-four children. The sailors were allowed to hold the children and gave the natives gifts of clothes, bells, mirrors, beads and medals. Records were also made of the language spoken, noting the difference between what Cook had recorded at Adventure Bay on Bruny Island during his earlier visit.

As with most of the French and British expeditions, scientific discovery was an important aspect of the voyage. This included an intense interest in the fauna of the Southland, for which purpose d'Entrecasteaux carried the botanist and gardener Felix Delahaye among his complement. Delahaye planted a European vegetable garden in what is now Pigsties Bay during their first visit. While William Bligh had earlier planted fruit trees on Bruny Island and Cook had left some pigs there, this is the earliest known instance of a planned European cultivation in Australia. Despite attempts to locate the garden, its whereabouts remain a mystery today.

The full story of the fate of La Perouse and his crews also remained unknown until 1964 when the wreckage of *L'Astrolabe* was discovered on a reef at Vanikoro in the present-day Solomon

Islands. D'Entrecasteaux had in fact sailed within miles of this location on his failed quest for the lost expedition. Nor did he ever return to France, dying at sea off the coast of New Guinea in July 1793.

The mystery of the Frenchman

The next French navigator sent to explore the Southland was the soon-to-be-famous Nicolas Baudin. Baudin's expedition in 1800–03 followed the same lines as those of d'Entrecasteaux and those before him; however, it will always be remembered for one crucial event—he left someone behind.

Baudin's corvettes, *Naturaliste* and *Geographe*, were at the southern extremity of the western Southland coast in May 1801 when Baudin sent a party of men ashore at what is now Geographe Bay, but he was unable to wait for their return when a storm forced him to put out to sea for safety. The shore party lost their longboat in the surf while landing, though a smaller skiff survived and a group of men attempted to row this back to their ships. They disappeared into the darkness, and those left behind spent a miserable night around a large fire on the unwelcoming sands.

When daylight came, the *Geographe* and *Naturaliste* were nowhere to be seen in the emptiness of the bay. Nor were their companions in the skiff. The survivors spent another day and night ashore, apparently warmed by an oversupply of alcohol. The following morning, through bleary eyes, they sighted their ships returning. A longboat was sent ashore, taking the first of two groups back to the ships. The men in the skiff had been safely found and picked up the night before.

The last group of men waited patiently for the longboat to return for them. It was night by the time it did. The men were dragged on lifelines one by one through the surf, anxious to get aboard the rescue boat and return to the safety of the corvettes. But a large wave dumped one of the struggling sailors deep in the sand and he was lost to their sight. When the longboat reached the ships, they had to report the loss of one man, drowned when he slipped into the water while trying to board. The *Geographe* and *Naturaliste*, perhaps mourning the loss of a sailor, sailed away.

But Thomas Timothée Vasse, helmsman on the *Naturaliste*, had not drowned. According to the considerable mythology surrounding this event and its aftermath, he managed to drag himself back to the beach. His fate is the subject of a number of wildly varying stories that illustrate the continuing power of myth in accounts of the Southland. The stories began almost as soon as Vasse disappeared. His shipmates believed he had survived and joined the natives. These rumours were amplified in the Paris newspapers in 1807 where it was also claimed that Vasse had somehow walked 'three or four hundred leagues south' where he was picked up by an American ship, then transferred to an English vessel which took him to England where he was imprisoned.

Thirty-or-so years later, the early settler George Fletcher Moore was given the indigenous version of the Vasse story:

Some natives of that neighbourhood recollect him. They treated him kindly and fed him, but he lingered on the sea coast, looking out for his vessel. He gradually became very thin from anxiety, exposure, and poor diet. At last the natives were absent for a time on a hunting expedition, and on their return they found him dead on the beach, his body much swollen (as they described it) perhaps dropsical.

The Aborigines offered to show Moore the bones but he had to leave.[10]

Moore was given these details in 1838. Only three years later, another settler told a different version of the sad story. Georgiana Molloy wrote that Vasse had come ashore to explore the area but 'was seized, strangled and the spear went in at the right side of the heart'. Molloy's more lurid version perhaps reflects the tense relations between black and white in the colony by that time.

The Vasse legends are a small but evocative example of the ease with which the Southland produced its own myths even after its supposed discovery. The appealing notion that Vasse survived and 'went native' is a comforting one. It also plays into stories such as that of William Buckley and others who lived for shorter or longer periods with Aboriginal people, speaking their language, practising their customs and sometimes intermarrying. This avoids the unhappy ending in which Vasse spends his days scanning the empty sea for a rescue ship and eventually dies of hunger, leaving his bleached bones on the sands of the Southland.

Despite what Moore was told by the local Aboriginal people, he did not sight Vasse's bones and it is not impossible that Vasse was drowned in the original rescue attempt and that all the survival stories are fantasies. Whatever his fate, Thomas Vasse is remembered in the name of the pretty river that flows through the thriving seaside town of Busselton.

The year after the inadvertent marooning of the forlorn Vasse, Baudin had arrived in Van Diemen's Land. One of the twenty-four scientists and artists in the expedition was zoologist, François Péron. He was influenced by the newly evolving 'science of man', eventually to be known as 'anthropology', and conducted fieldwork with the Aboriginal people, attempting to communicate with them, understand them and even measure them. Though now questionable, his attitudes were ahead of his time and he tried to see the people on their own terms rather than through the prejudices of most Europeans, including those of his captain. He noted the amazing speed at which the women could run through the bush, but also made much of the relatively poor physiques of the Aboriginal men who were always bested in wrestling competitions with the French midshipmen. Perhaps inevitably conflicted, Péron's view of the indigenous people is evident in his account of an attempt to measure their physical strength using an early dynamometer:

> Wishing at any cost to repeat certain observations which I had already begun in the Channel [d'Entrecasteaux] on the development of the physical powers of the people of these regions, I had Regnier's dynamometer brought from the boat, where I had till then left it. I hoped that the form and use of the instrument might perhaps fix the attention of the savages whom I wished to submit to its test. I was not mistaken. They admired the instrument; all wished to touch it at the same time, and I had great trouble in preventing its being broken. After giving them an idea of the object in view by a series of attempts ourselves, we began to make them act themselves on the instrument: seven individuals had already submitted, when one of them, who had previously tried, and had been unable to make the needle of the dynamometer go as far as I could, appeared indignant at this impotence, and, as if to give the instrument the lie direct, he seized my wrist angrily, and seemed to defy me to disengage myself. I succeeded, however, after a few efforts, and having in turn seized him with all my strength, he was unable, in spite of all his endeavours, to free himself, which seemed to cover him with confusion and fill him with anger.[11]

In another part of his account, Péron recalled:

> Nevertheless, all my [dynamometrical] observations having been made on the best constituted individuals of the nation, and the results being very decided and, above all, certain, one can, without fear of mistake, apply these results to the generality of the people of this race: they indicate a want of vigour truly remarkable: in fact, although my experiments had been repeated on the most vigorous class of the population—those from 18 to 40 years of age—not a single Van Diemen's Lander was able to press the needle beyond the 60th degree, and the mean of the twelve observations which I was able to make was only 50.6 kilogrammes.[12]

Here, in Péron's view, an instrument of European rationality was brought to bear on the 'savages' in the most enlightened manner of the time. But despite Péron's initially sympathetic stance towards the Aborigines, the results of his scientific measurement implicitly confirmed the negative comments made by almost all European navigators before him, from Willem Jansz to James Cook.[13] Conditioned by centuries of myth and ignorance, the newcomers could see the indigenous inhabitants only through biased eyes and the sensibilities of what they considered to be their 'civilisation'.

Baudin went on to chart the western coast and, probably for the first time, some of the south coast. In King George Sound in 1803 he saw Aboriginal fish traps made of stone and designed to catch fish as the tide retreated. But the only meeting with the local inhabitants took place when one of his officers encountered a group of eight local Aborigines on Bald Head. He attempted to trade with them, mainly for their fine looking dogs, probably dingoes, but all he came away with was a stone axe.

Sailing west, then north, Baudin's ships were at Shark Bay on 16 March 1803. Here, the local people were hostile and stayed hidden, though the French saw their huts and drew them in considerable if romanticised detail. The ships became separated at this point, with the corvette *Naturaliste* under Captain Jacques-Felix-Emmanuel Hamelin sending a party to Dirk Hartog Island, where they found the plate that Willem de Vlamingh erected in 1697 after recovering Hartog's original pewter plate. The French took their turn copying the inscription on the plate. Hamelin then ordered it returned to its position on the island, a decision with which his younger officers strongly disagreed. They argued that the plate should go back to France. They were overruled, but one of the officers, Lieutenant Louis de Freycinet, was determined to do something about the plate if he ever got a chance—and he would. Hamelin also left an inscription behind.

He had a lead plate made to commemorate the Baudin expedition. This was apparently erected on the island but has since disappeared.

As Baudin and his expedition progressed along the west coast, they bestowed French names on almost every natural feature sighted and referred to the land as 'Terre Napoléon'. They encountered a large fleet of *praus* trepanging near Broome, swapping biscuits for turtle eggs with the Macassans. Returning to Timor, Baudin's floating scientific laboratory and think-tank sailed for Mauritius in July 1803. Baudin died on the way home and his work was not given the recognition it deserved. Recent research has established that his South Seas expedition was one of the greatest scientific investigations to that time. He visited many other countries, his expedition returning to France with a menagerie of Australian, Indian, Molluccan and South African animals, anthropological information, charts, plant specimens and drawings. Baudin's activities also spurred the British, already established at Port Jackson, to settle Tasmania and Victoria earlier than they might have planned.

It would soon be the turn of another great navigator and explorer to write the next and final page of the secret atlas. This man was English and his work would be remembered in the many places he named and in the many named after him. He was Matthew Flinders.

11

The unknown coast

Was the Southland an island? Centuries of voyaging and charting had revealed many parts of the coast but no one knew if it could be sailed around completely. The question remained unanswered until an intrepid navigator and his men nursed their rotting boats around 'the Unknown Coast'.

Matthew Flinders, a Lincolnshire lad, joined the Royal Navy in 1789 and arrived at Port Jackson six years later. Often in company with George Bass, a naval surgeon and also from Lincolnshire, Flinders made several voyages around Botany Bay, incidentally confirming that the languages spoken by indigenous groups were often very different. Flinders and Bass circumnavigated Van Diemen's Land during a voyage from October 1798 to January 1799, proving that it was indeed an island. These exploits and his outstanding capabilities saw Flinders promoted to the rank of commander by 1801 and given orders from the Admiralty to explore the Unknown Coast—the southern shores of the continent, a large part of which are now known as the Great Australian Bight.

An island

Aboard HMS *Investigator*, Flinders sailed north from Port Jackson in July 1801 and sighted Cape Leeuwin that December. In King George Sound, Flinders and his men met with the 'indians'. After some early indications that the crew were not welcome, the local people, probably the King Ya-nup,[1] then accepted some gifts and remained on mostly friendly terms, frequently visiting the camp of the newcomers.

On the day of departure, the marines made a great impression when Flinders ordered them to parade in full uniform to the music of the fife and drum. The Aborigines admired the sailors' uniforms and were impressed by the military music. According to Flinders, 'When they saw these beautiful red-and-white men, with their bright muskets, drawn up in a line, they absolutely screamed with delight.' The Aborigines then became quiet as the marines began their drill 'to which they paid the most earnest and silent attention'. Some Aborigines moved in accord with the rhythm of the marines and an 'old man placed himself at the end of the rank, with a short staff in his hand, which he shouldered, presented, grounded as did the marines their muskets, without, I believe, knowing what he did'. Flinders was characteristically careful to demonstrate the sound and effect of musketry before the soldiers fired 'so that the vollies did not excite much terror'.[2]

On 3 January 1802 Flinders and his crew 'took leave of the natives' and the next day they left a bottle on Seal Island 'containing a parchment to inform future visitors of our arrival and intention to sail on the morrow'.

Flinders was in a good position to make some anthropological observations and comparisons with other indigenous people he had met:

> Our frequent and amicable communication with the natives of this country has been mentioned. The women were, however,

kept out of sight with seeming jealousy; and the men appeared to
suspect the same conduct in us, after they had satisfied themselves
that the most beardless of those they saw at the tents were of the
same sex with the rest. The belief that there must be women in
the ship induced two of them to comply with our persuasion
of getting into the boat, one morning, to go on board; but their
courage failing, they desired to be relanded, and made signs that
the ship must go on shore to them.

He was surprised to find the south-west people similar to those
of the east coast, observing that:

[They] do not extract one of the upper front teeth at the age of
puberty, as is generally practised at Port Jackson, nor do they
make use of the womerah, or throwing stick; but their colour, the
texture of the hair, and personal appearance are the same; their
songs run in the same cadence; the manner of painting themselves
is similar; their belts and fillets of hair are made in the same way,
and worn in the same manner. The short, skin cloak, which is of
kangaroo, and worn over the shoulders, leaving the rest of the
body naked, is more in the manner of the wood natives living at
the back of Port Jackson than of those who inhabit the sea coast;
and everything we saw confirmed the supposition of Captain
Vancouver, that they live more by hunting than fishing. None of
the small islands had been visited, no canoes were seen, nor was
any tree found in the woods from which the bark had been taken
for making one. They were fearful of trusting themselves upon the
water; and we could never succeed in making them understand
the use of the fish hook, although they were intelligent in compre-
hending our signs upon other subjects.

The navigator deemed their manners to be 'quick and vehement,
and their conversation vociferous, like that of most uncivilised
people'. His intrinsically colonial perspective was clear in his
comment: 'They seemed to have no idea of any superiority we

possessed over them; on the contrary, they left us, after the first interview, with some appearance of contempt for our pusillanimity; which was probably inferred from the desire we showed to be friendly with them. This opinion, however, seemed to be corrected in their future visits.'

Surgeon George Bass provided more detailed statistics of Aboriginal physiognomy, indicating that at least one 'indian' was prepared to allow close contact. According to Bass, the subject was 'one of the best proportioned' of the Aborigines, standing 5 feet 7 inches, and he was exactly 1 foot wide 'from the small rim of each ear across the forehead'.

On Middle Island on 16 January the crew found 'a piece of fir plank, with nails in it, which seemed to have been part of a ship's deck'. But there was no indication the island had been visited, either by Aborigines or Europeans. Where such an obviously European artefact originated can only be surmised. The most likely possibility was a wrecked whaler or sealer. By then, any number of such mostly undocumented private voyages had been undertaken and any number of sailors could have been cast away by misadventure or by malice, adding more inadvertent settlers on the southern continent.

A month after this discovery, Flinders was in Coffin Bay. He noted 'many smokes' and two bands of natives 'black and naked, differing in nothing that we could perceive from those of King George's Sound'.

At the aptly named Cape Catastrophe, six seamen, a midshipman and the master John Thistle (a personal friend of Flinders') were lost in an accident on 21 February. The party[3] had been sent ashore in the cutter to find water. It was seen returning at dusk but then no more. Flinders' redoubtable Lieutenant Fowler went out by lantern light but found only 'so strong a rippling of tide that he himself narrowly escaped being upset; and there was reason to fear that it had actually happened to Mr. Thistle'. They called out and fired muskets but no response came through the pitch-black night. Only two of the lost men could swim.[4]

Next day the search continued and the wreck was found and towed back to the *Investigator* 'bottom upward'. Flinders reported that, 'It was stove in every part, having to all appearance been dashed against the rocks. One of the oars was afterwards found, but nothing could be seen of our unfortunate shipmates.' They walked the shore looking for their lost companions, finding 'many huts and other signs that natives had resided there lately' but nothing more. The following day was spent searching again: 'All the little sinuosities of the coast were followed, and in one place I picked up a small keg which had belonged to Mr. Thistle, and also some broken pieces of the boat but these were all that could be discovered.'

Yet again, the next day, all searches proved fruitless and they feared the men had been taken by giant sharks. Running short of water, Flinders was forced to call off the search and set sail. This tragedy led to yet another message being placed on the remote shoreline of the southern continent. Before the *Investigator* left, Flinders 'caused an inscription to be engraven upon a sheet of copper, and set up on a stout post at the head of the cove, which I named Memory Cove; and further to commemorate our loss, I gave to each of the six islands nearest to Cape Catastrophe the name of one of the seamen'. The plaque read:

Memory Cove
His Majesty's ship Investigator—Matthew Flinders—
Commander, anchored here Feb 22 1802

Mr John Thistle, the master, Mr William Taylor,
midshipman, and six of the crew unfortunately
drowned near this place from being upset in a boat.
The wreck of the boat was found but their bodies
were not recovered.
Nautici Cavete! [5]

Although none of the men were found, it is not impossible that one or perhaps more of them did survive and somehow failed to be located by their comrades.

By March, Flinders was at Port Lincoln and reflected upon the natives he had encountered. His perceptive thoughts reveal a very different set of attitudes to those held by the earlier navigators. He found bark huts and also the evidence of extensive native coming and going to the English tents:

> But neither in my excursions nor in those of the botanists had any of the natives been discovered. This morning, however, three or four were heard calling to a boat, as was supposed, which had just landed; but they presently walked away, or perhaps retired into the wood to observe our movements. No attempt was made to follow them, for I had always found the natives of this country to avoid those who seemed anxious for communication; whereas, when left entirely alone, they would usually come down after having watched us for a few days. Nor does this conduct seem to be unnatural; for what, in such case, would be the conduct of any people, ourselves for instance, were we living in a state of nature, frequently at war with our neighbours, and ignorant of the existence of any other nation? On the arrival of strangers, so different in complexion and appearance to ourselves, having power to transport themselves over, and even living upon an element which to us was impassable, the first sensation would probably be terror, and the first movement flight. We should watch these extraordinary people from our retreats in the woods and rocks, and if we found ourselves sought and pursued by them, should conclude their designs to be inimical; but if, on the contrary, we saw them quietly employed in occupations which had no reference to us, curiosity would get the better of fear; and after observing them more closely, we should ourselves seek a communication. Such seemed to have been the conduct of these Australians; and I am persuaded that their appearance on the

morning when the tents were struck was a prelude to their coming down, and that had we remained a few days longer, a friendly communication would have ensued.

Flinders further contented himself with the thought that the way was favourably prepared for those who followed him, 'as it was to us in King George's Sound by Captain Vancouver and the ship Elligood'. Hoping to continue the goodwill to the benefit of those Europeans who came after him, he left gifts for the indigenous people: 'Some hatchets and various other articles were left in their paths, or fastened to stumps of the trees which had been cut down near our watering pits.' But even so sensitive a character as Flinders was apparently oblivious to the likelihood that leaving these gifts near the latrines may not have been the most positive way to encourage communication.

Like most before him, Flinders came across evidence of the indigenous use of fire to maintain their vast 'estate', as he called it. 'Upon Boston Island, however, there were abundant marks of fire; but they had the appearance, as at Thistle's Island, of having been caused by some conflagration of the woods several years before, rather than of being the small fire-places of the natives.'

After charting and naming Kangaroo Island and exploring further along the coast, the English came into contact with Nicolas Baudin's *Geographe* in what they consequently named Encounter Bay. At first, Flinders cleared for action until colours were hoisted on both the French and English ships. The British showed a white flag and Baudin flew the Union Jack, nautical signs that no aggression was intended. Nevertheless, the Englishman was not completely convinced of Baudin's good intentions: 'We veered round as Le Géographe was passing, so as to keep our broadside to her, lest the flag of truce should be a deception; and having come to the wind on the other tack, a boat was hoisted out, and I went on board the French ship, which had also hove to.'

The captains conversed through the translation of Flinders' naturalist, Robert Brown. There was discussion of explorations, voyages and charting, during which Baudin criticised a British chart of Bass Strait published in 1800. Unknown to Baudin, this chart was based on the necessarily constrained observations that George Bass and Flinders himself had made four years earlier. Before parting, Flinders cheekily presented Baudin with an updated version whereupon the Frenchman discovered that the British commander he spoke with was the maker of the chart he criticised. Baudin 'expressed not a little surprise, but had the politeness to congratulate himself on meeting me'.

Flinders was surprised that Baudin had not seemed very interested in what he was doing in these waters. But by the following morning, the Frenchman 'had become inquisitive, some of his officers having learned from my boat's crew that our object was also discovery'. Flinders had occasion to complain that his discoveries and names had been annexed by the French, who were then referring to the continent as 'Terre Napoléon'.[6]

The English and French navigators separated on 9 April and Flinders continued along the 'Unknown Coast'. He had friendly relations with the Boonwurrung people around Arthurs Seat in the Mornington Peninsula, and left paper with his ship's name beneath a small cairn of rocks at Indented Head. Here, the 'indians' hid while Flinders and his boat crew slept in their village. The inhabitants remained hidden until the British rowed away.

Flinders provided his views on possible settlement of the area:

Were a settlement to be made at Port Phillip, as doubtless there will be some time hereafter, the entrance could be easily defended; and it would not be difficult to establish a friendly intercourse with the natives, for they are acquainted with the effect of fire-arms and desirous of possessing many of our conveniences. I thought them more muscular than the men of

King George's Sound; but, generally speaking, they differ in no essential particular from the other inhabitants of the South and East Coasts except in language, which is dissimilar, if not altogether different to that of Port Jackson, and seemingly of King George's Sound also. I am not certain whether they have canoes, but none were seen.

At the end of his expedition, Matthew Flinders had circumnavigated the continent for the first time, proving that it was an island. He is also usually credited with naming it, writing to his brother in 1804: 'I call the whole island Australia, or Terra Australis.' Mapmakers had used the term as early as the sixteenth century[7] and Portuguese navigator Pedro Fernandez de Quiros used it around 1607, though Flinders seems to have been the first to apply it specifically to the land we know by that name today. The name, however, did not find much support during Flinders' lifetime, but was officially adopted in 1824.

The secret atlas of the Southland was now complete. Apart from a few details, the size, shape and nature of the once-mythical southern landmass was now clear to all and could be satisfactorily inscribed on sheets of paper. The continent was now 'known'.

But apart from small communities in New South Wales, Tasmania and some outposts here and there, it was not yet settled or even much explored. Australia existed, but still only as a shape upon a map. All around the shores of that shape were many more decades of discovery and danger.

The affair of the plates

Twelve years after Baudin left the western coasts, two Portuguese sailors joined the hundreds of others who had disappeared into the southern continent. The *Correio da Azia, a* dispatch vessel, was wrecked near what is now known as Ningaloo Reef in November 1816, thirteen years before the Swan River colony was founded. The crew escaped in the ship's boat, heading north and going ashore at least once on the journey. But two men were apparently left behind and although the survivors did not come into contact with any local inhabitants, there was a fear that the two had fallen victim to them or perhaps been eaten by wild animals.

The survivors in the boat were picked up by the American *Caledonia*, which had sailed out of Philadelphia, and so eventually reached Macau, their original destination. From Macau, a search for the lost ship was made by the brigantine *Emilla* in 1817. Aboard were some of the men who had been wrecked in the *Correio da Azia*. They were able to locate 'the exact site of their misfortune, with a bottom of rocks and a circle of rocks similar in appearance to a salt marsh'. Despite this, the *Emilla* was unable to locate the wreck nor any sign of the two missing men.[8] They joined the roll call of the many lost souls of the Southland.

Just two years after the *Correio da Azia* foundered, Louis de Freycinet was once again in Shark Bay, as master of the 350-ton corvette *Uranie*. This time there was no Captain Hamelin to block his desire to possess Willem de Vlamingh's plate. He had convinced the French government to fund an ambitious scientific expedition, and left France in 1817 on a voyage that would see him visit South America, the Pacific islands, East Timor and the Southland. Aboard his ship were 120 men and more than twenty officers, including the scientifically inclined artist Jacques Arago. Without permission of the authorities, de Freycinet had also secreted his 22-year-old wife, Rose, aboard *Uranie*. She would conduct her own observations during the three-year voyage, though these would not see the light of day for more than a century. But in their own lifetimes, the story of Rose and Louis de Freycinet became a sensation in France and they were feted and long remembered in many of the ports they visited during their global adventures.

On 13 September 1818, de Freycinet ordered his men to Inscription Point to recover de Vlamingh's plate. They returned with it a few days later, much to de Freycinet's satisfaction. He wrote later in justification of this deed:

> That such a rare plate might again be swallowed up by the sands, or else run the risk of being taken away and destroyed by some careless sailor, I felt that its correct place was in one of these great scientific depositories which offer to the historian such rich and precious documents. I planned, therefore, to place it in the collections of the Académie Royale des Inscriptions et Belles-Lettres de L'Institut de France.[9]

On reaching Shark Bay, Rose de Freycinet 'saw the low and arid coast of New Holland; there was nothing in the sight to ease our minds, for we knew we would find no water in this miserable land'. Her first contact with the local people came after she had to be carried ashore by two sailors because the beach waters were too shallow for their landing craft. A group of around ten Aborigines threatened the French with weapons and unmistakable signals to go back to their ship. 'I was afraid, and would willingly have hidden myself,' she wrote home.

But nothing happened and the natives retreated. Rose, de Freycinet and some officers were then able to lunch on the beach beneath a canvas shade. As well as the food provided for them from their ship, they enjoyed local oysters 'far tastier than all those I had, sitting at a table in comfort, in Paris'. What those who declined to welcome them made of this scene we can never know. Perhaps they thought that the picnicking strangers were not much of a threat after all. Some days later, contact was made with the local people when 'after much hesitation, they had come up to the men in the first camp and had exchanged their weapons for tin, glass necklaces and so on'.[10]

Despite this exchange of arms for gifts, quite commonly experienced during first contacts, relations could quickly turn difficult.

On one occasion, the ship's artist, Jacques Arago, defused some intercultural tension by rhythmically clacking a set of castanets together. The Aborigines were at first taken aback but then responded in kind with a traditional dance.

A few days later, *Uranie* sailed for Timor and eventual shipwreck in the Falkland Islands. But both Louis and Rose de Freycinet survived the wrecking and returned to France with their observations and artefacts, including de Vlamingh's plate. Louis de Freycinet faced a court martial for the loss of his command but was acquitted. Even the king was impressed with Rose's loyalty and daring. The couple had no children and were inseparable until Rose died in the Paris cholera epidemic of 1832.

The precious plate brought back by de Freycinet was duly delivered to the Académie Française. It then disappeared from public view until 1940 when it turned up in the basement of the building, tossed together with a collection of other metal items. The artefact is now housed and displayed in the Western Australian Maritime Museum after being gifted by France to Australia in 1947.

Settling parts unknown

There was more French activity in the southern seas at this time, motivating the British to confirm their control of the land they called 'New Holland'. Louis Duperrey served with de Freycinet as a marine hydrologist and in 1822 was back again with his own command. In 1824 Hyacinthe de Bougainville was also in south-western waters during an around-the-world trade and diplomacy mission. His father, Louis Antoine de Bougainville, had reached the Great Barrier Reef in 1768 but was forced to turn back, narrowly failing to discover the east coast of Australia. Neither the Duperrey or Hyacinthe de Bougainville expeditions seem to have landed, but another French voyager between 1826 and 1829 did make contact—of sorts.

Dumont d'Urville, commanding *L'Astrolabe,* was in King George Sound in October 1826, receiving a welcome from the King Ya-nup who were happy to take his gifts. However, it was not only indigenous people they met. Eight English-speaking men rowed out to the French ship. They were escaped convicts, deserting or marooned sealers, and were offered passage to Port Jackson.[11] Their numbers suggest how busy this stretch of coast had become, well before the settlement of the Swan River from 1829.

Two months after d'Urville's visit, Major Edmund Lockyer established a military and penal settlement at what is now Albany. Bearing secret instructions describing what he should do in the event of a confrontation with the French, Lockyer arrived aboard the brig *Amity* on Christmas Day 1826. He was accompanied by twenty soldiers from the 39th Regiment and twenty-three convicts. His main task was to let the French know that 'the whole of New Holland is subject to His Britannic Majesty's Government, and that orders have been given for the Establishment at King George's Sound of a Settlement for the reception of Criminals accordingly'.

Lockyer went ashore on Boxing Day and established initially friendly relations with the King Ya-nup. These did not last long. A few days later a party fetching water was attacked by Aborigines, who severely wounded a convict. Despite this, a more or less peaceful interaction was established between white and black. This was based to some extent on the generally favourable relations the indigenous people had experienced with earlier European visitors. Some of these must have introduced the custom of shaking hands to signify peace and friendship, as one of the King Ya-nup leaders, Mokare, retold a traditional account of friendship between his people and those voyagers who had come long before.

With a largely positive precedent like this, the settlers were able to push on with setting up camp, planting gardens and generally establishing themselves on the land. In early January a crew of sealers arrived. Under questioning they revealed that they had been abducting and even murdering local inhabitants. One of the Aboriginal men who had attacked Lockyer's watering party suffered deep wounds to his neck from the thrust of a sealer's cutlass. The British now knew why they were not welcomed by at least some of the local people.

The murderous sealers also reported the presence of d'Urville a few months earlier, giving Lockyer further incentive to establish a claim over the country of the King Ya-nup. To the sound of musketry, the British flag was raised over the little garrison on 21 January. The settlement was named Frederickstown after Frederick, Duke of York and Albany. By this ritual of possessioning, the land was formally claimed and occupied by a small detachment of the British army and a handful of convicts. But as the unexpected arrival of the sealers had proven, they were not there without diverse company. As well as visits from the now dispossessed local Aboriginal groups, they would experience ever-increasing numbers of whaling and sealing ships.

Sealers, pirates and settlers

The voyages and discoveries of Dutch, French and English navigators eventually led to European occupation and settlement of the southern continent from 1788. This was followed by the development of trade and commerce as the initial colony at Port Jackson grew and was followed by colonies around the country. But long before these events, visitors from many parts of the world were exploiting its abundant natural resources.

On a passage from Lima in April 1675, an English merchant trader was blown far south of his planned route around Cape Horn. He sheltered in the bay of a previously unknown island far to the south. He did not land. But exactly 100 years later, Captain James Cook did. He took possession of the island in the name of the British monarch and, patriotically, named it Georgia after the reigning king, George III. Cook's description of Georgia—now

South Georgia—was not positive but he did note the presence of large numbers of fur seals. British sealers were the first to officially arrive in 1786, followed rapidly by the Americans. By the early 1790s it is estimated that more than 100 ships were actively engaged in the southern ocean trade in seal fur and oil. The French entered the trade in 1802.

Although the French were not active in whaling until the 1830s, the industry was well established by then, adding further to the shipping activity in the region of the still largely unknown western and southern shores. It was not long before some of these ships began to visit. British and American sealers and whalers were along these coasts in the 1790s, all seeking the valued products of new waters. In 1792 the American whalers *Alliance* and *Asia* put men ashore at Dirk Hartog Island in search of water and food, while King George Sound and the surrounding waters were also popular, as well as the islands around Tasmania.

Sealing and whaling crews often established colonies of goats and rabbits on suitable islands, as well as vegetable gardens. They planned to return to these the following year, so ensuring access to vital supplies of meat and greens. Sometimes the animals and plants did not survive. Sometimes they flourished, forming colonies of European animals long before Europeans settled most of Australia. The notoriously desperate whalers and sealers were sometimes responsible for hostilities between the indigenous inhabitants and the settlers who arrived later. The oral traditions of these communities still hold tales of narrow escapes from one such identity known as 'Black Jack'.

The African-American John 'Black Jack' Anderson probably arrived in King George Sound in 1826 aboard the American whaler *The Vigilant*. Although the settlement at Albany was small, it had grog and, so the story goes, Black Jack and his crew soon got drunk. There were others like themselves ashore in this sailortown and it was not long before a fight broke out. One man died and Black

Jack was said to have been the killer. He escaped with his gang to the maze of islands that make up the Recherche Archipelago, eventually settling on Middle Island, from where he operated until well into the 1830s. He and his crew of cut-throats and rapists hunted seals, living off their meat and selling their skins. They were also said to have murdered a number of Aboriginal men and abducted their women.[12]

Piracy was an important part of Jack's lawless repertoire. Passing ships bound for Sydney or Hobart were robbed and he and his gang were rumoured to have carefully hidden away a horde of treasure in caves on their island. Legend has it that, despite the softening company of an English lover named Dorothea, Black Jack was almost as brutal towards his own men as he was to his victims. Eventually the gang members became sufficiently aggravated by this ill treatment and shot their leader in the head while he slept. But despite frantic searching, the murderers were unable to find where Jack had stashed his loot and so another lost treasure tradition began, attracting at least one modern-day hunt for his booty, believed to lie somewhere in 'Black Jack's Cave' on Middle Island.[13]

Apparently providing no hindrance to Black Jack's many felonries,[14] the garrison at King George Sound operated for almost five years. But the newly arriving Swan River settlers, 400 kilometres to the north, did not wish to have convicts in what was supposed to be a free colony. The recently appointed Governor James Stirling was also unhappy with even a small corner of his enormous territory being under the thumb of New South Wales— the start of ongoing colonial and state frictions between the east and west coasts. Stirling's influence in Britain and the fact that settlement of the west was now established at the Swan River led to the garrison being placed under his command, followed by a complete withdrawal in March 1831.[15]

Over the same period and beyond, the British made attempts to settle the northern coast. Fort Dundas was established on Melville

Island in 1824. It was abandoned after four years of unhappy relations with the Tiwi, illness among soldiers and convicts, and the difficulty of sustaining itself. In 1827 James Stirling founded Fort Wellington at Raffles Bay. Under the sensible and sensitive management of Captain Collett Barker, the enterprise did well, with Barker managing to balance the tensions between the colonists, local people and trepangers. But the garrison was closed in 1829. Another military settlement began at Port Essington in 1838. This was also promising at first, but after a troubled eleven years was abandoned. Then an ill-judged and badly managed settlement attempt at Escape Cliffs lasted for only three years to 1867. Two years after the closure of Escape Cliffs, though, the settlement that would become modern Darwin was finally planted on the continent's vast northern shores.

By the 1830s, the western coast was secured against threats from the French, or anyone else, though military defences were quickly constructed in Fremantle in case of attack. The northern approaches were settled, if shakily, by the 1860s. The southern and eastern seaboards were also in various stages of development. There was no more 'unknown coast' of the unexplored character that Matthew Flinders had been commanded to confirm. But there remained large distances between settlements—and between those distances would grow legends that still perplex us.

12

The last legend

Through the eighteenth and early nineteenth centuries, the great southern continent came more clearly into focus through charts, maps, journals and ever-increasing first contacts. It could, at last, be comprehended by the rational perceptions of the era. But it never completely emerged from its wreaths of myth and mystery. Legends of all kinds were spun from half-remembered events, lost and disappearing wrecks, and the persistent mysteries surrounding the fate of those Europeans known to have walked upon the continent long before its colonial settlement.

Fables and legends are cultural quicksilver. They form, fragment, join with other traditions and stubbornly persist as ephemeral stories that are as difficult to contain as they are to debunk. Often they are difficult to believe. Nevertheless, they live on stubbornly in the minds and mouths of many, mingling always with facts— where these can be found—yet providing a continual background of speculation and possibility that intrigues us across generations. Australia has produced many such myths through its pre-existence and into its eventual European settlement. Some of the most potent of these meld indigenous and settler traditions in legends that still whisper loudly to us. None are more compelling than the stories of the lost white tribes and the white Aborigines. Over time and space, these tales have had an existence of their own, as well as running together in surprising ways, as they did in the 1830s, and may one day do again.

A secret expedition

On 25 January 1834, a peculiar tale appeared in a British regional newspaper. The article was from an unnamed correspondent who wrote about the discovery of an unknown colony of Europeans on the north coast of New Holland. The author claimed that a friend had been with a group who landed at remote Raffles Bay on the north coast of the continent on 10 April 1832. The 'exploring party' undertook a two-month journey south into the then-unknown interior. The expedition was apparently promoted by a scientific society in Singapore, aided and patronised by the local government, and its object was both commercial and geographical; 'but it was got up with the greatest secrecy, and remained secret to all except the parties concerned'. The author's friend had allowed him to copy a section of his private journal of the secret expedition. This was followed with an extract from the unpublished manuscript of a journal kept by a 'Lieutenant Nixon', said to have been in command. The extract began with Nixon's account of the very unlikely sight that greeted him from the summit of a hill he climbed on 15 May 1832:

> On reaching the summit of the hill, no words can express the astonishment, delight, and wonder I felt at the magical change of scenery, after having travelled for so many days over nothing but barren hills and rocks, and sands and parching plains, without seeing a single tribe of aborigines excepting those on the sea coast, and having to dig for water every day.
>
> Looking to the southwards, I saw below me, at the distance of about three or four miles, a low and level country, laid out as it

were in plantations, with straight rows of trees, through which a broad sheet of smooth water extended in nearly a direct line from east to west, as far as the eye could reach to the westward, but apparently sweeping to the southward at its eastern extremity like a river; and near its banks, at one particular spot on the south side, there appeared to be a group of habitations, embosomed in a grove of tall trees like palms. The water I guessed to be about half a mile wide, and although the stream was clearly open for two thirds of the distance from the southern bank, the remainder of it was studded by thousands of little islands stretching along its northern shores: and what fixed me to the spot with indescribable sensations of rapture and admiration was the number of small boats or canoes with one or two persons in each, gliding along the narrow chanels [sic] between the little islands in every direction, some of which appeared to be fishing or drawing nets. None of them had a sail, but one that was floating down the body of the stream without wind, which seemed to denote that a current ran from east to west. It seemed as if enchantment had brought me into a civilized country, and I could scarcely resolve to leave the spot I stood upon, had it not been for the overpowering rays of a midday sun, affecting my bowels, as it frequently had done, during all the journey.

Having presumably dealt with his bowels, the beholder of this desert paradise was then given a very much larger surprise:

On reaching the bottom of the hill in my return to our party at the tents, I was just turning round a low rock, when I came suddenly upon a human being whose face was so fair and dress so white, that I was for a moment staggered with terror, and thought that I was looking upon an apparition. I had naturally expected to meet an Indian as black or brown as the rest of the natives, and not a white man in these unexplored regions. Still quaking with doubts about the integrity of my eyes, I proceeded on, and saw the apparition advancing upon me with the most perfect indifference: in another

223

minute he was quite near, and I now perceived that he had not yet seen me, for he was walking slowly and pensively with his eyes fixed on the ground, and he appeared to be a young man of a handsome and interesting countenance. We were got within four paces of each other when he heaved a deep and tremulous sigh, raised his eyes, and in an instant uttered a loud exclamation and fell insensible on the ground. My fears had now given place to sympathy, and I hastened to assist the unknown, who, I felt convinced, had been struck with the idea of seeing a supernatural being.

After the 'unknown' recovers and is assured that he has not encountered a ghost, Nixon claimed to engage him in conversation:

From a few expressions in old Dutch, which he uttered, I was luckily enabled to hold some conversation with him; for I had been at school in Holland in my youth and not quite forgotten the language. Badly as he spoke Dutch, yet I gathered from him a few particulars of a most extraordinary nature; namely, that he belonged to a small community, all as white as himself, he said about three hundred; that they lived in houses enclosed all together within a great wall to defend them from black men; that their fathers came there about one hundred and seventy years ago, as they said, from a distant land across the great sea; and that their ship broke, and eighty men and ten of their sisters (female passengers?) with many things were saved on shore. I prevailed on him to accompany me to my party, who I knew would be glad to be introduced to his friends before we set out on our return to our ship at Port Raffles, from which place we were now distant nearly five hundred miles, and our time was limited to a fixed period so as to enable the ship to carry us back to Singapore before the change of the monsoon. The young man's dress consisted of a round jacket and large breeches, both made of skins, divested of the hair and bleached as white as linen; and on his head he wore a tall white skin cap with a brim covered over with white down or the small feathers of the white cocatoo [sic].

After detailing his location, Nixon christened it Mount Singapore, 'after the name and in honour of the settlement to which the expedition belonged'. His journal then went on to describe the situation his party encountered when they entered 'the white village':

The joy of the simple inhabitants was quite extravagant. The descendant of an officer is looked up to as chief, and with him (whose name is Van Baerle), the party remained eight days. Their traditional history is that their fathers were compelled by famine, after the loss of their great vessel, to travel towards the rising sun, carrying with them as much of the stores as they could, during which many died; and by the wise advice of their ten sisters they crossed a ridge of land, and meeting with a rivulet on the other side, followed its course and were led to the spot they now inhabit, where they have continued ever since. They have no animals of the domestic kind, either cows, sheep, pigs or anything else; their plantations consist only of maize and yams, and these with fresh and dried fish constitute their principal food, which is changed occasionally for kangaroo and other game; but it appears that they frequently experience a scarcity and shortness of provisions, most probably owing to ignorance and mismanagement; and had little or nothing to offer us now except skins. They are nominal Christians: their marriages are performed without any ceremony: all the elders sit in council to manage their affairs; all the young, from ten up to a certain age, are considered a standing militia, and are armed with long pikes; they have no books or paper, nor any schools; they retain a certain observance of the Sabbath by refraining from their daily labours, and perform a short super-stitious ceremony on that day all together; and they may be considered almost a new race of beings.

This extraordinary tale of a secret expedition and a lost white colony somehow surviving in some of the most inhospitable terrain in the world—usually said to be Palm Valley in Finke

Gorge[1]—is the common stuff of New World exploration fantasy and folklore. But is it possible that this legend could be true? Some people believe it might be and have extensively researched the possibility.

The first mystery to be solved was the identity of the article's author. This turned out to be one Thomas J. Maslen. Although Maslen, an ex-officer of the British Indian army, never visited Australia, the country was his special object of study. In 1830 he published proposals for its exploration together with a largely fanciful map of the continent. In his personal copy, he hand-marked the alleged central Australian location of a Dutch colony on the map. The letter to the *Leeds Mercury* (Maslen resided in Yorkshire) was probably meant as a not very effective publicity stunt for the poor sales of his book.[2]

The next mystery was the identity of Lieutenant Nixon. Despite lengthy investigation of the relevant sources, researchers have not yet turned up such a person provably in the right place at the right time.

Other questions crowd in. Who sponsored such an expensive expedition and why? What was the rationale for equipping such an enterprise and dispatching it into what was literally the uncharted middle of nowhere? The usual reasons for clandestine undertakings of this sort are stories of fabulous riches, either in the form of gold, silver or prized products such as sandalwood and the like. But in this case, no motivating factor is given. Is there any independent evidence that might corroborate such an apparently fantastic tale? It seems that there might be.

Governor James Stirling established the Swan River colony on behalf of the British government, and at considerable benefit to himself, in 1829. The cities that were founded then, Perth and Fremantle, are still known as among the most isolated on earth. When the colony began, it truly was a frontier environment, with all the dangers, excitements and mysteries that might entail.

In June 1829 the 63rd Regiment of the British army arrived at the Swan River, first sighted by Willem de Vlamingh over 130 years earlier, and among them was nineteen-year-old ensign Robert Dale. Dale took part in exploration of the inland and of King George Sound, including the dense native forests of the south-west. He also became the owner of a good deal of granted property, as was common for this sort of colonial service. The young Dale judiciously pursued his various duties and was promoted to lieutenant in 1832.

Unfortunately, the new colony was soon in trouble economically and politically. Governor Stirling returned to England to seek increased government support, appointing Captain Fredrick Irwin as acting lieutenant governor. Irwin appointed Dale as his aide-de-camp at a very generous rate of pay, but the colonial office later abolished Dale's position. Possibly as a result of this, Dale and Irwin unexpectedly left the colony for England at the end of September 1833. At his farewell dinner, Dale stated that his reasons for leaving included 'motives of prudence and ulterior prospects'. What might these motives have been?

According to one interpretation, Dale may have been summoned back to England by Stirling to ensure his silence. The theory goes that Stirling had Dale lead a secret expedition in the early part of 1832. The party is said to have sailed to Fowlers Bay on the southern coast and then headed inland to the centre of the continent, somewhere south of the MacDonnell Ranges. The reason for this odd behaviour could be related to the existence of a lost Dutch colony, as mentioned in Maslen's letter to the newspaper. The details have been changed to disguise the fact that Dale's expedition would have been illegally entering another colony, New South Wales, and that as the British feared a Dutch claim on the continent, the authorities wanted to keep it all under wraps. It is claimed that Dale kept a journal of his mysterious mission, though this is, of course, missing.

There is also a suggestion that a Dutch harbourmaster in Java heard reports of this expedition from passing ships, but again these claims cannot be supported by documentary sources. There is some botanical evidence of grain-growing, the existence of palm trees and a water source in this part of the country. There are also a number of local indigenous traditions about a red-skinned people with long, fair hair who lived on fish caught by damming the river.[3]

Further possible evidence for this tale is found in some Dutch magazines where a version of the story appeared in 1837 and again in 1851. And there is also the disappearance of the ill-fated *Concordia*. Sailing out of Batavia in 1708, the 900-ton retours-chip was on her third homeward bound voyage with a cargo of ceramics and upwards of two hundred passengers and crew aboard. She was last sighted in filthy weather south of the Sunda Strait on 5 February. Almost three weeks later, wreckage believed to be from the *Concordia* was sighted. Otherwise, there has been no sign of her since then. The story goes that aboard the *Concordia* was a VOC official named Constantijn van Baerle, the same fairly unusual Dutch surname given in Lieutenant Nixon's account of his secret expedition.

While this all makes for a compelling yarn, it is difficult to square with the few known and likely facts. The *Concordia* is actually thought to have sunk near Mauritius, a very long way from Australia. Although one historian has identified a Constantijn van Baerle lost aboard the *Concordia*,[4] and it has been commonly asserted, there seems to be no supporting documentary evidence.

The intriguing story of the intrepid young ensign, Dale, journeying well beyond the known frontiers of the continent on a covert mission to a mysterious fertile valley in the desert fits some of the details given in Maslen's article. But it clearly has too many holes to be definitive. How did the British find out about the lost colony in the first place? How did the shipwreck survivors trek the vast and inhospitable distance from the coast to central Australia? And back again. How did the colonists manage to cultivate plantations in one of the driest parts of the most arid continent? What happened to the colony after Dale allegedly found it? Did he simply return to base and report to his superiors, leaving the white colony still lost? None of these questions can be answered,[5] though Robert Dale would later play a much better-documented role in another telling story.

Tales of lost tribes

There are other accounts of a white tribe wandering the interior of Australia. Woven through these tales would be discoveries of allegedly mysterious stone circles, rock paintings of European sailing ships and even a 'cathedral' in a cave. There are also testimonies from Aboriginal mythology and early settlers that refer to unusually light-skinned people. The Dieri people of the South Australian desert country have a legend involving light-skinned children and refer to the neighbouring Tangara people on the western side of Lake Eyre as *kana maralye*, or 'light-coloured men'.[6]

When George Grey led an expedition into the unknown north-west in 1838, he and his men became the first Europeans to sight the Wandjina rock paintings of the Kimberley region. They discovered what appeared to be carvings made in European style and apparently with metal tools. Grey also came across dwellings built in European style, a full-length depiction of what appeared to be a non-Aboriginal person dressed in robes, as well as stone arrangements that did not appear to belong to local indigenous culture. And he found what he called 'an alien white race' who were 'totally different, and almost white, who seem to exercise no small influence over the rest'.[7]

Around the same time, an officer aboard Grey's expedition ship *The Beagle*, moored in Roebuck Bay, came into close contact with some Aboriginal people:

They were about the middle age, about five feet six inches to five feet nine in height, broad shoulders, with large heads and overhanging brows; but it was not remarked that any of their teeth were wanting (as we afterwards observed in others); their legs were long and very slight, and their only covering a bit of grass suspended round the loins. There was an exception in the youngest, who appeared of an entirely different race: his skin was a copper colour, whilst the others were black; his head was not so large, and more rounded; the overhanging brow was lost; the shoulders more of a European turn, and the body and legs much better proportioned; in fact he might be considered a well-made man at our standard of figure. They were each armed with one, and some with two, spears, and pieces of stick about eight feet long and pointed at both ends. It was used after the manner of the Pacific Islanders, and the throwing-stick so much in use by the natives of the south did not appear known to them.[8]

Grey's was, however, not the only such sighting. In 1848, travelling through the hinterland near the wreck of the *Batavia*, the explorer A.C. Gregory came across a group of people who practised European-style agriculture and whose 'colour was neither black nor copper, but that peculiar colour that prevails with a mixture of European blood'.[9] Thirteen years later, there was talk of a mysterious tribe of fair-headed, pale and robust Aboriginal people along the northern branch of the upper Irwin River.[10] This sighting was in the same general region as another made more than thirty years later, when in 1895 it was reported that a prospector named Maitland Brown came across such a group east of Geraldton in the 'Virginia Range' (probably a mistake for the Victoria Range, the original European name for this area).[11]

An unidentified correspondent wrote to the *West Australian* newspaper in 1934 about a member of the 'Ingarra tribe' who sported a fine blond beard. He was known as Pieter and was considered to be of stocky Dutch appearance, rather than the more willowy local Aborigines, including all other known members of his family. Pieter's occupation was fishing from a boat, which he was said to handle very skilfully. At this time and place, Aborigines were not noted for these activities.[12] The Ingarra (a group name with various spellings) inhabited the coast at the northern end of Shark Bay, between the Gascoyne and Wooramel rivers and then inland to near Red Hill and Gascoyne Junction.[13]

Others also reported pale, fair-haired, blue-eyed or otherwise European-looking Aborigines on the west coast, most notably perhaps, the legendary Daisy Bates. While Bates remains a controversial figure, she has a claim to being the European with the most knowledge of that part of the country derived from her many years of close contact. In her book *The Passing of the Aborigines,* she describes what she considered to be Dutch-looking types among Aborigines 'as far out as the head-waters of the Gascoyne and the Murchison'.[14] The Gascoyne empties into Shark Bay and the mouth of the Murchison is near modern-day Kalbarri. Both rivers are in areas associated with castaways.

Most recently this theory has again been given an airing through claims that the *Vergulde Draeck* survivors did establish a colony near Karakin Lakes. The location of the evidence for this remains a secret as the site lies in private property. Among those who have examined the site and related evidence, opinions are divided, but there is considerable interest in the claim. It is further suggested that there was more than one 'white tribe' in Australia.[15]

All this evidence, of course, remains circumstantial, as with so many aspects of the Southland legends. Conclusions based upon it can only be conjectural until substantive documentary, physical or other unequivocal indications are discovered. [16] But legends sometimes turn out to be true—more or less.

White money

The year 1834 was a busy and exciting one in the fledgling Swan River colony. Less than six months after the secret expedition of

Lieutenant Nixon was reported, the *Perth Gazette* carried another strange story. Two Aboriginal men were telling of a wreck around thirty days' journey, or about 650 kilometres, to the north.[17] They had been told of this European maritime disaster by members of a northern tribe whom they seemed to call the *wayl* or 'wheel men'. According to the two Aborigines, there was 'white money' on the wreck. The newspaper reported:

> The story has been handed from tribe to tribe until it has reached our natives and runs as follows. We give it of course without implicitly relying on its accuracy, but the account is sufficiently authenticated to excite well-founded suspicions that some accident has happened. It appears the wreck has been lying on shore for 6 moons, or months, and the distance from this is said to be 30 days' journey, or about 400 miles. When the water is low, the natives are said to go on board, and bring from the wreck 'white money'; on money being shown to the native who brought the report, he picked out a dollar, as a similar piece to the money he had seen. Some steps should be immediately taken to establish or refute this statement: the native can soon be found. He is said to be importunate that soldier man, and white man, with horse, should go to the wreck, volunteering to escort them. We shall look with anxiety for further information upon this point.

There was some scepticism about this report, but the following Saturday the newspaper published another version of the same story. In this rendition, the wreck, or 'broke boat', as the Aborigines called it, also had survivors:

> The report we gave publicity to last week respecting the supposed wreck of a vessel to the northward, has met with some farther confirmation, and has attracted the attention of the local Government. A Council was held on Wednesday last (we believe) expressly for the purpose of taking this subject into consideration, and, after a diligent inquiry, it was thought expedient to make

arrangements for despatching an expedition to the northward, which will be immediately carried into effect. This, the winter season, rendering a land expedition both dangerous, and, in every probability, futile, it has been determined to charter the Monkey (a small vessel, now lying in our harbour) to proceed immediately to Shark's Bay, somewhere about the distance described at which the wreck may be expected to be fallen in with, where Mr. H.M. Ommanney [sic], of the Survey Department, and a party under his directions, will be landed to traverse the coast north and south, the Monkey remaining as a depot from whence they will draw their supplies, to enable them to extend their search in either direction.

The article went on to discuss the moral issues involved in the situation, and then continued with further details of the story as reported by a Mr Parker, a colonist living in the then-outlying settlement of Guildford:

About a week or ten days since, Tonguin and Weenat came to Parker's and gave him and his sons to understand, that they (Tonguin and Weenat) had recently learned from some of the northern tribes (who appear to be indiscriminately referred to under the name of Waylo men, or Weelmen) that a ship was wrecked ('boat broke') on the coast to the northward, about 30 (native) days walk from the Swan—that there was white money plenty lying on the beach for several yards, as thick as seed vessels under a red gum tree. On some article of brass being shewn, they said that was not like the colour of the money; but on a dollar being shewn, they recognised it immediately as the kind of money they meant: but laid the dollar on the ground and drawing a somewhat larger circle round it with the finger, said 'the money was like that'. They represented that the wreck had been seen six moons ago, and that all the white men were dead: none, as it is supposed, having been then seen by their informants, the Weel men. They added that, at low water, the natives could reach the wreck, which had blankets (sails) flying about it: from which it is presumed that the supposed vessel may not have entirely lost her masts on first striking, and they stuck up three sticks in a manner which led Parker's sons to understand that the wreck they were attempting to describe had three masts, but Parker himself did not infer the same meaning.

According to the report:

There were several white men, represented to be of very large stature, ladies and 'plenty piccaninnie' that they were living in houses made of canvas and wood ... there are five such houses, two large and three small—that they are not on a river but on the open sea ('Gabby England come')—that the sea coast, at the site of the wreck, takes a bend easterly into an apparent bay ... that the spot where the white money is strewed on the beach is some (indefinite) distance from the spot where the houses are and more within the bay; that the gabby (surf) breaks with very great noise where the money is.

The testimony of the Aborigines contained some intriguing details about contact between the castaways and the indigenous people, suggesting that the words they spoke were true: 'the white men gave the Weel men some gentlemen's (white) biscuit' while the latter gave in return spears, shields and other items. The wreck was said to be ten days' walk north, though this was interpreted by the colonists as a 'walk on horseback'.

The prospect of rescuing white people from the ravages of shipwreck and perhaps from the 'natives', together with the possibility of financial gain, electrified the small settler community on the Swan River. A few months earlier, some other Aborigines from the north carried some British coins into Perth, claiming they had received them from the 'Wayl men', fearsome indigenous inhabitants of the neighbouring territory. With this recent event as background, there was a strong incentive to find out more and plans were laid for a boat to sail northwards in search of the wreck.

While these preparations were being made, a local indigenous leader named Weeip entered the story. He had been recently outlawed for his resistance to colonial rule and his son effectively taken as a hostage by the colonial administration of Governor James Stirling. Hoping for the release of his son, Weeip volunteered to travel north to see what he could discover. He returned in early August, claiming the natives of the north had told him that there were definitely no survivors of the mysterious wreck, but that there was plenty of 'white money'. The settlers were inclined to disbelieve Weeip and it looked as though, despite his efforts, his son would not be released. But the following month the newspaper was able to report that the governor had indeed released Weeip's son, in return from a promise from Weeip to observe the settlers' laws and to ensure that his people did likewise.

The colonists also tried to rescue the survivors by sending the schooner *Monkey* north under Captain Pace. The party was led by Mr H.M. Ommaney of the Survey Department, with Mr Thomas Hunt as second in command, assisted by three volunteer privates from the 21st Regiment. With instructions to search around Dirk Hartog Island and Gantheaume Bay, they sailed from Fremantle on 18 July 1834. Eleven days later they sighted the Abrolhos and that evening, like many before them, 'saw a fire on the mainland, bearing N.E. by E, burn brilliantly for 6 or 7 minutes'.

On 11 August Ommaney and his group went ashore to trek along the coast. He described reaching 'a perpendicular, rocky, red cliff, 300 feet high, overhanging the sea' and noted that 'it was not blowing fresh, yet the surf was tremendous; large masses of rock were visible as each successive wave retired'. They continued to follow the coast south and then camped, still finding no water.

The next day they pushed on but one of the soldiers became ill from lack of water. Ommaney returned to the *Monkey* for water, finding another soldier in the same state when he arrived. It seems that the ship did not have sufficient water onboard and the whole company was placed on rations. On 17 August a crew member died and another was taken ill, either from lack of water or eating poisonous fish. They then found a water source and continued the search for survivors, trekking several kilometres east 'through a country superior, in point of soil, to any I had previously seen in this vicinity'. After this they reached a salt lake where they had a close encounter with the local Aborigines:

> [We] endeavoured to obtain a conference, but could not. Observing several striking round apparently to where we had left our watering party, I thought it prudent to make for the beach. We had not gone far, however, before we perceived they were following us. They hallooed and shewed a design to detain us, which we considered a scheme either to cut us off from, or to facilitate an attack upon, our watering party.

Ommaney and his crew walked another mile and a half to the beach where they found several natives assembled to confront them:

> They were violent in their gestures, and, as we supposed, in their language They would not allow us to approach them, neither did they advance towards us; but on our turning and proceeding in the direction of the boat, they appeared much pleased; one man came forward and threw down a shell, and retired. I picked it up, and laid down my handkerchief in its place, at which they all appeared delighted, but gave us to understand, by signs, that if we did not go away, they would throw their spears at us. Some of the natives seemed, at times, much disposed to molest us, but were apparently controled [sic] by others.

The natives, about thirty in all, 'had several very fine native dogs with them' and 'were tall, fine looking men'. Ommaney recorded their height in detail, with the shortest being about 5 feet 6 inches, five or six of them were 6 feet 1 inch, and the rest were 6 feet more or less. He added, 'Some of them had amazing large feet.'

Ommaney and his men reached the *Monkey* in safety, but next day went ashore again for water and were once more confronted by Aborigines. This time they were friendly and 'as much gratified with the flowers we offered them as with our European articles'. They became agitated when some of the soldiers went to gather oysters but subsequently 'brought some beautiful mullet, which they exchanged for paper, being annoyed when a sheet was divided, and giving a smaller fish in consequence'. Ommaney reported that, 'At length they seemed to get tired of exchanging their fish for articles they could not use, but continued a friendly conference to the last.'

On 26 August the *Monkey* was at Cape Ransonnet on the west coast of Dirk Hartog Island, where they made a surprising find: 'A great quantity of broken timber that had been washed up from some wreck, but many years since. Some was washed very high, and some was still washing among the reef: it seemed principally teak, with some fir, full of worms.' This evidence of an unknown wreck was not examined further. After failing to find sufficient water and facing a likely north-west gale, the *Monkey* returned to Fremantle on 2 October with no news of a silver trove.

Six weeks later, another rescue ship, the schooner *Ellen*, was despatched north but had no better luck than the *Monkey*.

But what was the older wreck whose timbers were still washing around the reef? Previous voyagers to the area, including Phillip Parker King and, even earlier, Louis de Freycinet, make no mention of wreckage. As with many other such tantalising asides that appear in the early journals, no one seems to have followed up sightings of this kind.

In the meantime, the Swan River settlers eventually determined, and it has been the belief since, that the stories were part of Aboriginal tradition and referred to events that had taken place not in 1834 but perhaps more than a century earlier. Compression of time is a common characteristic of oral tradition. In this case, it seems that the story of the 'broke boat' and the 'white money' did have a basis in fact, but it would be many more years before that could be shown to be so. This occurred when the wreck of the *Zuytdorp* was finally located, the site carpeted in silver coins from the ship's rich treasure trove of trading monies, a scene much like that described by the Aborigines in 1834.

While these events and speculations were playing out, other odd stories also began to circulate and were reported in the local and even the British press. In July 1834 some Aborigines reported they had contact with a party of whites living around 70 kilometres inland of the Swan River.[18] As there was little exploration and no settlement at this distance from the colony during this time, such news was astounding. Who these people might have been, if they ever existed, is a complete mystery. Although unlikely, it is just possible that a group of people had landed unnoticed on the southern shores of Western Australia and trekked inland in search of new homes in the wilds of the continent. If so, they were dangerously misguided.

Dutch Aborigines

Many Nunda and Malgana people of the Shark Bay area consider themselves to be Dutch. Some have even visited the Netherlands as an affirmation of this seemingly astonishing sense of identity. Nunda tradition includes stories 'about white fellas, going way back, that was walking up one of the rivers through where Mullewa is now'.[19] These stories are reinforced by suggestive evidence in addition to the eyewitness accounts of fair-haired, light-skinned and otherwise European-looking Aboriginal people in and around Nunda and Malgana country. There is also genetic evidence.

A rare skin disease known as *porphyria variegata* is especially prevalent among South Africans of Dutch ancestry. It is also found among Aboriginal people of the Kalbarri region. This has led geneticists to conduct studies to establish a link between VOC shipwreck survivors and local indigenous populations. They concluded, however, that the disease occurs spontaneously in the indigenous groups and so could not be connected with Dutch shipwreck survivors.[20] But there are other biological trails to follow.

An unusual genetic feature found among Nunda people is Ellis-van Creveld syndrome (EvC, also known as *chondroecto-dermal dysplasia*). This is characterised most visibly by extra fingers and toes, often causing enlarged feet, as noted by Ommaney. The occurrence of EvC worldwide is extremely low, except among Old Order Amish communities in Philadelphia, where the frequency is estimated at 13 per cent. Genetic studies have found that the second highest incidence of EvC is among Aboriginal people in south-west Western Australia.[21] The family groups who featured in this research were—and are—closely connected with the region of the *Zuytdorp* wreck and with its subsequent discovery and investigation. The extraordinary connection between these Australian Aborigines and the 'Plain People' of Philadelphia may be a man named Samuel King, descended from an Anabaptist family in seventeenth-century Switzerland.

In 1697 Abraham Küng's son Samuel married Anna Gnägi. They produced five daughters and two sons; one of these was the father of a Samuel King born in 1724. Twenty years later, Samuel and his brothers migrated to Philadelphia. They boarded the *Muscliffe Galley* in Rotterdam, arriving in Philadelphia just before Christmas 1744. About six years later, Samuel married Anna Yoder. By the time of his death, Samuel and Anna had begotten at least twelve and possibly fourteen children. Approximately 12 per cent of the Amish Mennonites in Lancaster County, as the successors of the Anabaptists are now known, and where the highest incidence of EvC is recorded, are the descendants of Samuel and Anna King.[22] It is thought that a member of the King family may have been among those aboard the *Zuytdorp*, either when she left the Netherlands or joining her when the ship was resupplied at Cape Town.

Unfortunately, the only surviving record of the voyage that might confirm this possibility is a list of the soldiers and tradesmen aboard, and this may well be incomplete given the dire circumstances of the *Zuytdorp*'s voyage to the Cape of Good Hope. So this intriguing genetic link remains speculative. A further attempt to confirm the EvC connection was made by geneticists, historians and folklorists in the mid-2010s, but the project has yet to report its findings.

Similar traditions about cohabitation of shipwreck survivors and Aboriginal people can also be found in the area where the *Vergulde Draeck* met her end. The lands of the people who now generally call themselves Nyungar[23] included the site of European settlement on the Swan River. From 1829 they were at the epicentre of colonisation. Some among them became leaders of local resistance to the increasing encroachments upon their traditional lands. In particular, the warrior known as Yagan came to represent the struggle of the Nyungar against the settlers. As usual in these cases, Yagan's story is one of confrontation, resistance and ultimate tragedy.

By all accounts, Yagan was an outstanding figure, not only as a leader but also physically. He is described as of greater stature than most of his people, 1.8 metres tall and 'head and shoulders above his fellows—in mind as well as in body'. In some accounts, Yagan had two sons; one was named 'Narli', the other 'Wille' or 'Willeim'.[24] In other sources Yagan is said to have been childless. Whichever the case, accounts of a Nyungar child with a Dutch forename at this early stage are intriguing.

From 1831 Yagan was the leader of a local resistance to European settlement. This was sparked when a farmer murdered a member of the warrior's group and Yagan revenged the killing. In 1832 he led another attack on the settlers and was outlawed with a reward of 20 pounds offered for his capture, which occurred later that year. The outlaw was sentenced to death but through the intervention of a settler named Robert Lyon was exiled to Carnac island under Lyon's supervision. A month later, Yagan and those imprisoned with him stole a boat and escaped. In this exploit, Yagan displayed boat-handling skills thought not to exist in indigenous culture. Despite this breakout, the Nyungar hero was seemingly judged to have served sufficient punishment as he was not apprehended. Later, he and his companions even provided corroborees within the Perth town site that were greatly enjoyed by the settlers. But violence between the original inhabitants and the newcomers soon flared again and in July 1833 Yagan was treacherously shot dead by a young settler he had befriended.

After his death, Yagan was skinned for his ceremonial decorations and tattoos. His head was severed from his body and smoked for preservation. When Frederick Irwin left the colony later that year, he was accompanied by the young ensign, Robert Dale, who allegedly led the secret expedition described by Maslen. Dale carried Yagan's head with him, probably as a grisly souvenir of his sojourn on the southern continent. In London he failed to sell the head for the desired 20 pounds and then entered into an agreement with a local surgeon and antiquarian to display the head at his fashionable soirees.

Dale received the head back in October 1835 and then gave it to the Liverpool Royal Institution.[25] It remained here and in successor organisations until it was buried in 1964.[26] During the 1980s Nyungar people began pressing the British and Australian governments for the head of their hero to be repatriated for proper burial according to custom. Following an intervention by then prime minister, John Howard, the skull was finally handed back to a delegation of Nyungar representatives in Liverpool in 1997 and returned to Western Australia. Community disagreements and the failure to locate Yagan's other remains delayed reburial of the skull until 2010. This important event took place in the specially created Yagan Memorial Park east of Perth.

Within the larger story of settlement and dispossession, this tale is a stark reminder of the tensions of colonisation. Its many ambivalences and apparent contradictions echo the first contacts at Cape York, the skin trade, as well as genuine efforts by black and white to live together. In Yagan's fate we confront the intersection of Australia's unavoidable history and necessary mythology. In Robert Dale's actions—real and folkloric—we see the threads unavoidably connecting black stories and white stories on the Southland.

13

Surviving the Southland

The date usually given for the European settlement of Australia is 1788. While this moment does mark the first known act of deliberate occupation, the tiny community clinging to Sydney Cove could hardly be said to have settled the continent. There was little expansion from the coastal region until the crossing of the Blue Mountains in 1813. Even then, the vast reaches of the continent remained virtually unknown to Europeans.

Settlements in other locations occurred slowly. Van Diemen's Land was not colonised until 1803. While the west had a small military garrison at Albany from 1826, a colony was not estab-lished until 1829 and it was a tentative enterprise for many years. Victoria and South Australia were colonised in the 1830s and although Queensland was opened up in the 1820s, free settlement was only permitted in 1842. The large area that is now the Northern Territory was not effectively settled until the 1870s and 80s.

Intrepid individuals and groups moved out into the hinterlands of their respective colonial capitals and in some cases sailed directly to other locations and other encounters. But Australia remained largely unknown until well after the heroic colonial feats of inland exploration that took place through much of the nineteenth century and even well into the twentieth. The last traditional group of Pintupi made their first contact only in 1984.[1] There has been a very long period in which unrecorded events may have taken place in many out-of-the-way locations. In terms of what is known and what can be reasonably argued, European occupation began long before the usually accepted date. Settlement entailed a process of myth, exploration, first contact and various forms of exchange that have given modern Australia its particular character.

This story is one of taking and leaving, of transactions between people in unfamiliar places and unfamiliar circumstances. It is usually called 'first contact', a brief term that conceals much more than it reveals. When Europeans—and some peoples from elsewhere—first came here, they brought with them goods to exchange. They may have called these items 'gifts', 'toys' or 'trinkets', but however named they were items of exchange, designed to smooth the difficulties they expected to experience in their initial encounters with native peoples. Some groups resisted the blandishments of the sea traders and voyagers. Others showed an inclination to trade for the items being held out to them. As time went on and interaction became more frequent, Aboriginal people often did trade with the newcomers, many of whom were keen to obtain what they considered to be exotic artefacts, weapons and handcrafts. Aboriginal people quickly identified what the newcomers valued and often began manufacturing such items to trade for those things that they now desired—including sugar, grog and clothing.[2]

These dealings highlight the distance between indigenous and European worldviews. Aboriginal people were, in many cases, unimpressed by the material items they were proffered, while Europeans wanted something in return, whether it was goods, scientific and cultural information and, ultimately, the land itself. These exchanges could hardly be equal. They were not 'trade' in any meaningful sense, as the Aborigines had no idea of the monetary value of European desires. Nor did they have the gold, jewels or other items commonly valued by the newcomers to their lands.

Initially, the continent seemed to hold nothing of any worth to the Europeans, and about the only thing they valued of the country was the possibility that it could provide labour, a concept and practice not to the liking of Aboriginal people. One of the earliest violent events between black and white occurred when the Dutch tried to make the Wik work for them in drawing water. Dampier also experienced an indigenous disinclination to serve him. The Europeans viewed it as ignorance of, and disdain for, work and their misunderstanding lay at the base of the violence fated to occur. It has also bedevilled relations since, as indigenous peoples were pressed into cheap labour in places such as the Kimberley, Cape York, the Torres Strait and elsewhere. These were all forms of exchange, cultural transactions and negotiation. But they were from the beginning an unequal exchange that usually favoured the newcomers and disadvantaged the original inhabitants.

Giving and taking

One of the many enigmas within the contemporary accounts of first contact involves clothing—or the lack of it. Most Europeans were struck by the nakedness of the Aboriginal people they saw and sometimes met, either on good terms or not. This was not necessarily a prurient interest. Instead, the journals suggest puzzlement at why people would choose to live without clothing, other than that needed for winter warmth in the southern reaches of the west and in Tasmania. Many of the newcomers simply assumed the Aborigines were so benighted that they had not invented clothing. It was not until James Cook that a European sensibility seemed able to grapple with nakedness as simply a factor of the minimal material needs of the indigenes.

In the European mind, clothes were immensely significant. They were not simply for concealing the body and, when necessary, warming or protecting it. As they do to a certain extent today, clothes spoke volumes about social status and power. The rich were determined to demonstrate their wealth and positions by the sumptuousness of their attire. Those at the other end of society had no such garb and often possessed only whatever they stood up in. Sometimes these were rags. Clothes were expensive anyway and the more one had and the more magnificent they were, the more one obviously possessed and the more one was to be respected. The *Batavia* mutineers capering murderously among the coral reefs in the robes and gowns of their departed skipper is a bizarre image but one that throws light on the European relationship between clothing and power.

Bringing these attitudes with them, the Europeans reasoned that when encountering other humans they, too, would desire such things. The Dutch, in particular, loaded their trading ships with bales of materials and clothing to use not only for trade but also as gifts for the natives they encountered. Their assumption was that these things would be valued, as they were in Europe. But clothing was often refused, ignored or briefly tried on then thrown away by many Australian Aboriginal groups. Some, notably in Tasmania and Western Australia, had an interest in the brighter colours and there was often considerable amusement expressed at military uniforms when first seen upon the French and English. On the whole, though, these prized European goods were simply meaningless to those for whom they were to be traded and gifted. Today, perhaps, this is not surprising, but to the newcomers it was inexplicable and formed one of the many gulfs of perception that lay between the oldest world and the newest.

As well as leaving things, the newcomers took them. It was necessary to take the wildlife for food, the water for sustenance and occasionally the timber for fires and even boatbuilding. Beginning seriously, perhaps, with William Dampier, there were concerted efforts to take samples of wildlife and plants, mainly for the purposes of scientific investigation. Enlightened though Dampier might seem by the general standards of the day, he was also a body trader. Although his victims were not Australian, he was happy to spirit away an islander from near the Philippines to England and then to make money from displaying him as a sideshow freak until he died of smallpox.

The VOC also deemed it necessary to take human beings away from their communities. These people were required for local intelligence that might lead to profitable trading for the company. While careful and pious instructions were given as to the abduction of these unfortunates, there were no directions about returning them from where they had been stolen. Occasionally we read, in passing, that one of these wretched hostages died of a tropical disease or simply of misery. Later, there was a large trade in skeletons, skulls and skins, the consequences of which are now being uncomfortably worked out in the museums, galleries and universities of the world as the descendants of those whose remains were appropriated demand their repatriation. Weapons, implements and sometimes highly sacred objects were also carted away by the curious and the enterprising. Many are still displayed in dusty irrelevance and, at best, usually pointless interpretation in museum cabinets around the globe. More lie in dark basements seen, if at all, by the occasional researcher.[3]

Not all those things taken by the Europeans were given freely or in exchange. When the *Endeavour* anchored in Botany Bay, Cook went ashore to stride upon the new land. He was met by a group of men who did not want the uninvited newcomers in their country. There was some stone throwing, gesturing and a few warning spears. Alarmed, Cook ordered his men to fire. Little physical damage was done, it seems, but one of the retreating Aborigines left behind a bark shield. Someone—possibly Joseph Banks—souvenired the artefact, took it home and it eventually became part of the British Museum collection, where it remains to this day.[4]

Like so many other taken objects, its existence is another mute testimony to the nature of pre-colonial and colonial exchange.

But there is also a less negative side to these transactions. In many cases, indigenous people were happy to trade their weapons and other items in return for almost worthless trinkets and junk. At least, they seemed worthless to those who offered them. Some of the earliest accounts of first contact show that indigenous people were able to see the practical value of a shard of glass or piece of metal. These were immediately adapted to their everyday needs. One thing learned through millennia of survival is the ability to make do, innovate and adapt anything that might appear useful. If it had some element of brightness or other beauty, even better. Aboriginal culture not only valued the artistic, it was integral to all they did, as we know from rock art, ceremony, song and the designs incorporated into everyday objects. The same event that garnered the shield for the British Museum was also recorded in oral tradition by the sons of those who encountered Cook and his men in 1770. When the British and the people of what he called Botany Bay did establish a workable relationship, Cook introduced them to rum and ship's biscuit, neither of which they cared for. But when Cook chopped a tree with a tomahawk, they were greatly impressed and took the tool for their own use.[5]

Another type of taking was the collection of Aboriginal speech. Many navigators, settlers and explorers had a positive mania for this form of possessioning. At one level, it had a purely practical function of allowing intercultural communication. At a deeper level, it could be seen as another deceit of colonialism—first take the land then take its languages. Whichever of these interpretations appeals, or not, the collected indigenous vocabularies of the early arrivals have often become the only records of now-dead languages and the cultures that spoke them. Indigenous Australians are able to use these records to resurrect their lost tongues. Again, acts in the past continue to shape what is thought and done in the future.

Today, trade in maritime and other archaeological artefacts and treasures is mostly illegal and booming. Wrecks and sites of historical and mythological significance are routinely plundered. 'Finders keepers', as the artefact hunter and writer Craig Childs put it in his thought-provoking book of that name.[6] Even when the dives and expeditions are legal and professional, are they still moral? Do we really need to fill the history zoos of the world with yet more captive relics of the past? Perhaps it would be better to simply locate them, document them and leave them where they lie—in their proper places. But such is our desire—even our need—not only to know the past but also to possess it, that the trade in treasure and antiquities will go on forever. The hard-nosed merchants of the VOC would have approved.

Inscribing possession

The earliest verified European artefact on the Southland is Dirk Hartog's improvised pewter marker. It was a common dinner plate, hastily beaten flat and shakily inscribed with a spontaneous message of arrival and, implicitly, of possessing. A glorified piece of seventeenth-century graffiti—today it might have said, 'Dirk was here'. Etched into its mildly malleable surface is the first writing we have. The plate was nailed to an oak post,[7] forced deep into a rock cleft, a symbolic insertion of the European into the Australian.

Hartog's plate and post withstood more than eight decades of wind, rain and salt. Then, in 1697, Willem de Vlamingh's upper-steersman found the battered oak timber still standing and the plate fallen at its base. Following Hartog's lead, de Vlamingh had a plate of his own fashioned and placed on a post that was probably made of Rottnest Island pine. He felt the need to remove Hartog's memorial and take it to the company through which it found its way to the 'nobilities' of the VOC in the Netherlands, eventually coming to rest in the Rijksmuseum. De Vlamingh's plate endured alone for more than a century until Jacques Felix

Emmanuel Hamelin arrived in 1801 as a member of Nicolas Baudin's expedition. Despite the urging of some of his officers, Hamelin decided the plate should remain as it was, a mute but evocative testament to the gradual revelation and appropriation of the mysterious Southland. He also mounted an inscribed lead plate or plaque to mark his coming.

Still coveting the de Vlamingh plate, Louis de Freycinet returned to Shark Bay in 1818 and stole it away to burnish the glory of the Académie Française. He may have taken Hamelin's plate as well. It was no longer there four years later. Phillip Parker King went to see it for himself but found only two empty posts 'and the nails by which they had been secured'.[8] King had his name and the day of his visit nailed into the remains.

By then, the Dutch, French and British had all found their own versions of *Terra Australis*. For the Dutch, it was a total disappointment and graveyard for some of their finest ships and a tiny fraction of their immense treasure. For the French, it was a land of intriguing indigenes, fascinating flora and fauna, and another potential territory. The British claim came last with Cook's commanded act of possession, followed by a penal settlement eighteen years later at Port Jackson. For them, it was a place to dump troublesome convicts, a possible source of masts for their mighty navy and a strategic southern outpost for an expanding global empire.

Others left tokens and deliberate signs of their presence. In April 1623, Jan Carstensz marked his coming to the river he named the Staten by nailing a wooden tablet to a tree. In 1772 Louis de Saint Aloüarn placed a bottle at Turtle Bay containing some French coins and a claim to the land. George Vancouver deposited two bottles in making his 1791 claim to the continent at what he named King George the Third's Sound. Even questing whalers felt the need to leave the evidence of their passing, as did the *Kingston* and *Elligood* at the same location in 1800. Matthew Flinders left a bottle and message at Seal Island in January 1802, as well as a commemorative inscription on a copper sheet at Memory Cove, Cape Catastrophe, a month or so later. The following year Nicolas Baudin had a commemorative inscription of his expedition's passing cut into a Kangaroo Island rock.

These, and other, more or less official inscriptions were complemented by individual acts of graffiti. In 1820 a sailor from Parker King's ship *Mermaid* carved 'HMC Mermaid' in a boab tree in Careening Bay. On Sweer's Island in 1841, Lort Stokes found the tree where Flinders' crew chipped 'Investigator' into the bark almost forty years earlier. Playing the same game as the makers and leavers of plates, Stokes had the name of his ship, *Beagle*, sliced into the other side of the trunk. There may have been many unrecorded messages to the future left in the desolate immensity that most early navigators experienced. That so many of those we know about have survived suggests the indifference of Aboriginal people to these peculiar acts of the strangers.

It is difficult to know what the Wik, Yolngu, Tiwi, Nunda and other indigenous groups thought of the first European wanderers and their strange customs. There is little more than the odd tantalising moment recorded by chance in a journal, diary or perhaps a surviving letter. But we know that the earliest arrivals thought of the first Australians as savages. The next wave of scientific navigators treated them as exotic specimens for study and archiving. Those who colonised the country soon came to see them as a nuisance and so mistreated them, despite usually genuine initial attempts to co-exist.

In between these swirling currents of global politics, trade and colonialism were cast away on the unknown shores upwards of three hundred souls, perhaps many more. What became of them? Did they meld into the indigenous population as some scientific evidence and much folklore suggests? Did they form a colony of some sort, a lost white tribe somehow surviving in the some of the harshest lands on earth? Incredible though this might seem, the legends are persistent. Or did they all perish—so far without a trace? And did at least some of these desolate wraiths leave their genes?

Whatever their individual or collective fates, the only words we have that can speak for the castaways are those functional few left on battered metal plates. The posts on which they stood are necessarily mute except for what archaeological speculation might suggest. Sparse though the artefacts of arrival, contact and perhaps pre-settlement might be, they are the true memorials to those who inadvertently settled, for however short—or long—a time.

In 2013, preparing for the 400th anniversary of Dirk Hartog's visit, the Western Australian Museum submitted de Vlamingh's dish to the telling beams of the Australian Synchrotron, a device that accelerates electrons to near the speed of light, deflecting them through magnetic fields and so allowing finely detailed inspection of surfaces. The tests proved that the 35-centimetre diameter pewter dinner plate was subjected to enormous environmental stress during its 121 years in the open. Winds so fierce that they embedded a grain of sand in the pewter were proof of a cyclone. The pewter had also reacted with the bronze nails that held it up and, eventually, with the acids leaching from the post on which it was erected. The synchrotron also revealed cutlery scrapes made while it was still being used as a dinner plate. From mundane implement to super-historical artefact, a change of status turbocharged with significance, not unlike fragments of the true cross or any number of other real and allegedly-so traces of the past. So great is our reverence of history and our need to connect with it that we display these few remnants in expensive monuments to the past. There, we imprint them with ever-greater meaning as the time since their imputed beginnings passes, making them evermore sacred. In the vast spaces of time and distance between these few leavings and markings, persist myths old and new.

Settling and surviving

We use the term 'settlement' and its variations to mean a straight-forward process of leaving an old land, arriving in a new one, establishing the conditions necessary for survival, maintaining and expanding those and, ultimately, staying. 'Settling down', forming 'settlements' and 'settling the country' are familiar phrases. But these necessities are only part of more complex symbolic, emotional and cultural interactions. When European people came to the Southland that was completely unknown to them, they entered into a profound set of new relationships, differing expectations and perhaps unexamined assumptions that determined the course of their futures. New settlers faced nameless dangers on the mountains, plains and deserts across which they eventually moved. They needed to learn and adapt to the many harsh environments. Some did; many did not and paid the price of failure.

As well as coming and staying, settling is also an act of possessioning, of taking over lands that were previously the preserve of those already there. In Australia, this is an incontrovertible fact—one of relatively few—about the nature of its modern settlement. The consequences of this act have been profound and, for Aboriginal people especially, almost completely negative. Australia has struggled with this reality since its inception and, judging by the history to date, will continue to do so for generations to come.

But from the earliest settlement by castaways, there has been one consistently bright thread within the relationship between black and white—that has been a product of unimaginably different cultures coming together, interacting and, little by little and unevenly, assuming something of the other into itself. Amid the misunderstandings, prejudices, violence and general bleakness of white and black relations can be found moments of something much more positive. There are many documented instances of indigenous people helping shipwreck survivors and we can reasonably infer that there were more such unknown acts of mercy.

The historical record also shows that there were instances where Aboriginal people attacked and murdered castaways, usually when in larger groups. Usually these acts were revenged with interest by settlers. Dreadful though these incidents were—and remain—they also bind black and white together in the story of the land. While they cannot be changed, they can be acknowledged in a mature balancing of the colonial record. We know that the relationships and interactions between indigenous people and newcomers were multifaceted, complex and varied greatly from place to place.[9] Just as it is inaccurate and unhelpful to think of indigenous Australians as a single group, so it is to think that all colonisers were heartless thugs intent on destroying the many different cultures and lifestyles they encountered in Australia.

These givings and takings, misunderstandings and conflicts, reprehensible though many of them now seem to us, were the basis of human intercourse on the new continent. But, as it was for indigenous people, so it was for those inadvertently settling—and surviving.

We know that more than 300 non-indigenous people were on the Southland at some point, beginning from several centuries before 1788. What happened to them after they stepped out of their sparsely documented presence in now-ancient journals and letters is only recorded, if at all, in the lineaments of the land itself. Perhaps in stone carvings and cave paintings. Certainly in the traditions of the first people. Melded with these ghostly memories are a few rusting fragments, buried coins and bleached European bones scattered along vast shorelines. Fitting then, that some important myths revolve around 'white Aborigines' and the likelihood of cohabitation.

In addition to the usually larger groups of shipwreck survivors that we know about, there are many small and mostly unnoticed incidents involving one, two or even more lost souls. The discrepancies in the journal of Francisco Pelsaert suggest that at least one survivor was unaccounted for when the remainder began their journey back from *Batavia*'s graveyard. Another five of Pelsaert's sailors disappeared off the coast. Two men went missing and remained unaccounted for on the western coast, which was not yet settled, during the wrecking of the *Correio da Azia* in 1815–16. It is also not impossible that Thomas Timothée Vasse cohabited with the indigenous people of south-western Australia. Other castaways certainly did, even if they declined to say so.[10]

If stories about other unverified wrecks, such as the Stradbroke Island Galleon, the Mahogany Ship and the Deadwater Wreck should turn out to be true, or even partly so, the potential number of Europeans straggling onto unknown shores increases dramatically. And there may well turn out to be wrecks as yet unlocated or unidentified[11], including *Ridderschip van Holland*, and *Aagtekerke* and possibly even the *Concordia*, supposed bearer of Constantijn van Baerle and the progenitors of the lost white tribe of central Australia. As always, fact and folklore flow together, making it difficult to discern one from the other. Sometimes it is impossible to do so. While the historical veracity of many of these legends and speculations is doubtful, their existence and persistence suggests a strong need to ask and investigate such questions.

Australia has been the point of connection between many of the world's great population movements, imperial expansion and conflict, trade and human perseverance, failings and triumphs. The Greeks were thinking about it, as were some early Islamic scholars. South Asian sailors visited seasonally to harvest trepang. The great mercantile explorations and empires of the early modern period made their way towards it. The Dutch finally walked upon it, followed by the English, the French and possibly the Portuguese. Others may one day be proven to have done so. When Europeans greeted, abducted, shot and eventually dispossessed the people occupying the continent for millennia, they made contact with the longest living tradition. A way of life that had persisted in one place for longer than any other. The human circle was now complete. The oldest reconnected with the newest and—as Europeans liked to think of themselves, their achievements and their technologies—the best.

While this book has told the story of inadvertent castaways, there is a sense in which even those who came here willingly and those descended from them are castaways still. It is possible to comprehend indigenous mythology, spirituality, living skills and creative expressions like rock art, dance and song. But that is about as far as the rational Western mindset can take us. That profoundly different way of understanding the universe and the place of human beings within it can only be approached through the notion of 'the Dreaming'—and this can never be completely perceived and appreciated by settlers.

Looking without seeing

The story of the Southland is the story of those already on these shores and that of those who came later. No matter how tentatively, Australia was finally encountered, revealed to some extent and settled long before the official date of non-Aboriginal occupation. The nature of that settlement, and of the more organised occupation that would come, resulted in the destruction of indigenous lifestyle and culture. While this was in part the result of greed, violence and dispossession, it was also the result of blindness.[12]

The relatively easy living that Aboriginal people appear to have made from their 'estate' left them time for other things. When this happened in Western societies, it led to the growth of extensive and intensive material infrastructures—government, churches, industrialism and labour. In Australia, people used their free time to develop a spiritual and cultural infrastructure of profound complexity. Mythologies, cosmologies, arts, law and ceremony that fused them as one with the land on which they lived. Those who came after the castaways hurled upon their shores could not know of this cultural infrastructure and its meanings. They could only see through European eyes what looked to be a shockingly sparse way of life. Alternatively, they saw a community of noble savages living in harmony with their land and free from the constraints that bound Europeans. This latter view was closer to the actuality, yet it was to be as destructive as the ignorance and prejudice of many newcomers. Both extremes denied the first Australians their rightful status as human beings.

The inability and unwillingness of Europeans to see how Aboriginal people husbanded the land has been powerfully demonstrated by historian Bill Gammage. Eons before the first Europeans arrived, the indigenous Australians had developed an efficient and effective management system of a continent-wide system of ecological management.[13] Intimately connected to these practicalities of firestick farming, fishing, finding water, hunting and gathering and the mythology and cosmology through which Aboriginal people preserved and passed on the secrets of survival—the Law and what Europeans called the Dreaming, having no other word to describe the concepts that were utterly alien to them. To Aboriginal people, though, all these things were simply self-evident and they were astonished, sad and sometimes angry at the failure of the Europeans to see and appreciate these things, let alone to understand what the ways of the newcomers were doing to them.

Many still are. In his exhaustively evidenced book, Gammage provides example upon example of Europeans looking but not seeing, of explorers and settlers simply imposing themselves on the land with no conception of how to manage it—and usually no interest in doing so outside the precepts and practices of northern hemisphere agriculture. Yet more instances could be given. How

could Europeans understand this, let alone become part of it—
even if they wished to?

Perhaps some of the forlorn souls who made it off their splintered
ships, across the reefs and rock platforms and onto the clifftops did
enter into this way of believing, seeing and living. Perhaps they
became Aboriginal. This, after all, is the implicit meaning in the
intermingling of white and black and, more metaphorically but
no less powerfully, in the long centuries of ignorance, speculation
and prejudice that made Australia what it was to be so long before
any European footfall. Here, the myth of lost white tribes reflects
xenophobia and that other deep fear once known as 'miscegena-
tion', the dreaded cross-breeding of black and white that features
so heavily in our pioneer experience, literature and folklore. The
Dutch descendants 'Lieutenant Nixon' allegedly met in central
Australia preserved their 'racial' purity by not intermarrying
with Aborigines.

Myths are potent receptacles of the often-unexpressed fears and
hopes of those who hold them. They are hard to change, no matter
what factual evidence is shown to undermine them. But they can
also be powerful in other ways. The stories of 'white Aborigines' are
almost certainly true, but they also draw on legend and speculations about cave drawings of sailing ships, stone circles, mysterious
carved heads and Phoenician voyages down under. These intersect
with history through the detritus of European mercantile exploration being literally washed up on these shores. History and myth
draw upon each other to inhabit complex cultural spaces where
stories are made, told and retold orally, in print and now most
potently on the great amplifier of delusion known as the World
Wide Web.

In the end, despite a mass of anecdotal, artefactual and genetic
evidence, the pre-1788 European settlement of Australia may
remain a legend. But it is a powerful and persistent one that reflects
the need for a richer mythology and history. Whatever might finally

be discovered—or rediscovered—about the truth of Australia's European occupation, one thing is inescapable: it is a communal story. With all its appalling realities of violence, dispossession and cultural desecration, the history and legends of the Southland are shared by indigenous people and those who came after. Nothing can change that past.

But perhaps we can shape the future. Bernard O'Dowd's line from 1900 describing the continent as the 'Last sea-thing dredged by sailor Time from Space' poses questions about the kind of place Australia would be once it came into formal existence at Federation in 1901. In the same poem, O'Dowd wondered whether the country would be just another place of greed or whether it would be a heaven on earth—a 'millennial Eden.'

AFTERWORD
With the bones

Inside the dimly lit shipwreck galleries of Fremantle's Maritime Museum lies the skeleton of one of Australia's first European settlers. It cramps in a shallow stone casket hewn from the rock shelf where the young man was hastily buried. His bones are bleached but also damaged, hacked with savage blows from the weapons of the castaways who killed him.

Looming over the remains is another set of bones. These are the splintered timbers of the ship that carried the young man and his murderers across the globe, casting them onto the jagged reefs of the great Southland. These skeletons of bone and wood—the hulking ship and her small sailor—are time's survivors. Dredged from the sea and its stone islands, these remains of incomprehensible violence are now officially 'artefacts'. They rest within a public museum and are legally protected by lawful acts of government. This gives them historical value that they did not have in the obscure past they inhabited. It was not until they were excavated from their next-to-last resting places by the finders and keepers of archaeological records and registers that they attained their value as *memento mori*. Now their remains can be preserved, interpreted and displayed for those who enter the purpose-built sepulchre that signifies the worth we accord them in the present. They are officially as well as technologically protected from further harm.

They need to be. The forces and interests that have turned a lost boy's bones and the *Batavia*'s once mighty timbers into artefacts have also imparted great monetary value. Their mortal remains, what they wore or carried, the spikes and pegs that held their floating world together and, of course, the treasure she carried, are prized by the unofficial plunderers of the past, the looters of lost lives and shattered ships. The demand for sunken relics from the history zoos and galleries of the world is insatiable, fuelling a fierce and almost invulnerable economy of illegal booty hunting and murky global transactions. The irony is that the thousands who sailed here in hundreds of vessels were also raiders as well as traders in skin and bone. Now we revere and commemorate them while we revile those who steal their remains.

Those who came to the unknown shores of the Southland, along with the great sailing craft that bore them, are now here forever. Australia is their home as well as their grave. Their remains and residues will continue to be sought by looters as well as by archaeologists, historians and other researchers. Our need to know about these ghosts and their stories is powerful and deep. Whether we call this 'heritage', 'history' or 'tradition', it is a compact we desire with those who have lived and died before us. The eighteenth-century French philosopher, Voltaire, famously said that history is only a pack of tricks we play upon the dead.[14] Less frequently quoted is the rest of his observation—if some useful end is served, it does the dead no harm as, in any case, they have tricks of their own.

Acknowledgements

I would like to acknowledge those who contributed in one way or another to the research and writing of this book, including Maureen Seal, Kylie Seal-Pollard, Rob Willis, Olya Willis, Nonja Peters, the late Rupert Gerritsen, Jack Goldblatt, John Mallard, John Longley and the dedicated keepers of the Sandwich Archives.

The Savage Shore is dedicated to the memories of my father, Des and my uncle, Jim—sailors both.

NOTES

1 Imagining the unknown Southland

1 Haveric, 2006.

2 Pugach, et al, 2013. See also Cavalli-Sforza, 2000.

3 Gilroy, 2008.

4 Khalaf, 2003.

5 Named after the VOC ship of the same name that visited in 1636.

6 Led by Dr Ian McIntosh, Indiana University–Purdue University Indiana-polis (IUPUI), 2013. See also La Canna, 2014: In August 2014 a Chinese coin was discovered on Elcho Island, dated between 1736 and 1795, leading to suggestions that the Chinese may have visited Australia for the trepang trade during the eighteenth century.

7 Major, 1859.

8 Major, 1859.

9 *Menzies, 2002.*

10 Finlay, 2004, p. 241ff.

11 Japan also has a contender in the form of Yamada Nagamasa, a pirate lord said to have visited Cape York Peninsula some time between 1628 and 1633. The Japanese were said to have referred to the unknown continent as the 'Coral Land of the South' (Goddard, 1933).

12 Tacon, et al, 2010.

13 Macknight, 1976. The ABC TV series *First Footprints*, broadcast in 2013, featured investigations and Aboriginal oral traditions about these extensive pre-1788 contacts.

14 Isaacs, 2005.

15 Ganter, 2013.

16 Wytfliet, 1598: '"Australia terra" is 'separated from New Guinea by a narrow strait', suggesting clear knowledge of the Torres Straits, not officially discovered until eight years later.

17 Jennings, 2013, confirms that de Gonneville's voyage is not mentioned before Paulmier made his claims.

18 Estensen, 1998, estimates no less than 25 books published on de Quiros' voyages 'in Spanish, Latin, French, English, Dutch and German.' (p. 108)

19 Apparently a mistranslation of Marco Polo's 'Lochac.'

20 On the Spanish voyages see Estensen, 2006. On claims for Spanish relics see Gilroy, 1985.

21 See Trickett, 2007, a recent addition to this approach, depending upon the discovery of a previously unknown map in the USA. See also McIntyre, 1977. There is a useful overview of the debate on the Portuguese discovery theory and the Dieppe maps at <http://en.wikipedia.org/wiki/Dieppe_maps>

22 Jefferys, n.d.

23 Poole, 2013.

24 There is also said to be a Spanish wreck at Long Island in the Whitsunday Passage, complete with Aboriginal traditions and a lost treasure legend, see http://www.stradbrokeislandgalleon.com/longislandwreck.html

25 Technically the United East India Company, or Verenigde Oost-indische Compagnie, from which the commonly used initials VOC are derived.

26 Originally known as the 'Assembly of the Seventeen.'

2 First encounters

1 There is some debate about whether Jansz actually landed on the Southland, though it is very likely that he did.

2 From the diary of Captain John Saris, 18 November 1605, quoted in Mutch, 1942.

3 Geoff Wharton, 'The Pennefather River: Place of Australian National Heritage', in Royal Geographical Society of Queensland Inc., 2005, p. 35. See also Henderson, 1998.

4 Heeres, 1899, p. 43.

5 It has been suggested that *Duyfken* made a second voyage to Australia. If so, it would have been in 1607. After further battles the following year, this time against the Spanish, the battered *Duyfken* was abandoned at Ternate (in the eastern Indonesian island group known as the Moluccas). A replica of *Duyfken* was launched in Fremantle in 2000 and the momentous voyage of Jansz and his men was reenacted.

6 Another version says the Aborigines took it for a large pelican, Henderson 1998, p. 158.

7 Henderson, 1998, p. 143ff; Peter Sutton, 'Stories About Feeling: Dutch-Australian Contact in Cape York Peninsula, 1606-1756', in Veth, 2008, p. 35ff.

8 This is from a number of versions of the story collected by Henderson from the Yunkaporta family and also, from a much older informant, Jack Spear Karntin, by Peter Sutton in 1976. See Hercus & Sutton, 1986. See also Miller, 2014, pp. 169–184 for further discussion of Wik oral traditions.

9 Though as early as 1597 it was known to some navigators that what we now call Papua New Guinea, was not part of the Southland. Wytfliet, 1598: 'The Australis Terra is the most southern of all lands. It is separated from New Guinea by a narrow strait. Its shores are hitherto but little known, since, after one voyage and another, that route has been deserted, and seldom is the country visited, unless when sailors are driven there by storms. The Australis Terra begins at two or three degrees from the equator, and is maintained by some to be of so great an extent that, if it were thoroughly explored, it would be regarded as a fifth part of the world.' But this fact was not known to Dutch navigators and it seems that the information came from Portuguese or even Spanish voyages to this region, possibly before 1530.

10 It has also been argued that the geographer and astronomer Petrus Plancius (1552–1622) was the first to suggest this route as a theoretical possibility.

11 The journal of *Mauritius* has been lost, fortunately Jansz's letter survived.

12 This was thought to be Exmouth Gulf, according to Mutch, 1942. Though after considerable surveying along the western coast, Henderson, 1998, p. 192, concluded that Yardie Creek on North West Cape was where Jansz went ashore in 1618.

13 It is not clear whether he went ashore or not.

14 All Brookes' quotations from Original Correspondence in Green, 1977.

15 Evidence of Thomas Bright, the *Tryall's* factor, in Green, 1977, p. 21.

16 See Green, 1977, referring to the work of Lee, 1934.

17 It is possible that one or more of those left on the wreck subsequently made it to the mainland, though there is no evidence that they did.

18 Major, 1859.

19 Quoted in Sankey, Margaret 'The Abbé Paulmier's *Mémoires* and Early French Voyages in Search of *Terra Australis*' in West-Sooby, 2013, p. 49. De Voutron is also referred to as Nicolas Gédéon de Voutron.

20 This term seems to have been first used by Wieder, 1942, p. 100. See also Slot, 1992, p. 93; Schilder, 1976, pp. 144–7, 149. Its use is here extended to

refer to the broad body of covert mercantile cartography based on charts, journals and now mostly irrecoverable word-of-mouth information.

21 A very rare copy of this chart, made by Willem Lodewijcksz, a clerk aboard one of de Houtman's ships, is held by the State Library of New South Wales.

22 Deinema, 2003.

3 'More like monsters'

1 In 1636, the VOC—at least officially—amended its policy to mention only willing natives were to be granted passage. See Ketelaar, n.d.

2 A man with overall command of a number of VOC ships was usually known as the 'Commandeur'.

3 Referred to in one translation as a 'slave'.

4 VOC jagts were smaller, faster craft with correspondingly small crews, sometimes said to be as few as 13. It seems that Pera and Aernem may have had substantially more aboard than this as their numbers lost would have rendered the survivors too few to sail the ships. If so, there would have been severe overcrowding, making life aboard especially uncomfortable, even in these more Spartan times.

5 Amboina was a Dutch possession from 1605 (taken from Portugal) and was VOC headquarters in the region from 1610–19, after which Batavia was established.

6 The journal of Jan Carstensz is in Heeres, 1899, p. 13. All page references refer to this volume.

7 Carstensz in Heeres, 1899, pp. 20–1.

8 At this point, it seems that they had not actually landed on the shore, despite Carstensz providing a description of the inhabitants and their weapons, including bows and arrows. While it is usually held that Australian Aborigines did not use the bow and arrow, this weapon was in use among Torres Strait Islanders and Aborigines around Cape York and possibly elsewhere along the northern coast where there had often been prolonged contact with New Guinea. Similarly with regard to body decoration, Aborigines and Torres Strait Islanders in the north did practise nasal septum piercing and wearing of animal bones and teeth, as often reported among New Guinean native inhabitants. On these points see McCarthy, 1953 and Soriano & Medina, 2009.

9 Carstensz in Heeres, 1899, pp. 27–9.

10 Possibly the board was made and inscribed on 24 April and not erected until later.

11 This river is thought to be either the modern Pennefather or Batavia rivers.

12 The journal entries (Carstensz in Heeres, 49) do not suggest *Leiden* landed anyone.

13 See Sutton in Veth, et al, 2008.

14 Konishi, 2013, p. 105.

4 Blood islands

1 Numbers estimated to be aboard *Batavia* at the time of the wreck vary.

2 Unless otherwise stated, all quotations from Pelsaert's journal are from Van Huystee, 1994.

3 Van Huystee, 1994.

4 Dash, 2002.

5 Van Huystee, 1994.

6 Cornelis Jansz, quoted in Dash, 2002, p. 252, see also pp. 400–1.

7 Dash, 2002, pp. 277–8.

8 Leys, 2010, and most recently FitzSimons, 2011.

9 Max and Graeme Cramer with Dave Johnson.

10 The original is in the Geraldton branch of the museum.

11 Western Australian Maritime Museum, n.d. In early 2015 archaeologists conducted further excavations, revealing another grave, the eleventh so far discovered.

5 Paper voyages

1 Not the island originally discovered by Tasman, but an early Dutch name for an area on the western side of the Arnhem Land Peninsula, after Maria van Diemen.

2 'Voyage of Gerrit Thomas Pool to the Southland', translated from Valentyn's 'Beschryvinge van Banda', in Major, 1859.

3 It is usually estimated that the mortality rates among those who ventured to the Indies and other tropical areas with the VOC were around 1 in 3.

4 Reynders, n.d.

5 For further details of the structure of the VOC, see Gaastra, n.d.

6 C J Zandvliet in Gaastra, n.d.

7 Possibly of the Vissher family of Amsterdam mapmakers.

8 Although the journal of Tasman's first voyage has been lost, two summaries have survived in other sources known as 'The Huijdecoper Journal' and the 'Sweers Journal.' Quotations are from these sources. There is no journal of Tasman's second voyage extant.

9 Major, 1859, p. 96.

10 Tasman's sailing orders in Burney, 1813.

11 Trustees of the Public Library of New South Wales, 1948. Though the Library's website gives the day as 1931 (March 2015).

12 National Library of Australia, 2007, pp. 30–1.

6 Death of the dragon

1 Also described as a 'pinnace', suggesting a smaller ship than she was.

2 See Major, 1859, for a translation of the relevant original documents.

3 It has been suggested that Leeman was aboard the *Vergulde Draeck* when she hit and that he was one of those who escaped in the ship's boat. There is some faint support for this in an account from 1705 included in Major, 1859, p. 94, the relevant section being: 'I am informed by a mate who about thirty or thirty-four years ago, lost his ship on the most westerly promontory of the south land, that he with some of the crew reached Batavia in the ship's boat, and was dispatched from thence to the place where he was shipwrecked with provisions and in order to deliver their shipmates they left these; but they found none of then though they saw impressions of large footsteps.' In the absence of supporting documentary evidence, the intriguing possibility that a man was twice wrecked on the unknown southland and twice escaped must remain speculation. Leeman is generally said to have been from the English sea town of Sandwich, though it has also been suggested that he came from a Dutch town called Sandwick.

4 Durrani Cooper, 1862, p. 15 and Vogel, 2000.

5 Henderson, 1982.

6 Green, 1973; Green, 1977; Green, 1983.

7 Gerritsen, 1994/2002.

8 Gerritsen, 2011.

9 Gerritsen, 2010.

7 Cliffs of fire

1 Unless otherwise stated, the quotations are from Dampier's published works. Any from his original journals are from Mitchell, 2010.

2 The indigenous people of South Africa were disparagingly referred to as 'Hottentots' by the early European settlers—this is Dampier's rendering of that term. The Monomotapa Empire was the Portuguese term for a Shona kingdom that existed from the fifteenth to the eighteenth centuries in what is now Zimbabwe and southern Zambia.

3 Van Den Boogaerde, 2011, pp. 75–6. It is possible that the ship was wrecked in the Houtman Abrolhos and that her wreckage was found on Pelsaert Island by the *Zeewijk* castaways.

4 This may have been from the *Vergulde Draeck* or from another wreck.

5 Not known to have been recovered or discovered.

6 'Some particulars relating to the voyage of Willem de Vlamingh to New Holland in 1696,' extracted from MS. Documents at The Hague and translated from the Dutch, in Major, 1859, p. 107ff.

7 For a brief overview see Aitken, 1897, p. 224ff.

8 The details of the little-known van Delft voyage are contained in a report from Batavia to the Seventeen Gentlemen, in Major, 1859, p. 165ff.

8 The ship of doom

1 Estimates of this number vary, but the VOC administrator at the Cape, Willem Helot, wrote on 30 March 1713 that 200 crew left the Cape aboard the *Zuytdorp* '. . . 86 eaters fewer than the number with which they put to sea.' There may also have been an unknown number of passengers. See Playford, 1996, p. 65.

2 Not an uncommon event. See Emmer, 2006, pp. 38–9.

3 Only the listing of the military men aboard the *Zuytdorp* has survived; the sailors' list is lost.

4 Gibbs, 2003.

5 Oldfield, 1865, pp. 234–5.

6 For an excellent overview of this evidence, see Gerritsen, n.d. See also Gerritsen, 1994/2002.

7 For an authoritative account see Playford, 1996, p. 82ff.

8 Playford, 1996, p. 179.

9 The full story—from various points of view—is told in a number of books as well as Playford's, including Robinson, 1980, and Henderson, 1980.

10 McDowell, 2012. See also Playford, 1996.

11 In 2015 an expedition was mounted to search for the *Fortuyn* off Christmas Island. The group also searched for another missing VOC ship, *Aagtekerke*, off the Cocos Islands.

12 Pownall, 2012.

13 See Amalfi, 2012.

14 Gregory, 1861, p. 482.

15 Wamaritimemyths.wordpress.com, 2007, referencing Busselton Historical Society, December 1979.

16 Gerritsen, 2010a.

17 Van Den Boogaerde, 2011, p. 75.

9 Skeleton coasts

1 A skin disease known as 'St Anthony's Fire' and, in extreme cases, potentially fatal. It can be contracted by eating bread infected with ergot, quite possible in a shipwreck situation. Consuming such bread may also induce hallucinations of the kind usually associated with psychedelic drugs such as LSD. It was treated before modern times by folk medicine in the form of charms and sympathetic magic. Today it is treated with antibiotics.

2 A measure of liquid ranging from 36 to 42 gallons, depending on the city in which the measuring was carried out.

3 Major, 1859, p. 176ff.

4 De Heer, n.d.

5 Preston 1833, pp. 78–9.

6 Ingelman-Sundberg, 1976 and Ingelman-Sundberg, 1977.

10 Empires collide

1 See Jack, 1921–2.

2 These animals have been identified as dingoes by later commentators, although the animal sounds more like a Thylacine, a species thought to be extinct on mainland Australia for 2000 years. Perhaps the beasts were a late hybrid strain?

3 Sydney Parkinson, botanical draughtsman and one of the first European artists known to have drawn the landscape and its inhabitants. He died on the *Endeavour's* return journey.

4 All quotations from Wharton, 1893.

5 Gammage, 2011.

6 All quotations from Furneaux are from Furneaux, 1779.

7 John Henry Martin's journal, <www.captaincooksociety.com>, accessed January 2015.

8 David Samwell's journal, <www.captaincooksociety.com>, accessed January 2015.

9 *Historical Records of New South Wales:* pt. 1 Cook, 1762–1780 v.1, pt. 2. Phillip, 1783–1792, p. 519.

10 Moore, 1884, pp. 340–41. See also Cullity, 1992.

11 Péron, pp. 285–286.

12 Péron p. 449.

13 See Anderson, 2001.

11 The unknown coast

1 Often referred to as the Mineng, a sub-group of the Nyungar people. See Shellam, 2009, pp. 31–3.

2 Flinders, 1814.

3 In some sources the total lost is given as six, though that seems to refer only to the crew minus the officers, Thistle and the midshipman, William Taylor.

4 In relation to this incident, Flinders also narrated a strange portent and the extent of superstition among his sailors. 'This evening, Mr. Fowler told me a circumstance which I thought extraordinary; and it afterwards proved to be more so. Whilst we were lying at Spithead, Mr. Thistle was one day waiting on

shore, and having nothing else to do he went to a certain old man, named Pine, to have his fortune told. The cunning man informed him that he was going out a long voyage, and that the ship, on arriving at her destination, would be joined by another vessel. That such was intended, he might have learned privately; but he added, that Mr. Thistle would be lost before the other vessel joined. As to the manner of his loss the magician refused to give any information. My boat's crew, hearing what Mr. Thistle said, went also to consult the wise man; and after the prefatory information of a long voyage, were told that they would be shipwrecked, but not in the ship they were going out in: whether they would escape and return to England, he was not permitted to reveal. This tale Mr. Thistle had often told at the mess table; and I remarked with some pain in a future part of the voyage, that every time my boat's crew went to embark with me in the Lady Nelson, there was some degree of apprehension amongst them that the time of the predicted shipwreck was arrived. I make no comment upon this story, but recommend a commander, if possible, to prevent any of his crew from consulting fortune tellers.'

5 This plaque is now in the South Australian Maritime Museum.

6 Flinders' journal was published after Péron's account of the Baudin expedition, enabling him to make his observation in a footnote to his own publication.

7 Clarke, 2014.

8 Erskine, 1997, and Green, 2003, which includes translations of the Captain's journals.

9 De Freycinet, 1825, p. 449.

10 Rivière, 1996, pp. 51–2.

11 Bloomfield, 2012, p. 155, referencing Rosenman, 1988, pp. xxx–xxxi.

12 *Perth Gazette and Western Australian Journal*, October 3, 1835, p. 575 (cumulative). See also *The West Australian*, August 3, 1929, p. 5. Research by Bob Warneke suggests Anderson did not arrive aboard the Vigilant, personal communication October 26 2015.

13 Hay, 2003. See also Hay, 2002.

14 *The Perth Gazette and Western Australian Journal* 3 October 1835, p. 575 for details of Black Jack's mode of operations.

15 Watson, 1923.

12 The last legend

1 Usually said to be the Palm Valley in the Finke Gorge, an area of remnant rainforest and difficult to access without a 4WD vehicle.

2 Cook, 2008 pp. 11–20.

3 Cook, 1999.

4 Gaastra, 1997.

5 It has also been suggested that Stirling fabricated the original letter and arranged for its publication in several places as an attempt to bolster flagging official support for his colony. See *Leeds Mercury*, 2014.

6 Howitt, 1902.

7 Modern expeditions to the area were carried out in 1990 (reported in *Australian Geographic* vol. 21 January-March 1991, pp. 39–40). More recently investigations by Les Hiddins have been inconclusive.

8 Grey, 1841.

9 This account does not actually appear in Gregory's published journal of his 1848 expedition, but does appear in an 1884 edition. We might wonder why he waited 36 years to mention this rather remarkable discovery, especially as he was unusually forthcoming about being offered sexual favours by Aboriginal women, a greeting custom of the time and place, and careful to indicate that these were not accepted.

10 *Perth Gazette* 8 August 1861, p. 2.

11 Hiddins, n.d. It seems more likely that it was his son, Maitland Howard Brown, who made this claim. In any case, no further information seems to be available.

12 Uren, 1940, pp. 233–4.

13 Usually as Inggarda, see South Australian Museum Archives, 2011.

14 Bates, 1938 p. 107. Bates began her long association with Aboriginal people in Western Australia from 1899.

15 Van Zanden, 2012.

16 The history and mythology of the 'lost colony' of Roanoke in Virginia is one well-developed example of similar traditions on a New World frontier. See The Lost Colony Centre for Science and Research, n.d. for connections to the extensive popular and academic research interest in Roanoke. Recent archaeological research has unearthed more clues, but still no solid conclusions, see Lawson, 1709, Milton, 2000 and Basu, 2013.

17 *Perth Gazette* 5 July 1834.

18 *Perth Gazette* 26 July 1834, p. 326.

19 John Mallard quoted in Peters, 2011. See also recordings of Nunda people made for the Western Australian Folklife Project, 2009, National Library of Australia and Jackson & de Gand, 1996.

20 Rossi et al, 2012.

21 Goldblatt et al, 1992.

22 Staker, 2013 (2014). See also Yoder, 1983, p. 2 and Hartzler, 1984. EvC is not found in other Amish groups.

23 A collective term for the various groups who peopled south-western Australia for many thousands of years before European settlement.

24 Peters, 2011.

25 Dale remained on leave in England and left the army in 1835. He became a timber merchant in Liverpool with a particular interest in the commercial prospects for West Australian jarrah, or 'mahogany' as it was known at that time. He never returned to Australia and died of tuberculosis at Bath, England in 1853. Some of his paintings of Western Australia have survived as valuable visual documents of colonialism.

26 Turnbull, 1998.

13 Surviving the Southland

1 See Mahony, 2014, although there may have been another group in 1986: see Sandford, 2010.

2 For an indication of the complexities involved in these interactions, on both sides, see Shino Konishi, 2013, and, in more detail, Konishi, 2012. See also Russell, 2012.

3 Daley, 2014, has written on this situation as it relates especially to Australian museums.

4 MacGregor, 2011, pp. 90–4.

5 See Warden, 2008, p. 213. The tradition was documented in 1833.

6 Childs, 2010.

7 No evidence for the species of the post exists, other than a statement by one of Parker King's officers, Cunningham, that it was oak. While this is a supposition, it is a reasonable one.

8 Phillip Parker King's diary aboard *Bathurst*, 21 January 1822. Despite archaeological searching, Hamelin's plate is still missing.

9 Shellam, 2009; Mulvaney & Green, 1992.

10 McCalman, 2013 includes several accounts of castaway European males living with indigenous groups in northern Queensland, marrying and fathering children. There were certainly other instances, including the well-known experience of William Buckley in Victoria. Female European castaways also lived with indigenous groups for lengthy periods. We know about these events because they came after 1788 and were documented, unlike much of what had passed previously.

11 Such as the old remnants of a 400-ton ship discovered by the survivors of the *Porpoise*, stranded on Wreck Island in 1803, see Australian Maritime Museum, 2009.

12 Smith, 1985.

13 Gammage, 2011.

14 'Tricks' is sometimes translated as 'lies.'

BIBLIOGRAPHY

Amalfi, Carmello, 2012, 'Finding WA's Lost Dutchmen', on the work of shipwreck hunter Hugh Edwards, Amalfi Publishing, <www.amalfipublishing.com.au/wp/2012/02/23/finding-was-lost-dutchmen> accessed August 2013.

Anderson, Stephanie, 2001, 'French Anthropology in Australia, the First Fieldwork Report: François Péron's 'Maria Island Anthropological Observations', *Aboriginal History*, vol. 25, pp. 228–4.

Arthur, Paul Longley, 2011, *Virtual Voyages: Travel Writing and the Antipodes 1605–1837*, Anthem Press, London.

Atherton Aitken, George, 1897, 'Alexander Selkirk' in Lee, Sidney (ed.), *Dictionary of National Biography, 1885–1900*, vol. 51, Smith Elder & Co., London.

Australian Maritime Museum, 2009, 'Wreck Reefs expedition: History of the area, <http://anmm.wordpress.com/2009/12/04/wreck-reefs-expedition-history-of-the-area>

Backhouse, Marcel, 1995, *The Flemish and Walloon communities at Sandwich during the reign of Elizabeth I (1561–1603)*, Royal Academies for Science and the Arts of Belgium, Brussels.

Basu, Tanya, 2013, 'Have We Found the Lost Colony of Roanoke Island?', *National Geographic*, 6 December <http://news.nationalgeographic.com.au/news/2013/12/131208-roanoke-lost-colony-discovery-history-raleigh> accessed January 2015.

BIBLIOGRAPHY

Bates, Daisy, 1938, *The Passing of the Aborigines*, John Murray, London.

Bloomfield, Noeline, 2012, *Almost a French Australia: French–British Rivalry in the Southern Oceans*, Halstead Press, Canberra.

Bowdler, Sandra, 1991, *In search of the Zuytdorp survivors: report on an archaeological reconnaissance of a site in the Shark Bay area, 1990*, preliminary report, Department of Archaeology, University of Western Australia, Perth.

Brown, Anthony, J., 2001, *Ill-Starred Captains: Flinders and Baudin*, Chatham, London.

Burney, James, 1813, *A chronological history of the voyages and discoveries in the South Sea or Pacific Ocean from the year 1620 to the year 1688*, Cambridge University Press, London.

Cavalli-Sforza, Luigi Luca, 2000, 'Genes, Peoples, and Languages', *Proceedings of the National Academy of Sciences of the United States of America*, vol. 94, no. 15.

Childs, Craig, 2010, *Finders Keepers: A Tale of Archaeological Plunder and Obsession*, Little, Brown & Co, New York.

Clarke, Philip & Clarke, Jacqueline, 2014, 'Putting "Australia" on the Map, *The Conversation*, 10 August, <http://tinyurl.com/llr4jga> accessed January 2014.

Clode, Danielle, 2007, *Voyages to the South Seas: In Search of Terres Australes*, Miegunyah Press, Melbourne.

Cook, Karen, S., 1999, 'A paper trail of discovery and deception: The report of the 1832 expedition that found a lost Dutch colony in central Australia', paper presented to Society for the History of Discoveries, Forty-First Annual Meeting, Washington, D.C.

——2008, 'Thomas John Maslen and "The Great River of Blessed Desire" on His Map of Australia', *The Globe*, vol. 61.

Cullity, Thomas Brendan, 1992, *Vasse: An account of the disappearance of Thomas Timothée Vasse*, T.B. Cullity, Perth.

Daley, Paul, 2014, 'Restless Indigenous Remains', *Meanjin*, August 2014, <http://meanjin.com.au/articles/post/restless-indigenous-remains>

Dash, Mike, 2002, *Batavia's Graveyard*, Weidenfeld & Nicolson, London.

De Freycinet, 1825, *Voyage Historique*, vol. 1, Chez Pillet Ane, Paris.

Deinema, Michaël, 2003, 'A maritime society: Friendship, animosity and group-formation on the ships of the Dutch East-India Company', unpublished student paper, University of Amsterdam, Amsterdam.

Donaldson, Ian & Donaldson, Tamsin (eds), 1985, *Seeing the First Australians*, George Allen & Unwin, Sydney.

Drake-Brockman, Henrietta, 1963, *Voyage to Disaster*, Angus and Robertson, Sydney.

Durrani Cooper, W.M. (ed), 1862, *Lists of foreign protestants, and aliens, resident in England 1618–1688. From returns in the state paper office*, The Camden Society, Westminster.

Duyker, Edward, 2006, *François Péron: An Impetuous Life*, Miegunyah Press, Melbourne.

Eisler, William, 1995, *The Furthest Shore: Images of Terra Australis from the Middle Ages to Captain Cook*, Cambridge University Press, Cambridge.

Emmer, Pieter (Chris Emery, trans.), 2006, *The Dutch Slave Trade 1500–1850*, Berghahn, New York and Oxford.

Erskine, N., 1997, 'Testing the waters: Some navigation problems of long distance voyages with particular reference to the wreck of the Portuguese ship *Correio da Azia* on the Western Australian coast, 26 November 1816', paper from the Australian Institute for Maritime Archaeology 17th International Conference, 5–13 September, Fremantle.

Estensen, Miriam, 1998, *Discovery: The Quest for the Great South Land*, Allen & Unwin, Sydney.

——2006, *Terra Australis Incognita: The Spanish Quest for the Mysterious South Land*, Allen & Unwin, Sydney.

ExLibris, n.d., *English Dissenters: Anabaptists* <www.exlibris.org/nonconform/engdis/anabaptists.html>

Finlay, Robert, 2004, 'How Not to (Re)Write World History: Gavin Menzies and the Chinese Discovery of America', *Journal of World History*, vol. 15, no. 2.

FitzSimons, Peter, 2011, *Batavia*, Random House, North Sydney.

Flecker, Michael, 2005, 'Unreported shipwrecks in Indonesia', *Nautical Archaeology* (newsletter of the Nautical Archaeology Society UK) vol. 4, pp. 6–7.

Flinders, Matthew, 1814, *A Voyage to Terra Australis,* vol. 1, G & W Nicol, London.

Forrest, Peter, 1995, *The Tiwi Meet the Dutch: The First European Contacts. An outline of the history of Tiwi Contact with European navigators, with special reference to the Tiwi encounter with Dutch seafarers in 1705*, The Tiwi Land Council, Winnellie, NT.

Franklin, D. & Freedman, L., 2006, 'An archaeological investigation of a multiple burial associated with the *Batavia* mutiny of 1629', *Records of the Western Australian Museum*, vol. 23, pp. 77–90.

Furneaux, Captain Tobias, 1779, *Captain Furneaux's Narrative, with some Account of Van Diemen's Land*, printed for W. Strahan and T. Cadell, London, available online at Project Gutenburg Australia <http://gutenberg.net.au/ebooks13/1306441h.html> accessed January 2015.

Gaastra, Femme, 1997, 'The Dutch East India Company: A Reluctant Discoverer', *The Great Circle*, vol. 19.

Gaastra, F.S., n.d., 'VOC Organization', TANAP (Towards A New Age of Partnership), an archive project covering the Dutch East India Company, The Netherlands, <www.tanap.net/content/voc/organization/organization_intro.htm> accessed July 2013.

Gammage, Bill, 2011, *The Biggest Estate on Earth: How Aborigines made Australia*, Allen & Unwin, Sydney.

Ganter, Regina, 2013, 'Histories with traction: Macassan contact in the framework of Muslim Australian history' in Marshall Clark and Sally K. May (eds), *Macassan History and Heritage: Journeys, encounters and influences*, Australian National University Press, Canberra.

Gerritsen, Rupert, 1994/2002, *And Their Ghosts May Be Heard*, Fremantle Arts Centre Press/Fremantle Press, South Fremantle.

——2006, 'The evidence for cohabitation between Indigenous Australians and marooned Dutch mariners and VOC passengers', in Nonja Peters (coordinating author) *The Dutch Down Under: 1606–2006*, pp. 38–55, Wolters Kluwer, Sydney.

——2010a, 'Geomorphology and the Deadwater Wreck', a modified form of a presentation given at the Eastern Australian Region of the Australasian Hydrographic Society Annual Symposium, 13 September, Sydney. <http://rupertgerritsen.tripod.com/pdf/unpublished/Geomorphology_and_the_Deadwater_Wreck.pdf>

——2010b, 'Marooned Mariners and Mudmaps: The Search for the Ring of Stones', *The Globe*, vol. 64, pp. 17–26.

——2011, *Selected Transcriptions, Translations, and Collation of Information for a Textual Analysis Relating to Material Evidence from the Vergulde Draeck and the 68 Missing Crew and Passengers from that Vessel, Reportedly Found on the Coast of Western Australia in the Period 1656–1658*, Batavia Online Publishing, Canberra.

——n.d., 'They Will offer all friendship: The evidence for cohabitation between indigenous Australians and marooned Dutch mariners and VOC passengers', <http://rupertgerritsen.tripod.com/pdf/published/Evidence_ of_Cohabitation_-_Book_Chapter.pdf> accessed January 2015.

Gibbs, Martin, 2003, 'The Archaeology of Crisis: Shipwreck Survivor Camps in Australasia', *Historical Archaeology* 2003, vol. 37, no. 1, pp. 128–45.

Gilroy, Rex, 1985, 'Carving Out A New History', *Australasian Post*, 19 December.

Gilroy, Rex & Gilroy, Heather, 2008, Uru: The lost civilisation of Australia, <www.rexgilroy.com>

Godard, Philippe & de Kerros, Tugdual, 2008, *1772: The French Annexation of New Holland: The tale of Louis De Saint Aloüarn.* (Odette Margot, Myra Stanbury and Sue Baxter, trans.), Western Australian Museum, Perth.

Goddard, W.G., 1933, 'First Pirate to Visit Australia', The Courier-Mail (Brisbane), November, p. 18.

Goldblatt, J.C., Minutillo, P.J. & Hurst, J., 1992, 'Ellis-van Creveld syndrome in a Western Australian Aboriginal community, Postaxial polydactyly as heterogenous manifestation', *Medical Journal of Australia*, vol. 157, pp. 271–2.

Green, Jeremy, N., n.d., 'Australia's Oldest Wreck: The historical background and archaeological analysis of the wreck of the English East India Company's ship Trial, lost off the coast of Western Australia in 1622', typescript, Western Australian Museum, Perth.

——1973, 'The wreck of the Dutch East Indiaman the Vergulde Draeck, 1656', *International Journal of Nautical Archaeology*, vol. 2, no. 2, pp. 267–89.

——1977, *The AVOC Jacht Vergulde Draeck wrecked off Western Australia 1656*, British Archaeological Reports, Supplementary Series 36, Oxford.

——1977, *Australia's Oldest Wreck: The Loss of the Trial, 1622*, British Archaeological Reports, Supplementary Series 27.

——1983, 'The Vergulde Draeck excavation 1981 & 1983', *Bulletin of the Australian Institute for Maritime Archaeology,* vol. 7, no. 2, pp. 1–8.

——2003, 'The search for the *Correio da Azia*', Department of Maritime Archaeology, Western Australian Maritime Museum, no. 179.

Gregory, F.T., 1861, 'On the Geology of a Part of Western Australia', *Quarterly Journal of the Geological Society of London*, vol. 17, pp. 475–83.

Grey, George, 1841, *Journals of Two Expeditions of Discovery in North-West and Western Australia, During the Years 1837, 1838 and 1839,* (2 vols), T and W Boone, London.

Hartzler, Harold, H., 1984, *King Family History*, H.H. Hartzler, Mankato, MN.

Haveric, Dzavid, 2006, *Australia in Muslim Discovery: Historical rediscovering of Australia by non-Muslims and Muslims*, Dzavid Haveric, Whittington, Vic.

Hay, Sarah, 2003, 'Adventures on Middle Island', *Net Work News*, Autumn 2003, pp. 22ff. (Rural, Regional and Remote Women's Network).

——2002, *Skins*, Allen & Unwin, Sydney.

De Heer, C., n.d., 'The wreck of the East Indiaman Zeewyk at the Abrolhos Islands in the year 1727', a translation of the ship's journal with a short introduction and notes, Western Australian Museum, <http://museum. wa.gov.au/maritimearchaeologydb/sites/default/files/no._282_translation_ de_graff_zeewijk_log_0.pdf>

Heeres, J.E., 1899, *The Part Borne by the Dutch in the Discovery of Australia 1606–1765,* Royal Dutch Geographical Society, London.

Henderson, Graeme, 1980, *Unfinished Voyages Vol. 1: Western Australian Shipwrecks 1622–1850.* University of Western Australia Press, Nedlands, WA.

Henderson, James A., 1993, *Phantoms of the* Tryall, St George Books, Perth.

——1998, *Sent Forth a Dove: Discovery of the* Duyfken, University of Western Australia Publishing, Nedlands, WA.

——1982, *Marooned: The wreck of the* Vergulde Draeck *and the abandonment and escape from the southland of Abraham Leeman in 1658*, St George Books, Perth.

Hercus, L.A. & Sutton, Peter (eds), c. 1986, *This is What Happened: Historical narratives by Aboriginals*, Australian Institute of Aboriginal Studies, Canberra.

Hiddins, Les, n.d., *The Dutch Colonisation of Australia*, Chapter 7, <www.ammerlaan.demon.nl/EARLY.HTM> accessed 17 June 2007 but since removed, see also <http://bushtuckerman.com.au/dutch-colony>

Howgego, Raymond John, 2003, *Encyclopedia of Exploration to 1800*, 4 volumes, Hordern House Rare Books, Potts Point, Sydney.

Howitt, Mary E.B. (comp.), 1902, 'Collectanea: Some Native Legends from Central Australia', *Folk-Lore*, vol. 13, no. 4 (December).

Indiana University–Purdue University Indianapolis (IUPUI), 2013, 'IUPUI led expedition seeks source of thousand-year-old coins in Aboriginal Australia' <http://newscenter.iupui.edu/5945/IUPUI-led-expedition-seeks-source-of-thousandyearold-coins-in-Aboriginal-Australia> accessed July 2013.

Ingelman-Sundberg, C., 1976, 'The V.O.C. Ship "Zeewijk", 1727 report on the 1976 survey of the site', *Australian Archaeology*, no. 5, pp. 18–33.

—— 1977, 'The V.O.C. ship Zeewijk lost off the Western Australian coast in 1727: An interim report on the first survey', *The International Journal of Nautical Archaeology*, vol. 6.

——1978, *Relics from the Dutch East Indiaman, Zeewijk, Foundered in 1727,* Western Australian Museum Special Publication No. 10.

——1978, 'The Dutch East Indiaman, Zeewijk, Wrecked in 1727: A report in the 1978 expedition to the site', unpublished paper, Western Australian Museum, Department of Maritime Archaeology.

Isaacs, Jennifer, 2005, *Australian Dreaming: 40,000 years of Aboriginal History,* New Holland Publishers, Sydney.

Jack, Robert Logan, 1921–2, *Northmost Australia: Three centuries of exploration, discovery, and adventure in and around the Cape York Peninsula, Queensland with a study of the narratives of all explorers by sea and land in the light of modern charting, many original or hitherto unpublished documents, thirty-nine illustrations, and sixteen specially prepared maps in two volumes,* George Robertson and Co., Sydney.

Jackson, Gavin & de Gand, Daniel, 1996, 'The Report of an Aboriginal Heritage Study of the Nanda Area Central, Kalbarri Region, Western Australia', prepared for the Nanda Aboriginal Corporation, Barrel Well Community, Anthropos Australia.

Jefferys, Greg, n.d., *The Stradbroke Island Galleon: The mystery of the ship in the swamp,* <www.stradbrokeislandgalleon.com> accessed August 2014.

Jennings, William, 2013, 'Gonneville's 'Terra Australis': Too good to be true?' *Australian Journal of French Studies,* vol. 50, no. 1, April, pp. 75–86.

Jones, Philip, 2007, *Ochre and Dust: Artefacts and Encounters on Australian Frontiers,* Wakefield Press, Kent Town, SA.

Ketelaar, Eric, n.d., 'Mapping for Societal memory: From Duyfken to digital', University of Amsterdam, <http://docs.exdat.com/docs/index-148029. html> accessed July 2013.

Khalaf, Salim George, 2003, Phoenicians in Australia? <www.phoenicia.org/ australia.html> accessed July 2013.

Konishi, Shino, *The Aboriginal Male in the Enlightenment World,* Pickering & Chatto, London, 2012.

——2013, 'Discovering the Savage Senses: French and British Explorers' Encounters with Aboriginal people' in John West-Sooby (ed), *Discovery and Empire: The French in the South Seas,* University of Adelaide Press, Adelaide, pp. 99–140.

La Canna, 2014, 'Old coin shows early Chinese contact with Aboriginal people in Elcho Island near Arnhem Land: expert', ABC Online, <www.abc.net.

au/news/2014-08-10/old-chinese-coin-found-in-arnhem-land/5660382> accessed August 2014.

Lawson, John, 1709, *A New Voyage to Carolina,* London.

Lee, Marriott, 1934, 'The First Sighting of Australia by the English', *Royal Australian Historical Society Journal and Proceedings* vol. 20, no. 5, pp. 273–280.

Leeds Mercury, 2014, 'Discovery of a White Colony on the Northern Shore of New Holland', transcription of article published in 1834, <www.wanowandthen.com/Leeds-Mercury-Article.html> accessed January 2015.

Leys, Simon, 2010, *The Wreck of the Batavia and Prosper,* Black Ink Books, Collingwood, Vic.

Lost Colony Centre for Science and Research, The, n.d. <http://www.lost-colony.com> accessed January 2015.

MacGregor, Neil, 2011, *A History of the World in 100 Objects,* Penguin, Ringwood, Vic.

Mahony, Alana, 2014, 'The day the Pintupi Nine entered the modern world', BBC News Magazine, 23 December <http://www.bbc.com/news/magazine-30500591> accessed January 2015.

Major, R.H. (ed.), 1859, *Early Voyages to Terra Australis, now called Australia: A Collection of Documents, and Extracts from Early Manuscript Maps, Illustrative of the History of Discovery on the Coasts of that vast island, from the beginning of the sixteenth century to the time of Captain Cook,* Hakluyt Society, London.

McCalman, Iain, 2013, *The Reef: A passionate history,* Viking, Sydney.

McCarthy, Frederick, D., 1953, 'The Oceanic and Indonesia [sic] Affiliations of Australian Aboriginal Culture', paper read at the Seventh Science Congress of the Royal Society of New Zealand, Christchurch, May 1951, Trustees of the Australian Museum, reproduced in *The Journal of the Polynesian Society,* vol. 62, no. 3, pp. 243–62, <www.jps.auckland.ac.nz/document/Volume_62_1953/Volume_62,_No._3/The_Oceanic_and_Indonesia_affiliations_of_Australian_Aboriginal_culture,_by_Frederick_D._McCarthy,_p_243-262/p1> accessed July 2013.

McDowell, Robin, 2012, 'Indonesia's Shipwrecks Mean Riches and Headaches', *Huffington Post* , 31 March, <www.huffingtonpost.com/2012/03/31/indonesias-shipwrecks-mea_n_1393473.html#s830149> accessed July 2013.

McHugh, Evan, 2006, *1606: An Epic Adventure,* Newsouth Publishing, Sydney.

McIntosh, Ian, S., 2013, 'Unbirri's pre-Macassan legacy, or how the Yolngu became black', in Clark, Marshall & and May, Sally K. (eds), 2013, *Macassan History and Heritage: Journeys, encounters and Influences,* Australian National University Press, Canberra.

McIntyre, K.G., 1977, *The Secret Discovery of Australia, Portuguese ventures 200 years before Cook,* Souvenir Press, Menindie, NSW.

Macknight, C., 1976, *The Voyage to Marege: Macassan Trepangers in Northern Australia,* Melbourne University Press, Melbourne.

Menzies, Gavin, 2002, *1421, The Year China Discovered the World,* Bantam Press, London.

Miller, Barbara, 2014, *The European Quest to Find Terra Australis Incognita: Quiros, Torres and Janszoon,* Barbara Miller, Sydney.

Milton, Giles, 2000, *Big Chief Elizabeth: The adventures and fate of the first English colonists in America,* Hodder & Stoughton, London.

Mitchell, Adrian, 2010, *Dampier's Monkey: The South Seas voyages of William Dampier,* containing transcripts of Dampier's original journals, Wakefield Press, Adelaide.

Moore, George Fletcher, 1884, *Diary of ten years eventful life of an early settler in Western Australia and also a descriptive vocabulary of the language of the Aborigines,* M Walbrook, London.

Morse, K., 1988, 'An archaeological survey of midden sites near the Zuytdorp wreck, Western Australia', *Bulletin of the Australian Institute for Maritime Archaeology,* vol. 12, no. 1, pp. 37–40.

Mulvaney, John & Green, Neville, 1992, *Commandant of Solitude: The Journals of Captain Collett Barker 1828-1831,* Miegunyah Press, Melbourne.

Mutch, T.D., 1942, 'The First Discovery of Australia With an account of the Voyage of the "Duyfken" and the Career of Captain Willem Jansz, *Journal of the Royal Australian Historical Society,* vol. 28, part 5.

Nash, Michael (ed.), 2007, *Shipwreck Archaeology in Australia,* University of Western Australia Press, Crawley, WA.

National Library of Australia, 2007, *Australia in Maps,* National Library of Australia, Canberra.

Oldfield, A., 1865, 'On the Aborigines of Australia', *Transactions of the Ethnological Society of London,* no. 3.

Paterson, Alistair & and Franklin, Daniel, 2004, 'The 1629 mass grave for Batavia victims, Beacon Island, Houtman Abrolhos Islands, Western Australia', *Australasian Historical Archaeology* vol. 22, pp. 71–8.

Penman, Leigh T.I., 'The *Batavia* Legacy: Implications of the *Batavia* Shipwreck (1629) in History and Imaginary', in Summo-O'Connell, Renata (ed.), 2009, *Imagined Australia: Reflections around the reciprocal construction of identity between Australia and Europe*, Peter Lang, Bern, pp. 153–70.

Péron, François, 1807–1816, *Voyage de découvertes aux terres australes* ('Voyage of Discovery to the Southern Lands'), three volumes, Paris.

Peters, Nonja, 2011, 'Snapshots of the Verenigde Oost Indische Compagnie (VOC) and influence in Australia', presentation to the Maritime Archeological Association of Western Australia, 18 October, <http://www.daaag.org/node/78> accessed January 2015.

Playford, Phillip, 1996, *Carpet of Silver: the Wreck of the Zuytdorp*, University of Western Australia Press, Nedlands.

——1995 (1959), 'The wreck of the Zuytdorp on the Western Australian coast in 1712', *Journal and Proceedings of the Western Australian Historical Society*, vol. 5, no. 5, pp. 5–41.

Poole, Fiona, 2013, 'Could this rewrite the history book?', ABC Mid North Coast NSW, 3 July, <www.abc.net.au/local/stories/2013/07/03/3794841.htm>

Pownall, Angela, 2012, 'Coins key to ship mystery', *The West Australian*, May 21.

Preston, William, 1833 (1980, UWAP), *Journals of Several Expeditions Made in Western Australia during the years 1829, 1830, 1831 and 1832*, London.

Pugach, Irian; Delfin, Frederick; Gunnarsdóttir, Ellen; Kayser, Manfred & Stoneking, Mark, 2013, 'Genome-wide data substantiate Holocene gene flow from India to Australia', *Proceedings of the National Academy of Sciences (PNAS)*, vol. 110, no. 5, pp. 1803–08.

Reynders, Peter, n.d. 'Why did the largest corporation in the world go broke? An economic review' (Abridged version), <http://gutenberg.net.au/VOC.html>

Rivière, Marc Serge (trans. & ed.), 1996, *A Woman of Courage: The journal of Rose de Freycinet on her voyage around the world 1817–1820*, National Library of Australia, Canberra.

Robinson, Alan, 1980, *In Australia Treasure is Not for the Finder*, A. Robinson, Perth.

Rosenman, Helen (ed. and trans.), 1988, *Two Voyages to the South Seas: Captain Jules S-C Dumont d'Urville*, University of Hawaii Press, Honolulu.

Rossi, E., Chin, C.Y.B., Beilby, J.P., Waso, H.F.J. & and Warnich, L., 2012, 'Variegate porphyria in Western Australian Aboriginal patients', *Internal Medicine Journal*, vol. 32, no. 9–10, pp. 445–50.

Royal Geographical Society of Queensland Inc., 2005, *Gulf of Carpentaria Scientific Study Report*, Royal Geographical Society of Queensland.

Russell, Lynette, 2012, *Roving Mariners: Australian Aboriginal Whalers and Sealers in the Southern Oceans 1790–1870*, State University of New York Press, Albany, NY.

Ryan, Simon, 1996, *The Cartographic Eye: How explorers saw Australia*, Cambridge University Press, Melbourne and Cambridge.

Sandford, Geoffrey, 2010, 'Larry Wells and the Lost Tribe', International Federation of Surveyors (FIG) Congress 2010, Facing the Challenges—Building the Capacity, Sydney, 11–16 April <http://www.fig.net/pub/fig2010/papers/ts05f%5Cts05f_sandford_4524.pdf> accessed January 2015.

Schilder, Günter (Olaf Richter, trans.), 1976, *Australia Unveiled: The share of the Dutch navigators in the discovery of Australia*, Theatrum Orbis Terrarum, Amsterdam.

Shellam, Tiffany, 2009, *Shaking Hands on the Fringe: Negotiating the Aboriginal world at King George's Sound*, University of Western Australia Press, Crawley, WA.

Slot, B.J., 1992, *Abel Tasman and the Discovery of New Zealand*, Cramwinckel, Amsterdam.

Smith, Bernard, 1985, *European Vision and the South Pacific*, Yale University Press, New Haven, CT.

Soriano, Dolors & Medina, Victòria, 2009, 'The Body as Language and Expression of the Indigenous Australian Cultural Identity', *Coolabah*, vol. 3.

South Australian Museum Archives, 2011. *Norman Tindale's Catalogue of Australian Aboriginal Tribes.*

Staker, J.P. (comp.), 2003 (2014), *Amish Mennonites in Tazewell County, Illinois*, <www.tcghs.org/links.htm>

Stephenson, P., 2007, *The Outsiders Within: Telling Australia's Indigenous-Asian story*, University of New South Wales Press, Sydney.

——2010, *Islam Dreaming: Indigenous Muslims in Australia*, University of New South Wales Press, Sydney.

Stevens, Henry N. (ed.), 1930, *New Light on the discovery of Australia as revealed by the journal of Captain Don Diego De Parado Y Tovar*, Henry Stevens, Son and Stiles, London.

Sutton, Peter, 'Stories About Feeling: Dutch-Australian Contact in Cape York Peninsula, 1606–1756', in Veth, Peter; Sutton, Peter & Neale, Margo (eds), 2008, *Strangers on the Shore: Early coastal contacts in Australia*, National Museum of Australia Press, Canberra.

Tacon, Paul S.C., May, Sally K., Fallon, Stewart J., Travers, Meg, Wesley, Daryl & Lamilami, Ronald, 2010, 'A minimum age for early depictions of Southeast Asian praus in the rock art of Arnhem Land, Northern Territory', *Australian Archaeology*, no. 71, pp. 1–10.

Tiley, Robert, 2006, *The Mermaid Tree*, ABC Books, Sydney.

Trickett, Peter, 2007, *Beyond Capricorn: How Portuguese adventurers discovered and mapped Australia and New Zealand 250 years before Captain Cook*, East St. Publications, Adelaide.

Trustees of the Public Library of New South Wales, 1948, *The Tasman Map of 1644*, The Mitchell Library, Sydney.

Turnbull, Paul, 1988, '"Outlawed Subjects": The procurement and scientific uses of Australian Aboriginal heads, ca. 1803–1835', *Eighteenth-Century Life*, vol. 22, no. 1, pp. 156–171.

Uren, Malcolm, 1940, *Sailormen's Ghosts: The Abrolhos Islands in three hundred years of romance, history and adventure*, Robertson & Mullens, Melbourne.

Van Den Boogaerde, Pierre, 2011, *Shipwrecks of Madagascar*, Strategic Book Publishing,

Van Huystee, Marit (ed. and trans.), 1994, *The Batavia Journal of François Pelsaert*, (ARA Document 1630: 1098 QQ II, pp. 232–316), Department of Maritime Archaeology, Western Australian Maritime Museum, no. 136.

Van Zanden, Henry, 2012, *The Lost White Tribes of Australia Part 1: 1656 The First Settlement of Australia*, Publishing Queen, Gosford, NSW.

Veth, Peter; Sutton, Peter & and Neale, Margo (eds), 2008, *Strangers on the Shore: Early Coastal Contacts in Australia*, National Museum of Australia Press, Canberra.

Vogel, Andrea, 2000, 'Huguenots-Walloons-Europe L-Archives', <http://archiver.rootsweb.ancestry.com/th/read/HUGUENOTS-WALLOONS-EUROPE/2000-04/0957085850> accessed October 2012.

Wamaritimemyths, 2007, 'Vergulde Draeck myth?' <http://wamaritimemyths.wordpress.com/2007/11/04/vergulde-draeck-myth> 4 November, accessed September 2013.

Warden, James, 2008, 'The Conciliation of Strangers' in Veth, Peter, Sutton, Peter and Neale, Margo (eds), *Strangers on the Shore: Early Coastal Contacts in Australia*, National Museum of Australia Press, 2008.

Watson, F. (ed.), 1923, *Historical Records of Australia*, Series III, Volume VI, Library Committee of the Commonwealth Parliament, Sydney.

Western Australian Museum, n.d. 'Excavation of the *Batavia* wreck site', <http://museum.wa.gov.au/research/research-areas/maritime-archaeology/batavia-cape-inscription/batavia/wreck-excavation> accessed July 2013.

Western Australian Folklife Project, 2009, National Library of Australia no. 4697366; ORAL TRC 6119.

Wharton, Captain W.J.L., R.N., F.R.S., (ed.), 1893, *Captain Cook's Journal During his First voyage Round the World Made in H.M. Bark 'Endeavour' 1768–71*, Elliot Stock, London.

Wharton, Geoff, 2005, 'The Pennefather River: Place of Australian National Heritage', in Royal Geographical Society of Queensland Inc., Gulf of Carpentaria Scientific Study Report (Royal Geographical Society of Queensland), p. 35.

Weaver, Fiona, 1990, 'Report of the Excavations of Previously Disturbed Land Sites Associated with the VOC Ship Zuytdorp, wrecked 1712, Zuytdorp Cliffs, Western Australia: A report to the Western Australian Maritime Museum', Fremantle, WA.

West-Sooby, John (ed), 2013, *Discovery and Empire: The French in the South Seas*, University of Adelaide Press, Adelaide.

Wieder, F.C., 1942, *Tasman's Kaart van Zijn Australische Ontdekkingen 1644*: '*de Bonaparte-kaart*', S-Gravenhage (The Hague), Martinus Nijhoff.

Willis, Rob; Willis, Olya & Curtin University, 2009, *Nunda oral history project,* sound recording, National Library of Australia, no. 4697366.

Wytfliet, Cornelius,1598, *Descriptionis Ptolemaicae Augmentum*, Gerard Rivius, Louvain.

Yoder, Don, 1983, 'The King-Gnagi Connection', *Pennsylvania Mennonite Heritage*, January.

Zandvliet, C.J., n.d., 'VOC maps and Drawings', TANAP (Towards A New Age of Partnership), an archive project covering the Dutch East India Company, The Netherlands, <www.tanap.net/content/voc/organization/organization_intro.htm>

INDEX